THE PSYCHOANALYST'S
AVERSION TO PROOF

AUSTIN RATNER

THE PSYCHOANALYST'S AVERSION TO PROOF

AUSTIN RATNER

International Psychoanalytic Books (IPBooks)
New York • http://www.IPBooks.net

Copyright © 2019 by Austin Ratner

Published by International Psychoanalytic Books (IPBooks)
Queens, NY
Online at: IPBooks.net

All rights reserved. No part of this publication may be reproduced, stored in a retrieval system, or transmitted in any form or by any means, electronic, mechanical, photocopying, recording or otherwise, without the prior written permission from the publisher.

Disclaimer
Every effort has been made to ensure that this book is free from error or omissions. Information provided is of general nature only and should not be considered legal or financial advice. The intent is to offer a variety of information to the reader. However, the author, publisher, editor or their agents or representatives shall not accept responsibility for any loss or inconvenience caused to a person or organization relying on this information.

Cover illustration by Austin Ratner
Cover inking and design by Kathy Kovacic
Author photo by Nina Subin
Book formatting services by Book Cover Cafe.com

ISBN: 978-1-949093-02-5

To Susan Ratner

Table of Contents

I. INTRODUCTION   1

II. FREUD'S AVERSION TO PROOF: A CASE STUDY   9

  1. Overview   9

  2. The Anxiety and Shame of Going Public with Forbidden Knowledge   11

  3. Three Defenses Against the Anxiety and Shame of Proof   14

    3.1. Projection of Inner Criticism onto the Audience   14

    3.2. Splitting and Avoidance   20

    3.3. Reversal: Giving Away Power to the Critics   35

  4. Summing Up the Diagnosis of Proof Aversion   38

  5. Freud's Oedipus Complex: Curiosity and Ambition   42

    5.1. Infantile Sexual Researches and Secrecy   42

    5.2. The Knowledge Contest with Jacob Freud   52

    5.3. Fate as a Psychological Construct   74

  6. The Role of Anti-Semitism in Proof Aversion   77

    6.1. The Character of Viennese Anti-Semitism   78

    6.2. Psychoanalysis as "Jewish Depravity"   84

  7. Freud's Authoritarianism as a Product of Proof Aversion   94

    7.1. Defenses in the Context of Dissident Criticism   99

    7.2. Projection of Rebellion and Its Attendant Inner Criticism   112

    7.3. Dogmatism as an Antidote to Doubt   116

  8. Case Study Conclusion   123

III. THE LEGACY OF FREUD'S AVERSION TO PROOF   127

1. A Brief History of Proof Aversion after Freud   127

1.1. Freud's Era: Ernest Jones   129

1.2. The Postwar American Heyday: Leo Rangell, Charles Brenner, Jacob Arlow, and Ralph Greenson   130

1.3. The Fifty-Year Decline: 1968 to 2018   136

1.4. The Psychoanalytic Community Today   139

2. Self-Fulfilling Prophecy: Proof Aversion as a Stimulus to Criticism of Psychoanalysis   143

2.1. Neglecting Research and Losing Academic Status   143

2.2. Faith-Based Psychoanalytic Rhetoric   146

2.3. Authoritarianism: An Unintended Consequence with Unintended Consequences   154

2.4. Treating Critics with Contempt   161

3. Conclusion: A Critique of Pure Resistance   180

IV. THE POSTMODERN AVERSION TO PROOF   185

1. Introduction: Postmodernism and Current Events   185

2. Postmodernism Is Narcissism   193

2.1. Disavowing Reality, Childhood, and Mortality   193

2.2. Radical Doubt Is Obsessional Neurosis   201

3. Postmodernism Is a Recrudescence of Ancient Skepticism   204

3.1. Ancient Skepticism Was Impractical   207

3.2. Skepticism Is a Defense Against the Anxiety of Influence   209

3.3. Knowledge and Doubt: Two Means of Relieving Anxiety   215

3.4. The Secret Desire of Radical Doubt Is Faith   226

4. Conclusion: The Postmodern Aversion to Proof   230

V. SOLUTIONS TO THE PROBLEM OF PROOF AVERSION   235

1. Further Study of the Hypothesis of Proof Aversion   236
1.1. The Analyst's Continuing Struggle to Look Inward   236
1.2. Transference in the Presentation-Criticism Dyad   240
1.3. Formal Investigations into Proof Aversion   244

2. Organizing in Support of Empirical Psychoanalysis   246
2.1. A New Endowment for Psychoanalytic Progress   248
2.2. Rebranding Psychoanalysis   251
2.3. More Psychoanalytic Researchers   257

3. New Research Strategies and New Study Designs   259
3.1. Digital Recording   260
3.2. Trigger Recording   262
3.3. Quantitative Psycholinguistics   264
3.4. Conclusion: Presenting Evidence to Critics   267

VI. CONCLUSION   271

1. Looking Back   271
2. You're Allowed to Cry There   272

ACKNOWLEDGEMENTS   275
REFERENCES   277

I. INTRODUCTION

When you're two years old, the world is full of good and bad magic. When I was two, my father got a fellowship to study disorders of the blood at the National Institutes of Health. He and my mother stuffed their luggage into an Oldsmobile Cutlass painted the metallic green of a bottle fly, tucked me into the back seat, and set forth from Cleveland to Rockville, Maryland. I thought I'd never see the rest of my family again.

It's my earliest surviving memory: my grandmother Eleanor, whom I called Grammy, appearing in the front doorway of our Rockville rowhouse as though she'd returned from the dead. My mother confirms that Grammy was in fact our first visitor in Rockville, but who knows whether I remember the details correctly? From later experience, I know my grandmother sometimes had a way of regarding small children as though she knew what they were thinking, and it's that knowing expression I recall on her face.

She had reason to guess my thoughts, and not only because she worked with young children as a social worker and child analyst. Her own life history had scarred her with the fear that love can vanish in an instant. One day when she was four years old, her father walked out of the house and never returned. Her mother had divorced him and, convinced it was best to make a clean start, forbade her father from seeing her again.

Eleanor found her father again in later life, but that couldn't put things right. Contrary to her mother's view, the wounds of childhood are not so easily outgrown or overlooked. When her own children were very small, my grandmother found herself crying all the time. At her middle daughter's nursery school, Hanna Perkins, which was founded by Sigmund Freud's disciple Anny Katan, a psychoanalyst asked Eleanor if she wanted some psychotherapy herself. She did.

It may seem obvious to a modern observer that the loss of Eleanor's father mattered. But her mother, who was born in the 19th century, didn't understand the inner life of children or the impact of early childhood in later life. By contrast, the psychoanalysts at Hanna Perkins not only understood that Eleanor's loss mattered, but understood that painful feelings can be hard to talk about, sometimes hard even to acknowledge. They understood that to know oneself better under conditions of pain and suffering usually requires help. My grandmother got a psychoanalysis that brought her relief and a new direction for her career in social work. The women who had come to Hanna Perkins from Anna Freud's Hampstead clinic gave Eleanor psychoanalytic training and she became one of the first child analysts and first lay analysts in the United States.

Freud might say that my memory of Grammy at our door is a "screen memory." (Grammy, who liked puns, might have said a "screen door memory.") The moment certainly acquired extra meaning given what happened soon thereafter. When my mother was six months pregnant, my father fell ill with a blood disorder of his own, a rare form of lymphoma. He died within months at the age of 29, 11 days before my third birthday and six weeks after my brother was born. My mother later told me a dream she had around that time in which a large tree fell on her house and destroyed it.

Having grown up beside a ghost, I think of another metaphor: a tree that grows up next to a chain link fence. Such a tree grows through the braided steel and incorporates the links into its trunk. I incorporated my dead father. Throughout my growing up any mention of him would arouse tempestuous feeling. When I became a teenager and went through periods of depression, however, I didn't know why. My grandmother and mother suggested a connection to my father's death. They introduced me to psychoanalysis, and over many years I explored that connection—at first its possibility, and then the ornate ways in which I had not only buried my father but, because of guilt and its devious manifestations, buried myself.

Sigmund Freud and his daughter Anna created my grandmother's profession, but their work also addressed my grandmother's personal experience in a way that no other branch of psychology or medicine did. The Freuds brought to our family the knowledge that childhood matters, and how it matters. Their knowledge of childhood and the ways of the heart helped my grandmother to understand her defense mechanisms, make rational choices, and live a better life. When I needed it, she opened the door to that knowledge for me so I could do the same.

Other schools of psychology do not account for a fact of human development that Grammy and I knew in our bones: childhood matters. The other schools of thought fail my grandmother and me because, as Freud writes in his case history of the "Wolf Man," other perspectives "are based on a low estimate of the importance of early infantile impressions and an unwillingness to ascribe such enduring effects to them." (Freud 1918, p. 49) My grandmother and I knew that childhood matters because we didn't have the luxury of pretending otherwise. And because childhood matters, Freud matters.

For that reason, public suspicion towards psychoanalysis has caused me dismay, and kindled hopes that psychoanalysts would do more to publicize its merits, and more to justify and defend psychoanalytic ideas and practices. Some analysts seriously aspire to those goals, but many remain pessimistic that efforts at validation can ever prevail when repression dooms the public to narrow-mindedness. Other analysts have abandoned hope of empirical justification on philosophical grounds, whether a postmodern skepticism toward objective knowledge or a dualist conviction that affairs of the heart cannot be understood through a scientific lens.

Freud made no secret of his own belief that repression makes implacable enemies of psychoanalysis and renders public validation practically impossible. As he wrote in his *History of the Psycho-Analytic Movement*: "I understood that from now onwards I was one of those who have 'disturbed the sleep of the world,' as Hebbel says, and that I could not reckon upon objectivity and tolerance.... I was prepared to accept the fate...." (Freud 1914, pp. 21-22) He has a point, but for the most part I disagree. I don't think the shrinking psychoanalytic community, or the world at large, can today afford to accept any fate other than progress. The world needs psychoanalysis now more than ever. And the world's most vulnerable population—children—needs an enlightened psychoanalytic voice to speak up on its behalf. The pharmaceutical and health insurance industries make themselves heard and so should psychoanalysts.

That said, this book does not attempt to dispute Freud's and other psychoanalysts' pessimism about public acceptance of psychoanalysis so much as to diagnose it. Pessimism cannot be disputed anyway, because it is a feeling. As such, it has a context, an origin story, and a psychodynamic architecture. Freud seldom scrutinized his feeling about public demonstrations of the validity of psychoanalysis; his writings express the feeling, but do not examine it. A survey of Freud's letters and papers, however, suggests his pessimism was complex, deep-seated, and deserving of further scrutiny. Gloomy passages on the topic of proof weave circuitous patterns of emotional interference into otherwise logical demonstrations and explanations. It's a central thesis of this book: Freud's writings on proof in fact exhibit irrational defense mechanisms, and the strength and consistency of those defenses suggest Freud had a genuine aversion to proving psychoanalytic ideas. The repetition of his rhetoric in later generations suggests that an aversion to proof has influenced the psychoanalytic community at large.

The proposition that emotion has interfered with psychoanalysts' reasoning about proof may sound brash. Freud is one of the great geniuses in history. If he was averse to proof, who am I to challenge him? A great many psychoanalysts have furthermore adopted Freud's approach to public validation. Are they all wrong? Postmodern analysts may consider proof a naïve or antiquated Enlightenment notion that ignores the complexity of epistemology and the special difficulties of psychoanalytic knowledge. Are those analysts also all wrong?

For the time being, I ask only that you consider the possibility that a feeling can intrude into the admittedly complex business of psychoanalytic validation for reasons specific to psychoanalysis, but also because of emotional conflicts attaching to proof and knowledge in general. And I ask you to consider whether these problems can perhaps be best understood and solved through the very strategies and theories that Freud invented.

My hope is that a study of proof aversion among psychoanalysts does not come across as scolding but rather as a useful, freeing insight, especially for those analysts who are already interested in pursuing scientific validation of psychoanalytic theories and efficacy— or are at least interested in the possibility of advancing psychoanalysis by demonstrating its merits to the public. A greater understanding of Freud's and other analysts' aversion to the public validation of psychoanalytic ideas could, I think, help the psychoanalytic movement in a number of ways: it could help to resolve some of the ambivalence about science and proof in the psychoanalytic community, help to free expositors of psychoanalysis from Freud's constraining precedent, and, more important, could help to free expositors of psychoanalysis from their own emotionally-laden aversion to the task of proof. Opposition from outside the psychoanalytic community makes the task of proof hard enough without aversions that arise from within.

If Freud had emotional conflicts about proving his theories, and if later psychoanalysts have exhibited similar conflicts, this of course raises the question *why?* Why should there be any particular emotional noise around the task of proof in a psychoanalytic context? I would assert that psychoanalytic knowledge, with all its affronts to polite society, is as charged to transmit as it is to uncover in the first place. "After all," Freud wrote in *The Interpretation of Dreams*, "there are many things which one has to keep secret from other people but of which one makes no secret to oneself...." (Freud 1900, pp. 212-213) If the instinctual contents of psychoanalytic knowledge inspire an urge to secrecy, then an aversion to proof and public demonstration may be all but inevitable for psychoanalysts. Furthermore, as I'll attempt to show, resistances to the task of proof are probably not limited to psychoanalysts. In later chapters I will psychoanalyze other forms of epistemic aversion.

But the problem of aversion to proof begins with Freud. As the first expositor of psychoanalysis, he faced enormous internal pressures as he went about explaining psychoanalytic ideas to others, and left behind a mountain of evidence of those pressures. Ernest Jones recounts, for instance, Freud's anxiety about lecturing at Clark University in Worcester, Massachusetts in 1909, and tells an anecdote that vividly reflects the need for psychological defensive measures when presenting psychoanalytic ideas in public. Jones writes:

[Freud] had made the interesting observation that, when faced with an anxious task, such as the present one of describing his startling conclusions to a foreign audience, it was helpful to provide a lightning conductor for one's emotions by deflecting one's attention on to a subsidiary goal. So before leaving Europe he maintained that he was going to America in the hope of catching sight of a wild porcupine *and* to give some lectures. The phrase 'to find one's porcupine' became a recognized saying in our circle. (Jones 1955, p. 59)

After the Clark lectures, Freud visited Harvard neurologist James Jackson Putnam's family camp in the Adirondacks and while there he in fact spotted a wild porcupine. "Having achieved his double purpose," Jones writes, "he was ready to return home." (p. 59) Freud's campaign to teach the world about psychoanalysis was far from over, however, and he would need more "porcupines" before he was through. The acquisition and perpetuation of knowledge has always been a Faustian bargain, especially for those who peer into the depths of the human heart and dare to repeat what they have seen.

II. FREUD'S AVERSION TO PROOF: A CASE STUDY

1. Overview

Freud learned from his patients and his self-analysis that what is unpleasant to see is also difficult to see. That is repression. But it could be added that what is unpleasant and difficult to see in private is also unpleasant and difficult to say in public. This in turn raises a question: If defenses interfere with private research into the psyche, could defenses also interfere with the public exposition of psychoanalysis? This case study attempts to answer that question by examining evidence of emotional interferences in Freud's public demonstrations of psychoanalytic ideas and in his discussions of the problem of public demonstration.

Correspondence, lectures, and papers dealing with proof and demonstration trace the following picture of Freud's emotions, a picture which I will shortly attempt to substantiate in more detail: Early on, Freud divulges not just excitement about his revolutionary discoveries, but also shame and anxiety. As time goes on and he forges ahead with the task of presenting his findings and theories publicly, he continues to fret over the reception of his antisocial discoveries and attests to an ungovernable feeling of rage at his unjust critics. He attempts to defuse his shame, anxiety, and anger by analyzing his critics' emotional resistances to his ideas, but he never completely succeeds at detaching his own feelings from the effort to present psychoanalytic theories to the public. Instead, these negative affects, and defenses against them, calcify over time into unexamined interferences with Freud's efforts to justify his own theories. "I am in no mood for presentations," Freud wrote to Wilhelm Fliess in 1896 (Masson 1985, p. 185), and in the years to come he would seldom feel in a mood to present his work to any audience that might criticize him.

Freud's case demonstrates that resistance to psychoanalytic knowledge can influence not just the audience but the public expositor of psychoanalysis. Declaring shocking psychoanalytic truths in public and conquering doubters with proof are bold, aggressive acts. If the expositor of psychoanalysis insufficiently analyzes his feelings in connection with these bold, aggressive acts, then the expositor's anxiety, shame, and compensatory indignation may stimulate defense mechanisms arrayed against the painful feelings. The result is distorted thinking about the business of proof, akin to the resistant arguments a patient makes against the continuation of psychoanalytic treatment.

Freud's writings contain evidence of the following defenses, all three of which hinder his efforts at proof, and all three of which Freud conceals behind critiques of external resistance to psychoanalysis:

1. Projection of inner criticism onto neutral or friendly figures, whom Freud then misinterprets as resistant to psychoanalysis.
2. Splitting of the audience into idealized allies and persecutory, resistant enemies, followed by avoidance of confrontations with enemies. Freud makes use of rationalizations and denials to support his avoidance of the task of proof, often by claiming that his audience's resistance makes efforts at proof futile.

3. Reversals in which the aggressive act of overpowering critics with proof is undone, or even displaced, by pessimistic discussion of the critics' power—their power of resistance or their power to abuse and harm psychoanalysis.

The public's fear of psychoanalytic ideas and its accompanying resistance were a real bête noire for Freud, but the diagnosis of public resistance to psychoanalysis was also Freud's favorite method of avoiding the task of proof or spoiling his own efforts at it.

2. The Anxiety and Shame of Going Public with Forbidden Knowledge

The discoveries of psychoanalytic research were hard to talk about from the beginning. Even before he published his findings, Freud worried over their reception. When Freud sent a draft of a paper on the sexual etiology of the neuroses to Fliess on February 8, 1893, he expressed trepidation about the paper's potential to scandalize, admonishing his friend, "You will of course keep the manuscript away from your young wife." (Masson 1985, p. 39) Likewise, the editors of the *Standard Edition* describe Freud's co-discoverer Josef Breuer as "a man half-afraid of his own remarkable discoveries."[1] The discoveries meanwhile filled Freud himself with excitement, but also induced a constantly interfering anxiety: "We shall not be shipwrecked. Instead of the channel we are seeking, we may find oceans," he wrote to Fliess on January 3, 1897, looking ahead to what discoveries the new year would bring. "[I]f we do not prematurely capsize, if our constitutions

---

1 S.E. 2:xxvi.

can stand it, we shall arrive.... When I happen to be without anxiety, I am still ready to take on all the devils." (p. 219) His adventuring in forbidden realms of the psyche even precipitated a "little hysteria" in Freud, as he put it in a letter to Fliess later that year.[2] In the same letter, Freud told Fliess that his self-analysis "paralyzes my psychic strength for describing and communicating what I have won so far." (p. 261) Psychoanalysis and the public communication of its discoveries clearly could be emotionally exhausting.

Fear of the judgments of polite society evidently contributed to this exhaustion and sense of paralysis. Having eaten from the tree of knowledge, Freud and Breuer acted a little as though their discovery were a crime to be concealed or blamed on somebody else. After publishing "On the Psychical Mechanism of Hysterical Phenomena: Preliminary Communication" (Breuer and Freud 1893), Freud and Breuer would each at times assign authorship of the theory to the other, as though simultaneously pointing a finger of blame at each other.[3] Freud also assigned "blame" to the eminent physicians Jean-Martin Charcot and Rudolf Chrobak, noting of the sexual etiology of the neuroses, "The idea for which I was being made responsible had by no means originated with me." (Freud 1914, p. 13)[4]

Wariness of society's judgments translated directly into apprehensions about publishing psychoanalytic discoveries. Writing to Fliess in a now-famous letter on September 21, 1897, Freud reports his landmark insight that the parental seductions described by his

---

2 Freud calls the hysteria "greatly accentuated by my work."

3 S.E. 2:xxvi-xxvii.

4 Soon afterward, Freud exonerates his mentors: "I have not of course disclosed the illustrious parentage of this scandalous idea in order to saddle other people with the responsibility for it." (p. 15) I.e., Freud's mentors bear no responsibility for the sexual theory of the neuroses because they only had glancing knowledge of it; meanwhile, Freud himself should not be blamed for a different reason—namely, that his theory isn't really "scandalous," but rather of "illustrious parentage."

hysterical patients were not facts but rather repressed wishes. (Masson 1985, pp. 264-266) This discovery cleared the path to recognition of infantile sexuality, the Oedipus complex, and the distorting power of defense mechanisms. Yet Freud's first impulse was to hide his insight, under the pretext that reversing himself could be embarrassing. "Of course I shall not tell it in Dan," he writes in the same letter, "nor speak of it in Askelon, in the land of the Philistines...." (p. 265) The apprehensions about publishing translated into real delays. "It was not for another eight years," the editors of the *Standard Edition* note, "that he did in fact publish the facts in the streets of Askelon—in the second of the *Three Essays* [*on the Theory of Sexuality*]."[5] Similarly, when Freud's friend Oscar Rie read the manuscript of the Dora case, "Fragment of an Analysis of a Case of Hysteria," Rie's discouraging feedback caused him to shelve it indefinitely. "At his request I let Oscar read 'Dreams and Hysteria,'" Freud writes to Fliess in 1901, "but I derived little joy from it. I shall make no further attempt to break through my isolation." (Masson 1985, p. 438) He didn't publish it for another 4 years.[6]

According to Freud, his controversial theories endangered his personal relationships—with friends and peers like Rie but also with mentors like Breuer, who was 14 years older, and had supported Freud inside and outside of work, going so far as to lend Freud money. (E. Freud 1961, p. 127) When Breuer deserted Freud in his psychological research, Freud thought he knew the reason why. "As Freud saw it," Peter Gay writes, "he was the explorer who had the courage of Breuer's discoveries; in pushing them as far as they would go, with

---

5 S.E. 1:261n. In a later chapter I will examine the possible meanings of Freud's biblical reference in greater detail.

6 Freud describes the delay in publication of the Dora case in the *History*. (Freud 1914, p. 22.)

all their erotic undertones, he had inevitably alienated the munificent mentor who had presided over his early career." (Gay 1988, p. 67) Freud invites this reading of the break with Breuer in *An Autobiographical Study*. "The development of psycho-analysis afterwards cost me his friendship," Freud writes. "It was not easy for me to pay such a price, but I could not escape it." (Freud 1925, p. 19) The Oedipal overtones are plain to see: Freud believed his sexual research had offended an important father-figure. Freud had not only discovered the Oedipus complex but, by choosing to share his discovery, had in a sense re-enacted it.

3. Three Defenses Against the Anxiety and Shame of Proof

3.1. Projection of Inner Criticism onto the Audience

The refrain sounds again and again throughout Freud's oeuvre: the audience is unfair to psychoanalysis, the audience withholds its sympathy from Freud's radical ideas, and Freud gives up trying to explain. "I am pausing," Freud wrote to Fliess in 1895. "I reported many of my neurotic findings in the psychiatric association and privately, and finally became annoyed at the small measure of understanding; I am withdrawing again." (Masson 1985, p. 120) Freud's disciples have long accepted his account of his relations with critics at face value. But is it accurate? Or is there an element of emotional distortion in it? Did Freud's internal shame and anxiety about his discoveries affect his perception of external criticism?

From the beginning, some critics were of course unfair to psychoanalysis, and critics continue to hurl unfair, irrational criticism at Freud to this day. In a letter to Fliess dated November 2, 1896, for example, Freud reports that a Würzburg psychiatrist named Konrad Rieger mocked Freud's essay with remarkable pique. Masson translates some of Rieger's harsh and unreasonable criticism:

> I cannot imagine that an experienced psychiatrist could read this essay without feeling total indignation. The reason for this indignation is that the author attributes the greatest importance to paranoid blather with sexual content [on the part of his patients] about purely chance happenings which, even if they were not based merely on imagination, are of no significance whatsoever. This kind of thing cannot possibly lead to anything but a simply dreadful 'old wives' psychiatry.' (Masson 1985, pp. 202-203n)

Dr. Rieger went on to accuse Freud's patients of suffering from the "poison of laziness" and to cure them of it Rieger prescribed them manual labor!

A close examination of the historical record, however, suggests that Freud was often unreliable in his estimation of criticism. He saw criticism where there was criticism, but he also saw it where there was none. Three critics to whom Freud calls attention in his writings illustrate the point: Adolf von Strümpell, Leopold Löwenfeld, and Richard von Krafft-Ebing. Freud repeatedly describes all three as though they opposed and damaged psychoanalysis when in fact they were his allies.

"Our book [Studies in Hysteria] had a vicious review by Strümpell in the Deutsche Zeitschrift für Nervenheilkunde," Freud wrote to Fliess on February 6, 1896. (Masson 1985, p. 170) Looking back on the review almost thirty years later, while writing An Autobiographical Study, Freud describes it as "a severe rebuff." (Freud 1925, p. 22) Ernest Jones and

THE PSYCHOANALYST'S AVERSION TO PROOF

other followers don't question Freud's account (Jones 1953, p. 252)[7], but it's inaccurate. Masson translates a passage from Strümpell's review in support of the many commentators who have attested Strümpell's review was "basically positive." (Masson 1985, p. 171) Gay agrees that Freud mischaracterized Strümpell's review with "a tenderness to criticism that was threatening to become a habit." (Gay 1988, p. 77)

In a letter to Fliess written on March 28 and April 2, 1895, Freud first complained about Löwenfeld: "Psychology is plaguing me a great deal. Löwenfeld launched the first attack on the anxiety neurosis in the *Münchener medizinische Wochenschrift*; I asked him for a reprint so that I can reply."[8] Masson quotes the following passage from Löwenfeld's review, which provides an opportunity to compare Freud's characterization with the reality:

> The Freudian theory may well be more or less justified in a large number of cases of anxiety states. My own observations also speak to the fact that anomalies in sexual life are of great significance in the genesis of obsessions and phobias. What I must object to is only Freud's claim of a specificity and a uniformity for the sexual etiology in cases of acquired anxiety states. (Masson 1985, p. 123n)

Freud's mischaracterization of Löwenfeld's article as an attack, "the first" in an anticipated sequence, looks more emotional than factual

---

7 Of note, Jones himself first became interested in Freud's work after reading a positive review of *Studies in Hysteria* in *Brain*. (Jones 1953, p. 252n)

8 Freud published "A Reply to Criticisms of My Paper on Anxiety Neurosis" that same year. In it he says that before Löwenfeld said a word, he'd already anticipated criticism of his theory of the sexual etiology of the neuroses and a "difficulty in the way of its acceptance ... a kind of reluctance to look squarely at sexual matters.... [O]ne had to be prepared to meet with resistance...." (Freud 1895, p. 124)

in light of what Löwenfeld actually said and who he turned out to be: a friend.

Yet Freud held onto the memory of this incident for years and used it as justification for avoiding direct engagement with his critics. Two decades after the Löwenfeld "attack," Freud cites it in his *Introductory Lectures on Psycho-Analysis* as one of the only "regular scientific dispute[s]" of his career. "It ended in our becoming friends and we have remained so to this day," Freud admits. "But I did not repeat the experiment for a long time, as I did not feel sure that the outcome would be the same." (Freud 1917, p. 245)

The Krafft-Ebing incident appears equally important, and perhaps equally distorted, in Freud's accounts of early resistance to psychoanalysis. This incident took place at a lecture Freud gave on April 21, 1896[9] to the Verein für Psychiatrie und Neurologie, on the sexual etiology of hysteria. In a letter to Fliess dated April 26, 1896, Freud expressed his bitterness about the reaction to his lecture: "A lecture on the etiology of hysteria at the psychiatric society was given an icy reception by the asses and a strange evaluation by Krafft-Ebing: 'It sounds like a scientific fairy tale.' ... They can go to hell." (Masson 1985, p. 184) Roughly a week later, on May 4, 1896, he wrote to Fliess, "I am as isolated as you would wish me to be. Word was given out to abandon me, for a void is forming all around me. So far I bear it with equanimity." (p. 185)

Just as the Strümpell and Löwenfeld incidents lingered in Freud's memory for years as symbols of unfair criticism, so did the lecture at the meeting chaired by Krafft-Ebing. Gay underscores the importance of this event for Freud: "It was an evening Freud chose never to forget; the traumatic residue it left became a ground for low expectations,

---

9   S.E. 3:190; Gay 1988, p. 93.

a justification of his pessimism." (Gay 1988, p. 93) The bitter language of the letters of 1896 echoes in Freud's account of the lecture in his 1914 *History*:

> But the silence which my communications met with, the void which formed itself about me, the hints that were conveyed to me, gradually made me realize that assertions on the part played by sexuality in the aetiology of the neuroses cannot count upon meeting with the same kind of treatment as other communications. I understood that from now onwards I was one of those who have 'disturbed the sleep of the world', as Hebbel says, and that I could not reckon upon objectivity and tolerance. (Freud 1914, pp. 21-22)

It's a legitimate question whether that lecture really created a "void" at all, or whether Freud imagined it in part or in whole due to paranoia. In the 1914 *History* and in the letter of 1896, Freud bitterly calls attention to the chair of the meeting, Krafft-Ebing, as though Krafft-Ebing were to some degree responsible for the prudish ostracism that Freud perceived during and after his lecture. But Krafft-Ebing was in truth neither a resistant prude when it came to sexual psychology, nor an enemy of psychoanalysis. On the contrary, he was at the time the world's foremost sexologist—Krafft-Ebing coined the terms *sadism, masochism,* and *homosexuality*—and whatever skepticism he expressed toward Freud's work that day, Krafft-Ebing extended crucial public support to Freud afterwards. In 1897, unsolicited by Freud, Krafft-Ebing wrote Freud a four-page, glowing recommendation for promotion to the rank of *professor extraordinarius*, citing Freud's "unusual talent" and expressing only the mild reservation that Freud's original and intriguing theories awaited more solid confirmation. (Masson 1985, pp. 229-231n) When Freud later asked Krafft-Ebing for help with his promotion in 1902, Freud tells Fliess that Krafft-Ebing "responded wonderfully." (Masson 1985, p. 456) Freud finally got the full professorship he'd long desired.

It so happens that Krafft-Ebing was also correct when in 1896 he referred to Freud's presentation as a "scientific fairy tale"; Freud had presented evidence for his seduction theory, which claimed that neurosis was caused by rampant child molestation. He was soon to abandon that idea as exactly what Krafft-Ebing had called it—a fairy tale, concocted by his patients to disguise their Oedipal feelings.

Nevertheless, as time went on, Freud's recollections of this "void" grew more extreme. In his *Autobiographical Study* he exaggerates and distorts the historical record by claiming, "For more than ten years after my separation from Breuer I had no followers. I was completely isolated. In Vienna I was shunned; abroad no notice was taken of me." (Freud 1925, p. 48) Here is Freud's "habit of dramatizing his intellectual isolation" (Gay 1988, p. 140) in full swing. Even when prominent voices praised *The Interpretation of Dreams*, a revolutionary work that was ahead of its time and bound to bewilder contemporaries, Freud "seemed determined to feel himself surrounded by a void, and to anticipate nothing but misunderstanding and neglect." (Gay 1988, p. 133) By the time Freud was writing *The New Introductory Lectures on Psycho-Analysis*, his early critics had become a medieval "mob" who'd cast him like an "evil-doer" into a "pillory." (Freud 1933, p. 137) It's a vivid image of what it meant to Freud to be one of history's "lonely discoverers" (Freud 1914, p. 23): harsh, moralistic opprobrium. His self-analysis never seems to have explored just how much of that opprobrium had arisen in his own superego due to the terrible facts of mental life he alone had dared to uncover—and due to the curiosity and ambition that had driven him to make those discoveries in the first place.

If Freud perceived a "void" and an "icy reception" when the reality was different, perhaps that's because he unconsciously felt that his shameful sexual ideas and hunger for recognition *deserved* an icy reception. By his own account, the discovery of sexual origins behind his patients' symptoms caused Freud anxiety and hysteria, the inevitable penalties for uncovering socially unacceptable facts of mental life. When he presented his research in public, it would appear that he got rid of some of that anxiety and inner criticism by projecting it onto reviewers and audience members like Strümpell, Löwenfeld, and Krafft-Ebing.

3.2. Splitting and Avoidance

Having been promoted at last to *professor extraordinarius*, Freud wrote his confidante Fliess on March 11, 1902 with a feeling of elation that psychoanalysis had been granted official sanction. The Emperor himself would soon ratify the appointment. "Congratulations and flowers already are pouring in," Freud writes, "as though the role of sexuality has suddenly been officially recognized by His Majesty, the significance of the dream certified by the Council of Ministers, and the necessity of a psychoanalytic therapy of hysteria carried by a two-thirds majority in Parliament." (Masson 1985, p. 457) It was a moment of vindication for Freud, but the fantasy of an up-and-down vote in Parliament also reflects a tendency that would come back to haunt him: Freud's inclination to split the world into rigidly defined camps, especially in relation to psychoanalysis. As Robert Holt has observed, "Whatever the nature of the critical dispute, Freud always took the uncompromising stance—my follower or my enemy." (Holt 2015, p. 339) Freud routinely divided the world into "opponents" and "adherents" of psychoanalysis, and seldom acknowledged middle grounds or potential for his audience to modify its views. The *History* pulses with the drumbeat of this black-and-white rhetoric.[10]

Where his rebel movement psychoanalysis was concerned, Freud saw officialdom as enemy territory. This was particularly true of academic medicine, about which Freud harbored ambivalence throughout his life. Here is a passage from the *History* where Freud expresses his bitter sense of alienation from the medical establishment:

> Meanwhile my writings were not reviewed in the medical journals, or, if as an exception they *were* reviewed, they were dismissed with expressions of scornful or pitying superiority. Occasionally a colleague would make some reference to me in one of his publications; it would be very short and not at all flattering—words such as 'eccentric', 'extreme', or 'very peculiar' would be used. (Freud 1914, pp. 22-23)

The examples of Strümpell, Löwenfeld, and Krafft-Ebing undermine or at least complicate these claims, but Freud tended to regard commentators like Strümpell with categorical mistrust. Freud in fact calls out his own tendency to demonize academic medicine in *The Question of Lay Analysis*. The fictional interlocutor in that work observes of Freud: "[Y]ou are dominated by a hostility against the medical profession." (Freud 1926, p. 233)

No doubt, psychoanalysis challenged the public with controversial and polarizing new ideas, but Freud's own psychology seems to have demanded that he split the world into opponents and adherents more rigidly than was necessary or factual. By splitting his audience

---

10 See Freud 1914, p. 34 for but one of countless examples of Freud's binary *opponent* vs. *adherent* rhetoric.

into idealized sympathizers and persecutory opponents and talking over his opponents' heads, he seems to have avoided confrontation. If Freud could label all of academia hopelessly biased against psychoanalysis, after all, then he could also excuse himself from academic settings where he was likely to encounter criticism. And that is so often just what he did. It was, perhaps, another way of "finding his porcupine."

Several different strategies for avoiding disputation with critics mark Freud's career: he would curate his audiences to try to insure that they were sympathetic to psychoanalysis; would decline invitations to medical conferences if a dispute seemed likely; and he would deploy surrogates to defend psychoanalysis on his behalf. Each of these evasive maneuvers may have relieved Freud's anxiety, but they did not aid in the task of demonstrating psychoanalysis and its merits to the public.

In the first place, Freud did not like public lecturing. The Clark lectures stressed him so much that he pretended he was only going to America to look for porcupines, not to teach the principles of psychoanalysis, and he diminished his *Introductory Lectures* as unimportant despite their resounding success. (Gay 1988, p. 369) In general, as he put it in 1896 (Masson 1985, p. 185), he was "in no mood for presentations" when it came to the undifferentiated public. He preferred to lecture to the comfy group he called the "Jewish academic reading circle" (p. 185) of young physicians, writers, and artists who gathered round him after 1902 "with the express intention of learning, practicing and spreading the knowledge of psycho-analysis." (Freud 1914, p. 25)

When Freud did give public presentations, he tried to purge opponents from his audience. One approach he used was to ask for sympathy and instruct those who were too resistant or unsympathetic with psychoanalysis at the outset to leave the lecture hall. "Where sympathy is lacking, understanding will not come very easily," he writes in his short essay entitled "A Difficulty in the Path of Psycho-Analysis." (Freud 1917, p. 137) In the first of the *Introductory Lectures*, given in 1915 at the University of Vienna, Freud advises his resistant critics to quit his lectures immediately: "I seriously advise you not to join my audience a second time…. [A]ll your habits of thought are inevitably bound to make you into opponents of psycho-analysis," he says. (Freud 1916-1917, p. 15) Freud also attempts to purge detractors from among his readers at the beginning of his *New Introductory Lectures on Psycho-Analysis*. They are not for just anyone, he says, but rather "are addressed to the multitude of educated people to whom we may perhaps attribute a benevolent, even though cautious, interest in the characteristics and discoveries of the young science." (Freud 1933, p. 6) Extracting a pledge of such benevolence from the audience cannot have had any real consequences for his presentation except to forestall his own anxiety.

When Freud had reason to believe he could be publicly subjected to criticism, he refused to show up. In a letter dated April 14, 1907, Freud explains to Jung why he declined an invitation to speak on psychoanalysis in Amsterdam, an invitation that consequently went to Jung instead:

> Shortly before your visit, I was asked to give that report in Amsterdam. I declined in haste for fear that I might talk it over with you and let you persuade me to accept…. Apparently a duel was planned between Janet and myself, but I detest gladiatorial fights in front of the noble rabble and cannot easily bring myself to put my findings to the vote of the indifferent crowd. (McGuire 1988, pp. 32-33)

It's clear from the letter that Freud wished to avoid confrontation, but it's not entirely clear there would have been one. Pierre Janet, like Strümpell, Löwenfeld, and Krafft-Ebing, was not exactly the avowed enemy Freud sometimes made him out to be. He objected to Freud's interpretations of sex behind every mental phenomenon, true, but Janet also accepted the existence of unconscious mental processes and had valued Freud and Breuer's "Preliminary Communication" enough to use it as the final chapter of his 1894 text on hysteria.[11]

Meanwhile, Freud deployed surrogates to defend psychoanalysis in public, often times Gentiles like the Swiss psychiatrists of the Burghölzli Asylum in Zürich—Carl Jung and his boss, Eugen Bleuler—and also the Englishman Ernest Jones, who eventually sparred with Janet in Freud's place at the 1913 International Medical Congress. Freud notes with satisfaction that "Janet had to submit to a number of corrections by Ernest Jones, who was able to point out to him his insufficient knowledge of the subject." (Freud 1914, p. 33)

Of course, Freud could not be everywhere all at once, but his reasons for deploying surrogates were by no means strictly rational. When Freud commends Bleuler's efforts on behalf of psychoanalysis, he explicitly notes that he needed Bleuler for disputation and demonstration because of his own emotional deficits:

The task to which I was not equal—that of demonstrating to the opponents of psycho-analysis *suaviter in modo* their injustice and arbitrariness—was undertaken and carried out most creditably by Bleuler in a paper written in 1910, 'Freud's Psycho-Analysis: A Defence and Some Critical Remarks.' (Freud 1914, pp. 40-41)

---

11 S.E. 2:xiv.

Bleuler and Jung were Freud's Teutonic knights, "championing the cause, holding the flag high, and meting out blows to our opponents," as he put it in a letter of praise to Jung in 1911. (McGuire 1988, p. 438) Freud's relationship with Jung exhibited from the beginning a heavy proportion of fantasy. Long before Freud grew old, he relished the idea that the young Swiss would take over the movement and defend psychoanalysis in his place. (p. 218)

Why did Freud feel himself unequal to the task of proving his critics wrong and require surrogates to do it instead? Freud's reference to the Jesuit credo *fortiter in re, suaviter in modo*—"boldly in substance, gently in style"—points to emotional causes. He felt he could be bold, *fortiter*, but not gentle, *suaviter*, with his critics. In other words, they made him so angry that he couldn't envision a civil disagreement. He admits as much in a previous passage:

> Perhaps I have been thought so good-natured or so easily intimidated that no further notice need be taken of me. This was a mistake; I can be as abusive and enraged as anyone; but I have not the art of expressing the underlying emotions in a form suitable for publication and I therefore prefer to abstain completely. (Freud 1914, p. 39)

A sublimated rage could fuel an effective confrontation rather than inhibit it, but the ungovernable emotion seems to represent a link in a psychodynamic chain that ends regrettably in silence and avoidance. Freud admits to this avoidance directly in the *New Introductory Lectures* when he considers arguing against his critics but "on second thoughts" concludes it "would become tedious and distressing and would be precisely what I have been so carefully avoiding all these years." (Freud 1933, p. 139)

Rationalization and Denial as Techniques of Avoidance

In letters and in more formal communications like the *History*, Freud makes it clear that he disliked justifying himself to enemies, to critics, or even to audiences whose allegiances were unknown to him. These expressions of the feeling *I don't want to prove* appear side-by-side in his writings with epistemological assessments of the external obstacles to proof of psychoanalytic concepts, assessments that often conclude pessimistically *I cannot prove*. When Freud draws a connection between the two types of statements, the direction of causation points from the epistemological to the emotional. He says in so many words: *I cannot prove*, therefore *I don't want to prove*.

But psychoanalysis urges the study of precisely the opposite direction of influence, wherein censorious emotion enforces epistemic limits, dictating what we are allowed to know, and what immoral knowledge we must repress, distort, or doubt out of existence. Freud does not consider the possibility that this sort of psychodynamic influence might apply to his statements about proof: *I don't want to prove because it makes me feel anxious and ashamed to declare my antisocial discoveries publicly, and therefore I convince myself that I cannot prove. I don't want to prove* would in that case be a motive of which Freud is not completely aware and *I cannot prove* a rationalization that conceals the motive and simultaneously fulfills the wish. This sort of thought transformation is commonplace according to Freud's model of dreaming and daydreaming, where latent wishes manifest as facts. (Freud 1900, p. 534, Freud 1901, p. 647)

Freud's writings on proof are filled with avoidant rationalizations of this kind. To identify them, closer examination of Freud's arguments is necessary, as is some disputation—not for the purpose of overturning his conclusions, but for the purpose of diagnosing whether his arguments are wholly rational or affected by emotional distortions.

First, let's consider the *History*. Early in that work, Freud makes the following comment on the problem of proof:

> How to compel these healthy people to examine the matter in a cool and scientifically objective spirit was an unsolved problem which was best left to time to clear up. In the history of science one can clearly see that often the very proposition which has at first called out nothing but contradiction has later come to be accepted, although no new proofs in support of it have been brought forward. (Freud 1914, p. 24)

What does Freud have in mind to rescue psychoanalysis from public resistance unless it's a method of proof or persuasion derived from future technology or future research or polemics on behalf of psychoanalysis? But he then expresses the hope that his ideas may one day be accepted without the help of any new proofs at all.

It's a puzzling *non sequitur*. For one thing, when it comes to his patients, Freud describes "a violent and tenacious resistance, which persists throughout the whole length of the treatment." (Freud 1917, p. 286) If the public's resistance is similar in character to his patients' resistance, as Freud himself suggests,[12] it's unlikely to go away on its own. Furthermore, Freud's assertion that objections to scientific theories often go away on their own without further evidence to support them is inaccurate. Revolutionary theories like heliocentricity, evolution, and relativity elicited furious resistance and gained traction only as more supportive arguments and evidence accumulated to overwhelm the opposition. For that matter, the radical theories continued attracting

---

12 "I made a first application of psycho-analysis by explaining to myself that this behaviour of the crowd was a manifestation of the same resistance which I had to struggle against in individual patients." (Freud 1933, p. 138)

objections long after new evidence had put them on a solid footing. Remarkably, in the case of evolution, the battle over validity continues to this day. Freud's wish for deliverance from his critics without a fight seems therefore futile. His assertion that his wish represents the actual state of affairs seems therefore like denial and rationalization.

Admittedly, the parallel to other scientific revolutions has limits. While they too were controversial, no principle of psychology necessarily obstructed the other theories' acceptance. Repression, by contrast, actively hides its existence from sight. Repression and resistance are the "peculiar conditions" that bedevil psychoanalysis alone in its pursuit of proof and which Freud cites again and again as reasons for pessimism:

> I made up my mind not to answer my opponents and, so far as my influence went, to restrain others from polemics. Under the peculiar conditions of the controversy over psycho-analysis it seemed to me very doubtful whether either public or written discussion would avail anything; it was certain which way the majority at congresses and meetings would go, and my faith in the reasonableness and good behaviour of the gentlemen who opposed me was not at any time great. (Freud 1914, p. 39)

This passage, however, also invites suspicion. While it attests accurately to Freud's feelings at one moment in time, it misrepresents his actual deeds over the long term. He did *not* give up on public or written discussions meant to prove the validity of psychoanalysis and to refute critics. In the end, Freud left behind a massive oeuvre of beautifully detailed empirical studies of his patients, of himself, and of quotidian phenomena like parapraxes, dreams, and jokes, along with theories that brilliantly explained his findings. It's not clear whether "the majority" of his audience really rejected him as he claims, either. His ideas in fact circled the globe during his own lifetime, as he himself points out in a lengthy footnote added to the *History* in 1923 (Freud 1914, pp. 33-34n), and again in a 1935 postscript to his *Autobiographical Study*, with even greater optimism for the future of psychoanalysis. (Freud 1925, pp. 71-74) Neither did Freud consistently restrain others from polemics or even consistently pretend that such restraint was necessary. A few pages before asserting the futility of polemics, Freud had in fact praised Ernest Jones's "skill in debate at [medical] congresses in America." (Freud 1914, p. 32)

When he's not fretting and rationalizing his proof aversion, the founder of psychoanalysis seems well aware that proving its merits to the public is both important and achievable. Less than a page after the outburst of pessimism quoted above, he in fact regrets that he didn't enter debate more often and more openly. It's a rare moment of acknowledgment that his reticence—not the public's resistance—might have contributed to the "hostile indifference" to analysis in Vienna:

> It may be that my policy of avoiding wide publicity is to some extent responsible for this. If I had encouraged or allowed the medical societies of Vienna to occupy themselves with psycho-analysis in stormy debates which would have brought into the open all the reproaches and invectives that were on its opponents' tongues or in their hearts—then, perhaps, the ban on psycho-analysis would have been overcome by now…. (Freud 1914, p. 40)[13]

---

13 The initial moment of insight into his own avoidance quickly yields to sarcasm towards his opponents, a typical display of ambivalence over the question whether "to prove or not to prove." The ambivalence is suggestive of internal emotional conflict: a wish to prove counteracted by an emotional resistance to the discomfort attached to proving.

When it comes to psychoanalytic theory (as opposed to efficacy), the whole of the *Introductory Lectures* in fact does everything Freud says he cannot do. The *Lectures* demonstrate the theory's empirical basis with beauty, detail, rational clarity, and explanatory power. As Gay suggests, the *Lectures* in fact succeeded in their aim of popularizing psychoanalysis: "They were widely read and widely translated: perhaps 50,000 copies in German were sold in his lifetime, and there were at least fifteen translations." (Gay 1988, p. 369)

When he's sailing along, deep in the middle of these lectures, Freud has few doubts about the possibility of proof. He knows he's provided it in ample quantities, he knows that still more may be provided with ease, and that resistance has no chance against the power of scientific observation: "And as to the other things that you are anxious not to believe, I will refer you to the findings of analysis and of the direct observation of children and will add that it calls for real ingenuity not to see all this or to see it differently." (Freud 1917, p. 316) "This and very much else of a similar nature will be shown to you by the direct observation of children and by the consideration of clearly retained memories from childhood uninfluenced by analysis." All of the information he has to impart "can be so easily obtained." (Freud 1917, p. 334)

But then doubts cause Freud to retreat from this confidence and to disavow his own efforts at proof. Especially at the beginning and in the end of the *Lectures*, Freud undermines his proofs with doubts about their prospects for success. He discontinues his efforts at proof and justifies having done so with more curious rationalizations and denials. "In medical training you are accustomed to *see* things..." he says at the outset. "In psycho-analysis, alas, everything is different." Freud goes on to declare of psychoanalysis that "it cannot be demonstrated" and "it is only by hearsay that you will

30

get to know psycho-analysis." This is because "you cannot be present as an audience at a psycho-analytic treatment." (Freud 1916-1917, pp. 16-18) The injunction against observation of an analysis is perhaps true in the narrow sense that the audience can't look on without seriously disturbing the process, but it's false that psychoanalytic ideas can't be demonstrated. Freud provides abundant justifications soon thereafter!

Furthermore, all scientists are accustomed to the sort of verification by inference upon which psychoanalysis depends.[14] At the same time that Freud was making his first inferences about unconscious processes, Richard Dixon Oldham was using seismographic records to make inferences about the composition of the earth's unseen core. The new field of virology was at the time proposing to study a germ invisible to light microscopes but inferred to exist because of its effects on plants and bacteria. Wilhelm Röntgen had just discovered an invisible radiation so mysterious he named it the X-ray. The reliance of psychoanalytic research on words and introspections, meanwhile, not seismographs or microscopes or vacuum tubes, made psychoanalytic observations nearer to hand and accessible without any instrumentation. As Freud says, "[T]hey can be confirmed by any observer who cares to see them." (Freud 1917, p. 325)

From the platform of this optimism about proof, Freud might have announced a plan for more research on the model of experimental psychology to verify his hypotheses and investigate the results of his treatments: more standardized studies, perhaps, yielding more codified and reproducible results. He had in fact once held out hopes that such methods could help support his theories:

---

14 Freud convincingly compares analytic inferences to those of archaeologists in his paper "Constructions in Analysis." (Freud 1937, p. 259)

The association experiments started by the Wundt School had been interpreted by them in a psycho-analytic sense.... By this means it had become possible to arrive at rapid experimental confirmation of psycho-analytic observations and to demonstrate directly to students certain connections which an analyst would only have been able to tell them about. The first bridge linking up experimental psychology with psycho-analysis had been built. (Freud 1914, p. 28)

But this work had been done by Jung, whom Freud came to despise, and Freud would show little enthusiasm for building further bridges. Saul Rosenzweig, who tested Freud's theories experimentally—and produced confirmatory results (Rosenzweig and Mason 1934)—describes Freud's reaction to the supportive research in Koch and Leary's *A Century of Psychology as Science* under the heading "Resistance to Experimental Verification." In a letter to Rosenzweig dated February 28, 1934, Freud writes:

I have examined your experimental studies for the verification of psychoanalytic propositions with interest. I cannot put much value on such confirmation because the abundance of reliable observations on which these propositions rest makes them independent of experimental verification. Still, it can do no harm. (Rosenzweig 1985, pp. 172-173)

Rosenzweig observes of Freud:

He came to regard any experimental approach to the verification of psychoanalytic concepts as harboring an undercurrent of personal "resistance" concealed by respectable scientific intent. He may also have rationalized his own resistance with the opinion that artificial laboratory conditions cannot reproduce the repressions of everyday life. (p. 174)

Freud later declined to support Rosenzweig's attempt to create a journal devoted to experimental psychopathology. The repudiation of Rosenzweig's help in proving the validity of psychoanalysis calls to mind what Freud says of his daughter in *The Interpretation of Dreams*: "If my little daughter did not want an apple that was offered to her, she asserted that the apple tasted sour without having tasted it." (Freud 1900, p. 141)

Studies of psychoanalytic efficacy fared no better with Freud. At the end of the *Lectures*, he summarily dismisses them. "Friends of analysis have advised us to meet the threatened publication of our failures with statistics of our successes drawn up by ourselves," he says. "I did not agree to this." (Freud 1917, p. 461) He then points out very real obstacles to the study of psychoanalytic efficacy with special emphasis on the public's irrational prejudice against psychoanalysis. This "prejudice" (*Vorurteil*) seems closely related to his idea of resistance (*Widerstand*), and it's Freud's ultimate reason for scuttling further efforts at proof of psychoanalytic efficacy: his audience is too biased for it to do any good.

But the strongest reason for holding back lay in the realization that in matters of therapy people behave highly irrationally, so that one has no prospect of accomplishing anything with them by rational means. A therapeutic novelty is either received with delirious enthusiasm—as, for instance, when Koch introduced his first tuberculin against tuberculosis to the public—or it is treated with abysmal distrust—like

Jenner's vaccination, which was in fact a blessing and which even to-day has its irreconcilable opponents. There was obviously a prejudice against psycho-analysis. If one had cured a severe case, one might hear people say: 'That proves nothing. He would have recovered on his own account by this time.' ... Nothing can be done against prejudices. (Freud 1917, pp. 461-462)

The reference to Edward Jenner, who developed the first vaccine against smallpox, is instructive. Freud takes comfort from the public's history of wrongheaded, violent resistance to Jenner's ideas, but he neglects to draw an obvious conclusion: proof is important. Without continued efforts at it, Jenner might not have prevailed, and smallpox might not have been cured. Public resistance to psychoanalysis clearly presents a serious obstacle to the task of psychoanalytic proof, but Freud treats resistance not as an obstacle but rather as the decisive, all-powerful factor in order to rationalize his wish to avoid proof and disputation.

Juxtaposing these pessimistic statements with all that Freud in fact achieved in the *Lectures* against resistant prejudices exposes "Nothing can be done against prejudices" as a distortion. He might just as well have said that everything can be done against prejudices. For who in human history did more to combat them than Sigmund Freud, the scientist who taught the world to deconstruct prejudice as a distortion of thought caused by defense mechanisms?

Yet, despite all that the University of Vienna lectures had achieved, Freud denigrated them. He "was inclined to be very severe with these adroit recapitulations of his thought," Gay says. "Unjustly slighting their felicities and their innovative formulations, Freud found little to like in his presentations." (Gay 1988, p. 369)

II. FREUD'S AVERSION TO PROOF: A CASE STUDY

3.3. Reversal: Giving Away Power to the Critics

Freud's critiques of audience resistance carry out another psychodynamic function: the critiques not only help to rationalize his avoidance, but often appear to substitute for efforts at proof. It was as though Freud liked to imagine that critiquing resistance and offering proof were the same thing. Rationally speaking, they are not the same thing, but emotionally speaking, the critique of resistance may have alleviated the stresses aroused by the task of proof. The hypothetical psychodynamic sequence would begin with Freud's desire to conquer his opponents by proof and to demonstrate the antisocial theories of psychoanalysis over their objections; this intention appears to trigger shame and anxiety in his superego; his ego purges the bad feelings by transforming the aggression of proof and the power of knowledge into deference before the unassailable powers of resistance; statements follow to the effect of *I cannot prove because resistance is too strong*; these rationalizations cover the defense's tracks but they don't eradicate all traces of their origins in the superego. The superego remains imprinted in the discussion in the form of moralistic language that is alien to the logic of proof but relevant to the anxiety of demonstrating forbidden knowledge.

The vocabulary of conscience has, for example, infiltrated the following rationalization of proof-avoidance from the *History*: "It was hardly to be expected, however, that during the years when I alone represented psycho-analysis I should develop any particular respect for the world's opinion or any bias towards intellectual appeasement." (Freud 1914, p. 24) Freud denies that anyone could "expect" him to "respect" or "appease" his critics through further dialogue or proof. *Expectations, respect, appeasement*—these are moral or legalistic words, not scientific ones, which imply that Freud has misconstrued the nature of proof according to emotion. He has projected onto his critics a power of moral judgment, a power of conscience, to which he must answer as though the criticism resided in him, and against which he then must rebel: *I will not meet your expectations, I will not respect your judgments, nor appease your demands.* If emotion is left out of the matter, however, proof needn't focus on answering critics' demands. Rather, it can and should focus on refuting critics' incorrect views and advancing one's own.

Consider Galileo, for example, who engaged Jesuit mathematician Christoph Scheiner in epistolary debate about the nature of sunspots in 1612 and 1613. Scheiner wished to defend the Jesuit ideal of the perfection of the sun and argued that sunspots were not imperfections on its surface but satellites. Galileo correctly contended that sunspots were irregularities belonging to the matter of the sun itself. Albert Van Helden writes, "Although he was polite to Scheiner, Galileo refuted his arguments and there was little doubt as to who was the winner of this dispute." (Van Helden 1995) Galileo may have been polite, but he and Scheiner disliked one another. Far from appeasing Scheiner, Galileo set out to destroy Scheiner's arguments and advance his own. Whereas world opinion on the validity of heliocentricity and psychoanalysis is important, critics' expectations are irrelevant.

The conscience vocabulary Freud uses suggests he has by contrast chosen to see proof as an act of obeisance to the powers that be, instead of the aggressive, competitive act of a Galileo at war with a benighted Christoph Scheiner. It's a view of proof that's fully comprehensible as a projection of inner criticism or a superego-determined identification with critics, but is not wholly commensurate with reality. Rachel Blass notes an instance of Freud's identification with "the external critic" in a passage from *Moses and Monotheism.* (Blass 2003, p. 672) "Once again I am prepared to find myself blamed for having presented my reconstruction of the early history of the people of Israel with too great and unjustified certainty," Freud writes. "I shall not feel very severely hit by this criticism, since it finds an echo in my own judgment." (Freud 1939, p. 41) Dismissal of inner and outer criticism, Blass suggests, helped unfetter Freud's introspective research. When Freud dismisses external critics' expectations instead of challenging critics' arguments, however—as though the two acts were the same—he misses an opportunity to strengthen psychoanalysis's public standing. And if he misses opportunities to advance his life's work, he must do so according to an unconscious motive.

It's a valid question whether Strachey's translation has perhaps introduced superego connotations. Freud's original German word choices, however, focus even more directly on who is permitted to say and do what. Where Strachey has "It was hardly to be expected," Freud originally wrote "*wird wohl niemand erwarten dürfen.*"[15] *Dürfen* means "allow" or "permit" so a more literal translation might be, "surely no one has a right to expect." Where Strachey has "world's opinion," Freud originally wrote "*Urteil der Welt.*" "Opinion" may be a soft translation of *Urteil*, which can mean "verdict" or even "sentence." Where Strachey has "intellectual appeasement," Freud originally wrote "*intellektuellen Nachgiebigkeit,*" which can also be translated as "intellectual compliance." *Nachgiebigkeit* is used in physics, for example, to mean "compliance" or "squishiness." It's as though for Freud proof meant softening himself and conforming to judgments, as opposed to continuing the advance of his unyielding ideas into enemy territory.

---

15 I do not speak German. A number of reviewers of my paper on proof aversion became preoccupied by my use of German. I had the impression that this somehow made them feel insecure or competitive with me. Because I don't speak German, I have relied on help from German-speakers and on Google Translate and Google Search in order to test my observations about Freud's word connotations in German.

Similarly, when Freud speaks of "demonstrating to the opponents of psycho-analysis *suaviter in modo* their injustice and arbitrariness" (Freud 1914, p. 40) his concept of proof seems again infiltrated by an alien concern with fairness and conscience. He didn't need to demonstrate to the critics that they were unjust and arbitrary; he needed to demonstrate to the public that his critics were wrong. Galileo didn't debate Christoph Scheiner to make him sorry, nor to persuade Scheiner to accept heliocentricity; the "debate" in fact took place in letters addressed to a third party, the Augsburg scholar Marc Welser. Galileo wanted to persuade the public that Scheiner was wrong, and he did, even if it meant he had to spend the remainder of his life under house arrest reciting the Seven Penitential Psalms—and it did. Despite Freud's material successes demonstrating psychoanalysis, despite his real experiences with Welser-like figures who did give psychoanalysis a fair hearing, he could not think of public resistance as anything but universal and monolithic in nature. If Freud unconsciously identified with his critics, perhaps that's why he couldn't imagine not being criticized.

4. Summing Up the Diagnosis of Proof Aversion

To sum up the thesis thus far: Freud exhibits shame and anxiety when he attempts to demonstrate psychoanalytic knowledge to the public, and he exhibits a consequent aversion to proving, characterized by defense mechanisms such as: projection of inner criticism; avoidance of criticism covered over by rationalizations; and a reversal in which the power of scientific proof is transformed into the critics' power of resistance to psychoanalysis.

In *The Interpretation of Dreams*, Freud actually acknowledges that conscience may corrupt the presentation of psychoanalytic ideas. Freud explains dreams' censorious distortions of wishes, then elaborates:

> I will try to seek a social parallel to this internal event in the mind. Where can we find a similar distortion of a psychical act in social life? Only where two persons are concerned, one of whom possesses a certain degree of power which the second is obliged to take into account. In such a case the second person will distort his psychical acts or, as we might put it, will dissimulate. The politeness which I practise every day is to a large extent dissimulation of this kind; and *when I interpret my dreams for my readers I am obliged to adopt similar distortions*. The poet complains of the need for these distortions in the words:
>
> *Das Beste, was du wissen kannst,*
> *Darfst du den Buben doch nicht sagen.*
> ['After all, the best of what you know may not be told to boys.']¹⁶
>
> A similar difficulty confronts the political writer who has disagreeable truths to tell to those in authority. If he presents them undisguised, the authorities will suppress his words— after they have been spoken, if his pronouncement was an oral one, but beforehand, if he had intended to make it in print. *A writer must beware of the censorship, and on its account he*

---

16 The editors of the *Standard Edition* tell us how often in letters, speeches, and books Freud quoted this line from Goethe's *Faust*. He quotes it twice in *The Interpretation of Dreams* alone, the second time on p. 453, just after this statement: "I reflected on the amount of self-discipline it was costing me to offer the public even my book upon dreams—I should have to give away so much of my own private character in it."

must soften and distort the expression of his opinion. (Freud 1900, pp. 141-142)[17]

Public demonstration of psychoanalysis is precisely one of those situations "where two persons are concerned, one of whom [the critic] possesses a certain degree of power which the second [the expositor of psychoanalysis] is obliged to take into account." It's also a situation where Freud "has disagreeable truths to tell to those in authority." He feels "obliged" to censor his dream interpretations. As Goethe said, the best of what Freud knows cannot be told—or so he feels.

Countless times in *The Interpretation of Dreams* Freud notes the interference of self-censorship. When, for instance, he breaks off the interpretation of his dream about his patient Irma's injection, he gives this excuse:

[C]onsiderations which arise in the case of every dream of my own restrain me from pursuing my interpretative work. If anyone should feel tempted to express a hasty condemnation of my reticence, I would advise him to make the experiment of being franker than I am. For the moment I am satisfied with the achievement of this one piece of fresh knowledge. (Freud 1900, p. 121)

Freud has prevailed against his own resistance to acquire complete knowledge of the latent meaning of the dream, but self-censorship prevents him from sharing it all. Therefore, we must settle for a partial demonstration of what he knows and the rest we must take on faith. Similarly, in his analysis of his dream of Count Thun he remarks:

---

17 Emphasis added.

I must also refrain from any detailed analysis of the two remaining episodes of the dream.... It will rightly be suspected that what compels me to make this suppression is sexual material.... After all, there are many things which one has to keep secret from other people but of which one makes no secret to oneself.... (Freud 1900, pp. 212-213)

It's chastity and embarrassment that cause Freud to break off the public pursuit of knowledge at these moments, and this is of course understandable. In other contexts, however, I'm inclined to think that Freud engaged in self-censorship without knowing it; in other words, I suspect that defense mechanisms curtailed or interrupted his public presentations because of an unconscious sense of chastity and embarrassment. And that's in essence Freud's whole problem with proof.

Freud tells us that his one-time colleague Wilhelm Stekel had a name for unexamined "complexes" and distortions of judgment among psychoanalysts: *blinde Flecken,* or blind spots. (Freud 1912, p. 116) If Freud never thoroughly examined the distortions and inhibitions affecting his efforts at proof, the reason would seem to be just that: a blind spot in the field of his otherwise perspicacious vision. Given the charged emotional phenomena with which all psychoanalysts must deal, such blind spots and proof aversions may very well be a professional hazard. The abundant repetition of Freud's patterns among later psychoanalysts would suggest as much.

That said, particular historical and personal circumstances must also have contributed to Freud's proof aversion—first among them his unique position as the founder of psychoanalysis and discoverer of the unconscious. A closer look at some of those particular circumstances may help to explain the nature and the strength of Freud's proof aversion, and may help to justify contemporary expositors of psychoanalysis in moving beyond him.

5. Freud's Oedipus Complex: Curiosity and Ambition

In his *Autobiographical Study*, Freud names two personal qualities that propelled him to his great discoveries: curiosity and independence of mind. This chapter examines the ways that Freud's strongly developed *Wißtrieb*, or epistemophilic instinct, (Freud 1909, p. 245) informed both his curiosity and his ambition, and how it may have shaped his inner conflicts. Autobiographical passages in his writings suggest that his own infantile sexual researches shaped him into the scientist he became and instigated in him a compulsion for secrecy as he went about his adult sexual research. Other autobiographical material suggests that Freud measured his powers against his father's, specifically in the domain of knowledge; and that his prowess as a scientist made him feel "wrecked by success" when he compared himself to his humble, relatively uneducated father. Both the compulsion for secrecy in research and the guilt about outshining his father in the realm of knowledge may have contributed to Freud's ambivalence about public demonstrations of his revolutionary discoveries.

5.1. Infantile Sexual Researches and Secrecy

It's a touching motif that recurs throughout the Freudian oeuvre: the figure of a small boy who asks his father and his pregnant mother where babies come from and is told a lie about a stork. References to the child questioner and the duplicitous tale of the stork appear in *The Interpretation of Dreams* (Freud 1900, p. 251); in "On the Sexual

Theories of Children" (Freud 1908, pp. 213-214); in the "Little Hans" case history (Freud 1909, p. 10); in "Leonardo Da Vinci and a Memory of his Childhood" (Freud 1910, p. 78); and in the section on "The Sexual Researches of Childhood" that Freud added to *Three Essays on the Theory of Sexuality* in 1915 (Freud 1905, p. 194).

Even when Freud describes this parable of infantile sexual research in connection with others, it seems to allude plainly to Freud's personal biography. Freud was the eldest child of Amalia and Jacob Freud, and Freud generally tells the story of infantile sexual research from the perspective of an eldest child researching the birth of a younger sibling. Furthermore, Freud assigns a special role to infantile sexual researches in the personal development of all daring scientists, like himself and Leonardo Da Vinci.

> When we find that in the picture presented by a person's character a single instinct has developed an excessive strength, as did the craving for knowledge [*Wißbegierde*] in Leonardo, we look for the explanation in a special disposition.... We consider it probable that an instinct like this of excessive strength was already active in the subject's earliest childhood, and that its supremacy was established by impressions in the child's life. We make the further assumption that it found reinforcement from what were originally sexual instinctual forces, so that later it could take the place of a part of the subject's sexual life. Thus a person of this sort would, for example, pursue research with the same passionate devotion that another would give to his love, and he would be able to investigate instead of loving....
>
> The core of his [Leonardo's] nature, and the secret of it, would appear to be that after his curiosity had been activated

43

in infancy in the service of sexual interests he succeeded in sublimating the greater part of his libido into an urge for research.... (Freud 1910, pp. 77-80)

Freud proposes that Leonardo's scientific curiosity was a sublimation of his childhood sexual curiosity, even though little is known of Leonardo Da Vinci's childhood; it seems conspicuously autobiographical, as Ernest Jones has observed: "[M]uch of what Freud said when he penetrated into Leonardo's personality was at the same time a self-description; there was surely an extensive identification between Leonardo and himself." (Jones 1955, p. 432) Freud himself admits, "[B]iographers are fixated on their heroes in a quite special way. In many cases they have chosen their hero as the subject of their studies because—for reasons of their personal emotional life—they have felt a special affection for him from the very first." (Freud 1910, p. 130) If Freud saw infantile sexual research as an influential factor in Leonardo's development into a scientist, such research was clearly just as influential in Freud's own development.

After all, the adult Freud's specific variety of research was even more closely related to infantile sexual research than Leonardo's. Leonardo may have sublimated childhood sexual curiosity into all kinds of researches, but as an adult scientist Freud conducted specifically sexual research that aimed to penetrate society's disguises and subterfuges in order to learn human beings' most closely guarded secrets. This sort of scientific curiosity doesn't just derive its motivation from the sexual curiosity of childhood, it actually resembles the sexual curiosity of childhood.

Freud's biographers have noted as much. Jones cites Freud's memory of "penetrating into his parents' bedroom out of (sexual) curiosity and being ordered out by an irate father" (Jones 1953, p. 7) and traces Freud's scientific interests back to such sexual curiosity.

II. FREUD'S AVERSION TO PROOF: A CASE STUDY

Freud's later discovery of the Oedipus complex, Jones suggests, owed more than a little to the mysterious and troubling family relations of his infancy and "the spur it gave to his curiosity." (p. 11) At the end of the first chapter of his biography, Jones sums up the connection between Freud the scientist and Freud the infantile sexual researcher:

> He had a veritable passion to *understand*. At the outset this need to understand was stimulated in a way from which there was no escape. His intelligence was given a task from which he never flinched till, forty years later, he found the solution in a fashion that made his name immortal. (p. 14)

That is, Freud began the task of understanding human sexuality in infancy and completed it as a mature scientist "forty years later," in the late 1890s, when he conducted his self-analysis. Gay agrees with Jones's analysis:

> While he chose medicine freely, he wrote in his "Autobiographical Study," he "felt no particular partiality for the position and activity of a physician in those early years, nor, by the way, later. Rather, I was moved by a sort of greed for knowledge."[18] This is among the most suggestive autobiographical passages Freud ever published. Freud the psychoanalyst would later point to the sexual curiosity of youngsters as the true source of scientific inquisitiveness. (Gay 1988, p. 25)

Gay then follows Jones in interpreting Freud's incursion into his parents' bedroom as a "straightforward, rather coarse expression

---

18 The German word Freud uses to describe his scientific "greed for knowledge" is identical to that which he uses for curiosity in children, *Wißbegierde*, and close to his word for the epistemophilic instinct, *Wißtrieb*.

of such curiosity," which Freud the adult scientist "later refined into research." (p. 25)

In order to further appreciate the significance of childhood sexual researches in Freud's early life, consider Freud's first lengthy discussion of the subject, which appears in his 1908 paper "On the Sexual Theories of Children." The passage begins with Freud's speculation that pregnancies are generally the instigator of children's curiosity about the male-female gender difference:

> A child's desire for knowledge on this point ... is aroused under the goad of the self-seeking instincts that dominate him, when—perhaps after the end of his second year—he is confronted with the arrival of a new baby.... The loss of his parents' care, which he actually experiences or justly fears, and the presentiment that from now on he must for evermore share all his possessions with the newcomer, have the effect of awakening his emotions and sharpening his capacities for thought. The elder child expresses unconcealed hostility towards his rival, which finds vent in unfriendly criticisms of it.... (Freud 1908, p. 212)

Freud acknowledges that children may of course begin their sexual researches for numerous reasons, but as he tells and retells the parable of the child sex researcher, he almost always returns to the conspicuously autobiographical detail of the birth of a younger sibling. The "unfriendly criticisms" of the elder toward the younger child also seem to point to one of the serious problems of Freud's own childhood—the death in 1858 of his younger brother Julius, when Freud was not yet 2 and Julius was 7 months old. In a letter to Fliess dated October 3, 1897, Freud remembers "that I greeted my brother (who was a year my junior and died after a few months) with ill-wishes and genuine childish jealousy, and that his death left the germ of self-reproaches in me." (Masson 1985, p. 268) Another sibling, Freud's sister Anna, arrived when Freud was two-and-a-half, but in the letter Freud gives Julius pride of place over Anna in determining "what is neurotic, but also what is intense, in all my friendships."

The account of childhood sexual curiosity in "On the Sexual Theories of Children" continues:

> At the instigation of these feelings and worries, the child now comes to be occupied with the first, grand problem of life and asks himself the question: *'Where do babies come from?'*...
>
> ... Where a child is not already too much intimidated, he sooner or later adopts the direct method of demanding an answer from his parents or those in charge of him, who are in his eyes the source of all knowledge. This method, however, fails. The child receives either evasive answers or a rebuke for his curiosity, or he is dismissed with the mythologically significant piece of information which, in German countries, runs: 'The stork brings the babies; it fetches them out of the water.' I have reason to believe that far more children than their parents suspect are dissatisfied with this solution and meet it with energetic doubts, which, however, they do not always openly admit. I know of a three-year-old boy who, after receiving this piece of enlightenment, disappeared—to the terror of his nurse. He was found at the edge of the big pond adjoining the country house, to which he had hurried in order to see the babies in the water. I also know of another boy who could only allow his disbelief to find expression in a hesitant remark that he knew better, that it was not a stork that brought

babies but a heron. It seems to me to follow from a great deal of information I have received that children refuse to believe the stork theory and that from the time of this first deception and rebuff they nourish a distrust of adults and have a suspicion of there being something forbidden which is being withheld from them by the 'grown-ups,' and that they consequently hide their further researches under a cloak of secrecy. With this, however, the child also experiences the first occasion for a 'psychical conflict,' in that views for which he feels an instinctual kind of preference, but which are not 'right' in the eyes of the grown-ups, come into opposition with other views, which are supported by the authority of the grown-ups without being acceptable to him himself. Such a psychical conflict may soon turn into a 'psychical dissociation.' The set of views which are bound up with being 'good,' but also with a cessation of reflection, become the dominant and conscious views; while the other set, for which the child's work of research has meanwhile obtained fresh evidence, but which are not supposed to count, become the suppressed and 'unconscious' ones. The nuclear complex of a neurosis is in this way brought into being. (pp. 212-214)

The last line seems to imply that all neuroses arise from the foundation of unhappy infantile sexual researches. Perhaps they do; but that's a narrower explanation of the etiology of neurosis than Freud generally employs. He describes neuroses arising from myriad childhood impressions, and the common denominator in those formative experiences is not frustrated knowledge per se, but frustrated instinct. Neurosis occurs, Freud teaches, when instincts meet with forces of reality that compel the instincts into an association with anxiety, guilt, or shame, such that the ego represses the instincts and distorts their expression and thereby evades the feelings of anxiety, guilt, and shame.

If in this instance Freud overstates the role of sexual researches in the genesis of neurosis, perhaps it's because curiosity was so vital to the organization of his own early conflicts. In his Leonardo study, Freud asserts:

> [Leonardo] was confronted in his early life with one problem more than other children—[and] began to brood on this riddle with special intensity, and so at a tender age became a researcher, tormented as he was by the great question of where babies come from and what the father has to do with their origin. (Freud 1910, p. 92)

Some eldest children it seems, like Freud and Leonardo, are burdened more than others with the problem of where babies come from.

And if *Where do babies come from?* was "the first, grand problem" of Freud's life, then the second problem appears to have been, *How do you get rid of them?* Freud speaks to the close connection between the two questions in his Leonardo essay: "Researches are directed to the question of where babies come from, exactly as if the child were looking for ways and means to avert so undesired an event." (Freud 1910, p. 78) It stands to reason that a child of Freud's intelligence would research the origins of his unwelcome siblings with an eye toward eliminating them, and it furthermore stands to reason that Freud might reproach himself for his anti-baby research because he had a baby brother who actually died.

Freud's recollection of seeing his mother undressed on a train provides another small scrap of evidence that his infantile sexual curiosity played a role in the formation of his own neurosis. He writes to Fliess:

> [L]ater (between the ages of two and two-and-a-half) my libido was stirred up towards *matrem*, namely on the occasion of a journey with her from Leipzig to Vienna, during which we must have spent the night together and I must have had an opportunity of seeing her *nudam*. (Masson 1985, pp. 261-262)

It was on a trip to Leipzig, Ernest Jones tells us, that Freud first developed "a 'phobia' of travelling by train, from which he suffered a good deal for about a dozen years (1887-99) before he was able to dispel it by analysis." (Jones 1953, p. 13) Was there a connection between the phobia and the excitement and confusion of seeing his mother naked?

In *The Interpretation of Dreams*, Freud tells us of another bit of travel neurosis. He says he's always yearned to see Rome but has forbidden himself from going, and he gives this peculiar excuse— "for at the season of the year when it is possible for me to travel, residence in Rome must be avoided for reasons of health." Then, in two footnotes added in 1909 and 1925, he says, "I discovered long since that it only needs a little courage to fulfil wishes which till then have been regarded as unattainable; and thereafter became a constant pilgrim to Rome." (Freud 1900, p. 194) Gay summarizes the deep emotional meanings with which Freud invested the city of Rome: "A charged and ambivalent symbol, Rome stood for Freud's most potent concealed erotic, and only slightly less concealed aggressive wishes, and glanced at their secret history." (Gay 1988, p. 132)

The story of seeing his mother undressed on a train and his irrational hesitancy to visit Rome suggest that perhaps Freud's travel phobia arose in order to subdue his curiosity to see new places—both geographical and anatomical—because the curiosity made him anxious. Like the infant Freud's fantasy that he killed his baby brother with his malignant and "over-powerful"[19] curiosity, the travel anecdotes point to the dangers of knowing, or wanting to know too much. And if the pleasure and power of seeing and knowing felt too shameful or dangerous to pursue in the open, perhaps Freud as a child developed a strategy of researching in private, just as other children, Freud asserts in "On the Sexual Theories of Children," "consequently hide their further researches under a cloak of secrecy." (Freud 1908, p. 214) Jones describes Freud's well-known penchant for privacy and secrecy in his adulthood (Jones 1955, pp. 408-410), and indeed traces it to "Freud's earliest years," in which Jones surmises "there had been extremely strong motives for concealing some important phase of his development—perhaps even from himself." (p. 409)

Freud's penchant for secrecy, rooted perhaps in his infantile sexual researches, is of course more than a little germane to understanding his later attitude to research and proof. To put it more directly: it seems reasonable to suppose that Freud's need for secrecy in his infantile sexual researches demanded similar secrecy in his adult sexual researches. Maybe the presentation of proof was for Freud akin to admitting publicly to the secret researches he'd done as a child in order to rid himself of his siblings and to restore himself to his mother's exclusive affections. Maybe sexual research could not be discussed too openly, or before too large an audience, without compromising the necessary secrecy of it. Often in his public demonstrations, Freud

---

19 After asserting that "the craving for knowledge [*Wißbegierde*]" had "an excessive strength" in Leonardo (Freud 1910, p. 77), Freud reiterates that Leonardo possessed in childhood "an over-powerful instinct for investigation" [*des übermächtigen Forschertriebes*] which was at first sexual in nature. (p. 78)

will tell what he knows, but will not say exactly how he came to know it. Thus, when he writes in *The Interpretation of Dreams*, "After all, there are many things which one has to keep secret from other people but of which one makes no secret to oneself," (Freud 1900, p. 213) it's as if he's saying, *I know where babies come from, but I can't tell you how I learned it*. To tell how he knows would be to admit to his "over-powerful" appetite for sightseeing in such forbidden lands as one sees on trips to Leipzig and Rome.

5.2. The Knowledge Contest with Jacob Freud

Freud had a young mother who was constantly pregnant in his early life, and a baby brother who died. Sexual researches aimed at reclaiming his mother and killing off his siblings could on their own account create guilt, anxiety, and shame. And a small boy's curiosity to see his mother naked could of course create castration anxiety if, in seeing his mother nude, he invented alarming theories to explain to himself why her body was so different from his own. And then there's the particular kind of father Freud had. Jacob Freud had two sons by a previous marriage and was already in his forties by the time Sigmund was born and Julius died; Freud's mother Amalia had scarcely entered her twenties. Jones tells us that Freud once thought his half-brother Philipp was his father and "tearfully begged" Philipp "not to make his mother again pregnant." (Jones 1955, p. 434)

When Freud describes the child sex researcher forming theories to explain "the obscure part played by the father" in procreation (Freud 1910, p. 79) and pondering "what the father has to do with" the origin of babies (p. 92), one wonders if he refers not only to the disproportionate role of mothers in making babies but to the "obscure" figure of Jacob Freud, the mild-mannered, older father whom Freud once doubted had the potency to impregnate his young mother. The following famous story seems emblematic of the troubling way that Freud sometimes thought about his father: with a disappointed and perhaps guilty sense of his father's impotence.

> 'When I was a young man,' he [Jacob Freud] said, 'I went for a walk one Saturday in the streets of your birthplace; I was well dressed, and had a new fur cap on my head. A Christian came up to me and with a single blow knocked off my cap into the mud and shouted: "Jew! get off the pavement!" ' 'And what did you do?' I asked. 'I went into the roadway and picked up my cap,' was his quiet reply. This struck me as unheroic conduct on the part of the big, strong man who was holding the little boy by the hand. (Freud 1900, p. 197)

When Freud compares his father to himself, however, the competition does not take place in the street; it takes place in the realm of knowledge. Consider Freud's covertly autobiographical discussion of childhood sexual researches in the Leonardo essay. As a snapshot of Sigmund Freud asking his own parents about babies, it suggests a parallel disappointment in their cowardice or their inability to explain:

> [Children] date their intellectual independence from this act of disbelief, [and] they often feel in serious opposition to adults and in fact never afterwards forgive them for having deceived them here about the true facts of the case. They investigate along their own lines, divine the baby's presence inside its mother's body, and following the lead of the impulses of their own sexuality form theories of babies originating from eating, of their being born through the bowels, and of the obscure part played by the father. (Freud 1910, p. 79)

Isn't this Freud talking about his own childhood? Leonardo would have had little opportunity to divine a baby's presence inside his mother's body since he had no siblings until he was at least an adolescent. Then there's the matter of the child's "intellectual independence" [*geistige Selbständigkeit*], which follows his rejection of the stork theory. Intellectual independence was certainly Freud's defining trait—in others' eyes, but also in his own. (Freud 1925, p. 9)

Assuming the passage does provide an accurate window onto Freud's own sexual researches as a child, it would appear that his intellectual independence originated in a disappointment with his parents, who either declined to explain babies or told an unconvincing story about storks, but in either case were a poor source of information. As the discussion of Leonardo's intellectual emancipation continues, Freud singles out the "obscure" figure of the father as the more important of the two parents in forging the son's recognition of his own intellectual powers.

In most other human beings—no less to-day than in primaeval times—the need for support from an authority of some sort is so compelling that their world begins to totter if that authority is threatened. Only Leonardo could dispense with that support; he would not have been able to do so had he not learnt in the first years of his life to do without his father. His later scientific research, with all its boldness and independence, presupposed the existence of infantile sexual researches uninhibited by his father, and was a prolongation of them with the sexual element excluded. (Freud 1910, pp. 122-123)

Surely, Freud identifies with Leonardo when he asserts that the great Renaissance man "escaped being intimidated by his father during his earliest childhood," and when he asserts that this condition enabled Leonardo to "cast away the fetters of authority" in all his researches. (p. 123) In this account of scientific genius, a father like Ser Piero Da Vinci or Jacob Freud who does not "intimidate" his son helps incubate the self-reliance necessary for the later flowering of the son's intellectual prowess. But then it's a bittersweet celebration; these exhilarating early researches also bring frustration and despair: "Where a child is not already too much intimidated, he sooner or later adopts the direct method of demanding an answer from his parents or those in charge of him, who are in his eyes the source of all knowledge. This method, however, fails." (Freud 1908, p. 212) "The impression caused by this failure in the first attempt at intellectual independence appears to be of a lasting and deeply depressing kind." (Freud 1910, p. 79)

A child's parents fail to answer his questions despite being "in his eyes the source of all knowledge." If Freud asked his father Jacob to explain babies, but Jacob wouldn't or couldn't, perhaps it left Freud feeling adventurous and self-reliant but also exposed. One wonders if young Freud did not feel on some level that a man who cannot explain babies *is* a baby, and that in consequence of his own superior powers of explanation and independence of judgment, he was more intellectually powerful than his father. Freud knew more than the "big, strong man" who was supposed to know everything. His father seemed old, uninvolved with babies, and incapable of explaining them, and so Freud believed his brother Philip had sired Julius. In the world of Freud's early childhood, it seems, sons are the ones who make both babies and explanations, not fathers.

That could be a heavy burden of power and responsibility for a child. "Knowledge is power," as Francis Bacon said, and it would seem that Freud intuitively perceived that connection from an early age and measured his own intellectual power in comparison with his father's lack of sophistication. Feeling so "over-powerful" in curiosity and knowledge could of course foster an equally over-powerful guilt, a guilt opposed to further triumphs in the domain of knowledge. When Freud, exhilarated by his own intellectual powers, launched his self-reliant researches into the origins of babies, did he also perceive in that lonely task his father's haunting absence? Did he believe in a childlike way that he'd killed his father with his powerful and competitive intellect? Was that why intellectual independence was "of a lasting and deeply depressing kind"?

When Freud writes about other events in his own past, he continues to underscore the idea that Jacob Freud was unhelpful or even opposed to his son's education and his son's preparations to become a great scientist. And in turn he underscores the pain and guilt his father caused him by failing to support his pursuit of greatness through learning. While analyzing his "Dream of the Botanical Monograph," for example, Freud recalls this scene from his early childhood, which triangulates the relationship between himself, his father, and his learning in a striking way:

> It had once amused my father to hand over a book with *coloured plates* (an account of a journey through Persia) for me and my eldest sister to destroy. Not easy to justify from the educational point of view! I had been five years old at the time and my sister not yet three; and the picture of the two of us blissfully pulling the book to pieces (leaf by leaf, like an *artichoke*, I found myself saying) was almost the only plastic memory that I retained from that period of my life. (Freud 1900, p. 172)

The scene casts his father as a Philistine who does not respect books and has a backwards attitude to secular learning and travel.[20] Freud then reports how he contradicted his father's Philistinism with his own lifelong bibliophilia, a close relative of his epistemophilia:

> Then, when I became a student, I had developed a passion for collecting and owning books, which was analogous to my liking for learning out of monographs.... I had always, from the time I first began to think about myself, referred this first passion of mine back to the childhood memory I have mentioned. (p. 172)

Immediately, another memory surfaces in which Jacob Freud again thwarts Freud's bibliophilia. "I had early discovered, of course, that passions often lead to sorrow," Freud writes a sentence on. "When I was seventeen I had run up a largish account at the bookseller's and had nothing to meet it with; and my father had scarcely taken it as an excuse that my inclinations might have chosen a worse outlet." (p. 173)

In Freud's recollections of his university years and medical training, he depicts financial insecurity as one of the chief antagonists in his struggle to educate himself, and he blames his father for the money problems. Freud describes his father's financial ruin as a hindrance to his own growth and development in his paper "Screen Memories": "When I was about three, the branch of industry in which my father was concerned met with a catastrophe. He lost all his means and we were forced to leave the place and move to a large town. Long and difficult years followed, of which, as it seems to me, nothing was

---

20 Jacob Freud was a secular, enlightened Jew but he had little education apart from reading the Bible and the Talmud and had exhausted his worldliness in immigrating to Vienna. (Richards 2014, pp. 989, 992; Freud 1936, p. 247)

worth remembering." (Freud 1899, p. 312) But he did remember one thing from that period: destroying a book under his father's Philistine influence. Thus Freud seems to represent the whole period of his father's business failure with that memory of his father seducing him to damage a book—as if his father's ruin has created a psychological necessity that he should imagine the ruin of his own education, the destruction of his own growing power in the sphere of knowledge. It's as though he must sacrifice his own greatest strength, his knowledge and intellect, precisely because he feels guilty about possessing it when his father possesses so little in the way of either education or business success or money.

This pattern also shows up in a letter to Martha Bernays dated January 10, 1884, in which Freud says, "Yesterday I met Father in the street, still full of projects, still hoping. I took it upon myself to write to Emanuel and Phillipp [Freud's older half-brothers] urging them to help Father out of his present predicament. He doesn't want to do it himself since he considers himself badly treated." (E. Freud 1961, p. 86) Directly after Freud relays to Martha this dismaying news of his father's persistent money troubles, Freud launches into a prolonged, abashed confession that he that day accepted money from his old religion teacher Samuel Hammerschlag. The juxtaposition of his father's impecunity in one sentence with his shame at having to accept money in the very next clearly demonstrates the association between the two things. Unstated, perhaps, is Freud's disappointment that his father has never been able to help him financially, and that he consequently has to turn for help to other father figures, like Hammerschlag. A repressed hatred for his father and anxiety about his father's impotence must, in other words, have played some background role in his shame about accepting money.

In "Screen Memories," Freud describes his father's failed attempt to rectify the financial insecurity he bestowed upon his son. The plan is harebrained and once again interferes with Freud's pursuit of knowledge: "[M]y father and my uncle had concocted a plan by which I was to exchange the abstruse subject of my studies for one of more practical value, settle down, after my studies were completed, in the place where my uncle lived, and marry my cousin." (p. 314) Obviously, Freud did not capitulate to his father's parochial stratagems, but instead persevered against his father, and against his own inner resistance, in order to become a scientist.

In Freud's dreams he celebrates his own intellectual powers in defiance of the limitations he feels emanating from this financially and intellectually weak, Philistine, and censorious *imago* of his father. The dream-thoughts behind Freud's Dream of the Botanical Monograph, and behind his dream of Count Thun, in particular illuminate Freud's wishes to know more than his ignorant father alongside wishes to honor him by knowing less.

It's the interpretation of the latter dream that yields Freud's famous memory of his father's prediction that "the boy will come to nothing." Besides being a standout in the history of failed prognostication, the episode sticks in Freud's memory as an emblem of his father's opposition to his success in becoming a great scientist:

When I was seven or eight years old there was another domestic scene, which I can remember very clearly. One evening before going to sleep I disregarded the rules which modesty lays down and obeyed the calls of nature in my parents' bedroom while they were present. In the course of his reprimand, my father let fall the words: 'The boy will come to nothing.' This must have been a frightful blow to my ambition,

59

for references to this scene are still constantly recurring in my dreams and are always linked with an enumeration of my achievements and successes, as though I wanted to say: 'You see, I *have* come to something.' (p. 216)

The Count Thun dream redresses this insult by a reversal of the urination scene in his parents' bedroom:

Once more I was in front of the station, but this time in the company of an elderly gentleman.... He appeared to be blind, at all events with one eye, and I handed him a male glass urinal (which we had to buy or had bought in town). So I was a sick-nurse and had to give him the urinal because he was blind. (p. 210)

Freud makes the following interpretation:

The older man (clearly my father, since his blindness in one eye referred to his unilateral glaucoma) was now micturating in front of me, just as I had in front of him in my childhood. In the reference to his glaucoma I was reminding him of the cocaine, which had helped him in the operation, as though I had in that way kept my promise. Moreover, I was making fun of him; I had to hand him the urinal because he was blind, and I revelled in allusions to my discoveries in connection with the theory of hysteria, of which I felt so proud. (pp. 216-217)

By juxtaposing himself in the dream with an older man who can't see, Freud seems to have created a pictogram of his triumph over his father in the domain of knowledge. Freud has far-reaching vision and a knowledge of hysteria which surpasses even that of his fellow clinicians, while his father is half-blind and helpless; the dream-work has encoded differences in intellectual power through an ocular metaphor.

But the reference to blindness and sight is more specific and more dramatic than that, as Freud explains here and also in his interpretation of the Dream of the Botanical Monograph. In his interpretation of the botanical monograph, Freud says the monograph represented his paper on cocaine, which led directly to Karl Koller's demonstration of its anesthetic properties in the eye. Shortly after Koller's study was published, Freud says, Jacob Freud had in fact required surgery for glaucoma and Koller himself had administered the anesthesia. (pp. 170-171) So in dreaming about an old man's blindness in his dream of Count Thun, Freud explains that he was dreaming about his father's glaucoma surgery and the heroic role that his own intellect had played in rescuing his father from blindness. His father (or anyway his superego's introjection of his father) had darkened Freud's world with his opposition to Freud's curiosity and ambition; but Freud's research literally helped to save his father's vision with ophthalmic anesthesia.

Dreams that concern Jacob Freud's death and burial return to the theme of vision and blindness, knowledge and ignorance. Jacob Freud died on October 23, 1896, and on the night after the funeral, Freud dreamed about it, as he told Fliess in a letter dated November 2, 1896. In the dream, Freud says he saw a notice posted in his barbershop saying, "You are requested to close the eyes." (Masson 1985, p. 202) Freud notes in the letter and in *The Interpretation of Dreams* that the notice has several meanings; the manifest meaning instructs Freud that he should perform a funeral rite and close his dead father's eyes. But because the notice says *"the* eyes" instead of "his eyes," Freud also interprets the message as an instruction that he should close his own eyes, i.e. that he should overlook something. (Freud 1900, pp. 317-318)

61

Neither in the letter nor in *The Interpretation of Dreams* does he say what he's meant to overlook; it would seem that in closing his eyes, Freud has either overlooked the meaning of the dream or censored it from the letter and the published account.

In any case, as often happens in dreams, the answer seems to be hiding in plain sight: doesn't the dream underneath instruct that Freud, on the occasion of outliving his father, should blind himself, just as his father was blinded by glaucoma? And by blinding himself, is he not essentially pledging to forfeit the lifelong contest of vision and knowledge he carried on with his father? Is he not obliging his father by a cessation of looking and knowing, a cessation of the curiosity and ambition that met with his father's disapproval (at least in his own imagination)? By 1896, Freud had gazed on vistas previously unknown to psychological science, and had become so much greater than his father in the realm of knowledge. It seems to be this act of patricide and domination over his father which Freud himself has censored or "overlooked."

All of this material suggests that knowledge was for Freud an instinctual affair, a sublimation not only of sexual curiosity but of Oedipal ambition to know more, and in this way to be bigger and more powerful than his father who "had no secondary education." (Freud 1936, p. 247) And in accord with the Oedipal character of Freud's pursuit of knowledge, he must have felt guilty about "out-knowing" his father and consequently convinced that his father opposed him in the acquisition of this power.

If this is so, consider how the dramatic success of Freud's career may have reverberated in his unconscious. From early on, Freud harbored soaring ambitions to become a "great man" who would expand the frontiers of human knowledge. In 1873, writing to his friend Emil Fluss about his final exams at school, Freud noted that a professor had compared his writing style to that of the great German philosopher Johann Gottfried von Herder:

> I was suitably impressed by this amazing fact and do not hesitate to disseminate the happy event, the first of its kind, as widely as possible—to you, for instance, who until now have probably remained unaware that you have been exchanging letters with a German stylist. And now I advise you as a friend, not as an interested party, to preserve them— have them bound—take good care of them—one never knows. (E. Freud 1961, p. 4)

The tone is facetious, but the ambition palpably real—as Freud then attested soon after with pure terror of mediocrity: "You take my 'worries about the future' too lightly. People who fear nothing but mediocrity, you say, are safe. Safe from what? I ask. Surely not safe and secure from being mediocre?" (p. 5)[21] Five years later, while in medical school, Freud wrote half-jokingly to Wilhelm Knöpfmacher, "I am also sending you herewith my collected works, not my complete ones as I have reason to suspect, for I am awaiting the correction of a third." (p. 6) He'd just published his first two scientific papers. Years later, while writing *The Interpretation of Dreams*, Freud described to Fliess his fantasy of a plaque honoring the house where he'd discovered the secret of dreams. (Freud 1900, p. 121n) Freud and Fluss couldn't know it for sure in 1873; Freud and Fliess didn't even know it in 1900; but we all know it now: Freud's letters and papers really would be collected. His career really would end up realizing his ambitions for

---

21 Freud's pride after winning the 1930 Goethe Prize underscores the sincerity of his lifelong ambition to be a great writer. In a 1935 postscript to his *Autobiographical Study*, Freud describes winning the prize as "the climax of my life as a citizen." (Freud 1925, p. 73)

fame and intellectual conquest—so profoundly that in 1917 he could justly rank himself in the elite company of Copernicus and Darwin. (Freud 1917, pp. 139-141)

Many people of talent and ambition wish to do great deeds, to outshine their fathers, and to win international fame, but Freud's wishes were answered in a spectacular way. Ernest Jones illustrates the unusual drama of Freud's professional wish-fulfillment with the following anecdote: when Freud was a student at the University of Vienna, he fantasized that his bust too would someday join the ranks of the great professors memorialized in stone in the University's inner courtyard. Eventually, it really happened. The University of Vienna bust of Sigmund Freud, Jones writes, "was unveiled on February 4, 1955. It is a very rare example of such a day-dream of adolescence coming true in every detail, even if it took eighty years to do so." (Jones 1955, p. 14)

If Freud's career satisfied the ambitions and sexual curiosity of his youth in a striking way, perhaps the successful realization of those wishes uniquely predisposed him to feelings of anxiety and shame. He must have felt like Oedipus, who'd attained his crown and his knowledge at too great a cost. Along those lines, Ernest Jones tells a second story in connection with Freud's student daydream of adding his bust to the colonnade at the University of Vienna:

In 1906, on the occasion of his fiftieth birthday, the little group of adherents in Vienna presented him with a medallion, designed by a well-known sculptor Karl Maria Schwerdtner, having on the obverse his side-portrait in bas-relief and on the reverse a Greek design of Oedipus answering the Sphinx. Around it is a line from Sophocles' *Oedipus Tyrannus*: ["Who divined the famed riddle and was a man most mighty."] ...

II. FREUD'S AVERSION TO PROOF: A CASE STUDY

At the presentation of the medallion there was a curious incident. When Freud read the inscription he became pale and agitated and in a strangled voice demanded to know who had thought of it.... Freud disclosed that as a young student at the University of Vienna he used to stroll around the great Court inspecting the busts of former famous professors of the institution. He then had the phantasy, not merely of seeing his own bust there in the future, which would not have been anything remarkable in an ambitious student, but of it actually being inscribed with the *identical words* he now saw on the medallion. (Jones 1955, p. 14)

Both Oedipus and Freud embarked upon heroic quests[22] for knowledge. Oedipus sought answers first to the Riddle of the Sphinx and then to the riddle of King Laius's death and his own birth, and Oedipus's solutions brought him power and sexual fulfillment of a horrific kind, soaked in blood, bereft of wholesome maternal love, ruined by loss and ostracism. Likewise, Freud's curiosity and his ambition to conquer forbidden realms of knowledge were the twin engines of progress in his career. Whether or not he explored all the psychodynamic ramifications of his powerful *Wißtrieb*, his epistemophilic instinct, Freud satisfied that instinct in profound ways that most other scientists do not. He had committed no crimes in doing so, but he may have felt that he had. Perhaps that's the trouble with proof that's most specific to Freud: in order to solve the riddle of repression, he had to violate its injunctions, and in so doing he not only discovered the Oedipus complex but in a sense re-enacted it.

---

22 Both the word *question* and the word *quest* derive from the same Latin root—*quaestus*, past participle of *quaerere*, meaning "to seek" or "to ask." For Freud as for Oedipus, asking *was* seeking and questioning *was* questing.

Expecting Ostracism, Avoiding Fame

Having acquired the fame he long sought, it would seem that his Oedipal guilt sometimes turned that fame into its opposite: ostracism. Even before he became famous or said anything too controversial or groundbreaking, the hunger for fame alone seems to have instigated in him an expectation of ostracism. Freud's idea of a persecutory "void," for example, originated more than ten years before he proposed a sexual etiology behind mental suffering.

A comparison of his nearly identical accounts of two very different lectures illustrates this point. The first took place in Vienna in 1886, before he proposed a sexual etiology to hysteria. The second took place in Vienna in 1896 after the formulation of the sexual etiology— the lecture to Krafft-Ebing and the "asses" at the psychiatric society. Freud says repeatedly that people criticized him for his sexual theories, but he complains of the exact same neglect before he ever presented them—another piece of evidence that his perception of neglect depended less on external realities and more on his inner state of mind.

"[A]ll my old papers have at last appeared," Freud wrote to his fiancée Martha in 1884, when he was still studying neuroanatomy. He felt ignored and abused by critics even in the context of those conventional studies: "The most recent one I sent you was an amplification of a previous work, the best I have ever done, although so far I haven't received one word of recognition for it, nothing but reproaches for the alleged lack of references to the relevant literature." (E. Freud 1961, p. 122) At the Salpêtrière in Paris the following year, Freud recalls with typical indignation that he had "little attention paid me to begin with." (Freud 1925, p. 12) He then explains that he won entry into Charcot's circle because of his fluency in French and German, and after studying with Charcot, he returned to Vienna in 1886 to lecture on his experiences treating hysteria at the famous French neurologist's side.

At the time of the 1886 lecture on Charcot, Freud had not yet formulated his theories of a sexual etiology behind hysteria or neurosis. The most controversial part of his lecture appears to have been neither sexual nor even original to Freud, but rather his report on Charcot's use of hypnotic suggestion and on Charcot's belief that hysteria could affect men as well as women. Yet Freud describes the reaction to the Charcot lecture in terms almost identical to those he uses after the lecture to Krafft-Ebing, which met with "an icy reception." Of the Charcot lecture in Vienna, Freud has this to say in his *Autobiographical Study*:

> I met with a bad reception. Persons of authority, such as the chairman (Bamberger, the physician), declared that what I said was incredible.... At length, outside the hospital, I came upon a case of classical hysterical hemi-anaesthesia in a man, and demonstrated it before the 'Gesellschaft der Aerzte.' This time I was applauded, but no further interest was taken in me. The impression that the high authorities had rejected my innovations remained unshaken; and, with my hysteria in men and my production of hysterical paralyses by suggestion, I found myself forced into the Opposition. As I was soon afterwards excluded from the laboratory of cerebral anatomy and for terms on end had nowhere to deliver my lectures, I withdrew from academic life and ceased to attend the learned societies. It is a whole generation since I have visited the 'Gesellschaft der Aerzte.' (Freud 1925, pp. 15-16)

The similarity between Freud's account of his "bad reception" in 1886— before he ever proposed a sexual etiology—and his account of the "icy reception" in 1896—after the formulation of the sexual etiologies—

suggests that he carried a sense of persecution around inside him, from Vienna to Paris and back again. And if Freud felt persecuted over a period of decades and across a wide variety of circumstances, then one can only conclude that he himself authored some of that persecution in his own superego. And if he consistently attributed all of the perceived criticism to others, then this once again implies that he projected some of it onto them from within his own superego.

If his superego prompted him to expect ostracism even when he wasn't presenting anything particularly sexual, perhaps it was because of the current of patricidal ambition that went into his presentations before the authorities. He expected their ostracism, perhaps, because he wanted to rise above them and dwarf them with his fame and accomplishments—because he wanted to usurp their authority and feared their reprisal for his filial ambition. A letter to Martha Bernays dated January 29, 1884 illustrates Freud's ardor to become greater and more famous than the senior faculty at the University of Vienna medical school and also his hesitancy to move forward, perhaps until he can decisively amaze them all:

> I am soon going to choose a topic for a paper from among the problems concerning nervous diseases. I am not worried about failing to find a topic, and I can evidently continue working on this subject on my own. Today the Club met; I sat behind Billroth and Nothnagel and was naughty enough to think: Just wait till you welcome me as you are welcoming the others now! Billroth doesn't know me; Nothnagel, by the way, was rather patronizing last time. Meynert continues to treat me with great respect and advised me to give a lecture at the Medical Society as well, which I don't intend to do just now. (E. Freud 1961, pp. 95-96)

Later, when Freud began to publish more controversial theories, it wasn't only the controversy that led him to expect and even imagine criticism. It seems that it was also a fear of senior faculty revenging themselves upon him for the challenges he'd hurled their way. Freud's misperception in 1896 of Adolf von Strümpell's reaction to his book *Studies in Hysteria* illustrates this point very clearly. He interpreted Strümpell's review as "vicious" criticism when it was not. In reality, it was Freud who had in fact challenged and criticized Strümpell five years earlier, in 1891! Freud and his friend Oscar Rie had that year published a monograph on cases of pediatric hemiplegia and in it they "cast doubt on Strümpell's view that acute poliomyelitis can cause a cerebral hemiplegia...." (Jones 1953, p. 216) It's a striking case of reversal: Freud imagined Strümpell criticizing him after he'd criticized Strümpell.

Just as Freud anticipated ostracism and criticism even before devising his controversial sexual theories, he also suffered inhibitions about publishing from the very beginning of his career. "[E]ven in the first years of my scientific work," Freud writes in *The Interpretation of Dreams*, "it happened that I allowed a discovery of mine to lie fallow until an energetic remonstrance on [Brücke's] part drove me into publishing it." (Freud 1900, p. 454) It's telling that Freud required the encouragement of a father-figure like Ernst Brücke, Freud's laboratory supervisor and first idol among scientists. Only the support of a powerful man of knowledge like Brücke, perhaps, could relieve Freud's anxiety about killing off his intellectual forebears by publishing greater discoveries than they had. Then in 1884 in the letter excerpted above, Freud expresses reluctance to give a lecture he'd been invited to give. In this period, Freud also failed to publish on the anesthetic properties of cocaine in the eye; he instead told his colleague Koller about the insight into cocaine, and let Koller do the demonstration and publish the results. "I had myself indicated this application of the alkaloid in my published paper, but I had not been thorough enough to pursue the matter further." (Freud 1900, p. 170) These inhibitions about publishing, which antedate Freud's sexual researches and theories, suggest that his Oedipal ambitions alone were enough to hinder his efforts at proof and publication.

Freud's break with Breuer illustrates in highly personal terms his dread of being ostracized by a father-figure in retaliation for ambitious research. Freud writes in the *History* that "[Breuer] was the first to show the reaction of distaste and repudiation which was later to become so familiar to me, but which at that time I had not yet learnt to recognize as my inevitable fate." (Freud 1914, p. 12) He attributes the loss of his "munificent mentor" Breuer, as Gay puts it, to Breuer's prudery. But it was surely more than that; Freud had also seized an opportunity for fame and discovery that his mentor Breuer failed to seize himself. He had surpassed Breuer and part of him was undoubtedly thrilled to do so. Freud had killed him in the annals of science, where Breuer would forever cling to Freud's towering name as a footnote. When Freud recalls Breuer's "retirement from our common work" in the *Study*, and adds, "I became the sole administrator of his legacy" (Freud 1925, p. 22), he sounds indeed like a son speaking of a father who has not just retired but actually died. Surely, Freud's guilt about killing off one of his intellectual fathers contributed to his conviction that Breuer had repudiated him. Breuer, who was obviously no slouch at psychology himself, evidently noticed Freud's distress and even supplied a diagnosis: "paranoia scientifica." (Masson 1985, p. 175)

All the rivalry and paranoia embroiled in Freud's challenges to his senior colleagues surely derive their true power from rivalry with his own father in the realm of knowledge, and the paranoia that follows from that primordial rivalry. Having taught Freud lessons from the

Bible, Jacob Freud was in fact both father and first teacher to Freud (Richards 2014, p. 990)—all the more reason that Jacob Freud should loom behind other academic figures of authority in Freud's mind. And if Freud's guilt about surpassing his father held him back with a fear of ostracism, perhaps it's no coincidence that Freud's greatest discoveries and publications follow his father's death in 1896. It was the analysis of his feelings about losing his father that enabled Freud to write his masterwork *The Interpretation of Dreams*, as he notes in his Preface to the Second Edition:

> For this book has a further subjective significance for me personally—a significance which I only grasped after I had completed it. It was, I found, a portion of my own self-analysis, my reaction to my father's death—that is to say, to the most important event, the most poignant loss, of a man's life. (Freud 1900, p. xxvi)

Even after Freud's self-analysis and the publication of *The Interpretation of Dreams*, however, his emotional struggles with research, and the fame such research brought, were far from over. The hunt for palliative "porcupines" had not yet commenced in earnest.

To Tell It in Dan

On September 21, 1897, as the one-year anniversary of Jacob Freud's death approached, Freud wrote to Fliess about his decision to abandon the seduction theory of hysteria in favor of the even more controversial theory of infantile sexuality, and in the letter Freud makes an interesting slip: "Of course I shall not tell it in Dan, nor speak of it in Askelon, in the land of the Philistines," Freud writes, "but in your eyes and my own, I have more the feeling of a victory than a defeat (which is surely not right)." (Masson 1985, p. 265) The *Standard Edition* editors clarify: "Freud is misquoting II Samuel i, 20: 'Tell it not in Gath, publish it not in the streets of Askelon; lest the daughters of the Philistines rejoice, lest the daughters of the uncircumcised triumph.' "[23]

These words of sorrow belong to the biblical figure of David and they weigh heavy with Oedipal guilt after the death of the Israelite King Saul; in the Books of Samuel, David diminishes his king and adoptive father Saul in a bitter rivalry that renders Saul vulnerable to the Philistines, who then kill him. Yosef Hayim Yerushalmi points out that Freud knew the quotation's context very well; Freud also cites this line in an 1880 letter to Karl Koller and there notes that it refers to the death of Saul. (Yerushalmi 1991, pp. 65-66) Furthermore, Freud attests to how well he knew the Bible in his *Autobiographical Study*: "My deep engrossment in the Bible story (almost as soon as I had learnt the art of reading) had, as I recognized much later, an enduring effect upon the direction of my interest." (Freud 1925, p. 8) Yerushalmi interprets Freud's parapraxis—"I shall not tell it in Dan" instead of "Tell it not in Gath"—as an unconscious reference to the Samson story. (Yerushalmi 1991, pp. 66-67) Freud may very well be thinking of Samson, the great Jewish hero from the Tribe of Dan whom the Philistines robbed of his strength, and who then sacrificed his life to defeat the Philistines.

But Freud's parapraxis in quoting this biblical verse may have another meaning. When David says "publish it not in the streets of Askelon" in order to suppress rejoicing at Saul's death, he's quite clearly suppressing his own joy in finally defeating his rival and tormentor. David in other words suppresses public knowledge of his

---

23 S.E. 1:260n. In the preceding verse, 2 Samuel 1:19, David laments Saul's death with the famous exclamation "How the mighty are fallen!"

Oedipus complex, and it's indirect evidence of the Oedipus complex—the fact of infantile sexuality—that Freud doesn't want to publish in the streets of Askelon. In quoting the Oedipal figure of David on the occasion of discovering infantile sexuality, Freud speaks not only to his enemies but evidently to himself: *I shall not publish the news that I wished to kill my father.*

The parapraxis "Dan" instead of "Gath" furthermore may be pointing directly at Freud's father, Jacob, through another biblical association. Dan is a place like Gath in the Bible, and also a Tribe—but before Dan became a Tribe, he was a person. Indeed, Dan is one of the twelve sons of the great biblical patriarch, Jacob, and is the firstborn son of Jacob's second concubine, Bilhah—just as Freud was the firstborn son of Jacob Freud's second wife Amalia. Coincidence? Perhaps. But Jacob Freud was clearly on Freud's mind during the composition of the letter to Fliess in which the parapraxis appears. Freud refers to his father in the letter's second paragraph, and as I mentioned, the one-year anniversary of Jacob Freud's death was just a month away at the time Freud wrote the letter to Fliess.

While alive, Freud's father had disappointed him and engaged both his pity and his competitive ambition with traits of meekness before anti-Semites, impecunity, parochialism, limited education, and unemployment. Sigmund far outdid Jacob, and after Jacob's death Freud began uncovering his own childhood wishes not only to worship his father but to destroy him, to conquer the old man with his own young, powerful mind and to take his young mother for his own. To "tell it in Dan" was perhaps, for Freud, to speak the forbidden Oedipal language of the son of Jacob, and at the moment of Freud's momentous discovery of infantile sexuality, his conscience apparently instructed him not to "tell it in Dan." He was tempted instead to tell it in the inhibited language of Jacob, his father, who had once had his cap knocked off by an anti-Semite and had picked it up without a word. Such docility before the repressive forces of conscience would of course meet with conflict in Freud's mind; Freud's ferocious curiosity and ambition would not give in to his filial piety without a fight and his powerful intellect equipped him to unleash that curiosity and ambition through the elegant method of self-analysis. But having unleashed those affects of sexual curiosity and patricidal ambition, he would continue to pay a price. Freud himself showed the world what follows the eruption of affects and self-knowledge so unwelcome to the superego: defense mechanisms.

5.3. Fate as a Psychological Construct

One of those defenses was evidently a despairing sense of "fate." In the *History*, Freud says that when he dared to report on taboo facts of instinctual life, he was subjected to ostracism, an "inevitable fate" ("*unabwendbares Schicksal*") fomented by public resistance to the unwelcome truths of psychoanalysis. (Freud 1914, p. 12) In the *Lectures*, the phrase "inevitable fate" or a near relative of it ("*unabwendbares Verhängnis*") comes up again, this time in reference to Oedipus. It was Oedipus's inevitable fate to kill his father and marry his mother, and it is psychoanalysts' inevitable fate, Freud says, to know the relevance of this tale to every human heart. It was Freud's particular fate not only to know of the Oedipus complex but to announce it to the world. He clearly derived enormous pride and satisfaction from having done so, and his conscience evidently rebelled against that pleasure and pride, collecting its debts from Freud like the Devil come to take Faust's soul as payment for the glorious knowledge he'd acquired. If Freud foresaw doom in the world's reaction to psychoanalysis, perhaps it was because discovering the Oedipus complex and proclaiming it to the world felt, as I've said, like performing the terrible deeds that Oedipus did, living out Oedipus's "inevitable fate" in all its instinctual pleasure and pride, and in all its corresponding horror and loneliness.

Freud in fact admits that his sense of "fate" is a construct of his own conscience in one of his last papers, "A Disturbance of Memory on the Acropolis." Writing in the 1930s, Freud recalls a 1904 trip to Athens he took with his brother, whereon he had a feeling of pessimism that they wouldn't make it there to see the Acropolis. Once he was standing at the Acropolis, he felt disbelief and asked himself why he'd been in such "a gloomy state and foreseen nothing but obstacles and difficulties" in the way of getting there. (Freud 1936, p. 241) He concludes that sometimes it seems that Fate has only woe in store because one feels deserving of nothing else. "For, as has long been known," he writes, "the Fate [*Schicksal*] which we expect to treat us so badly is a materialization of our conscience, of the severe super-ego within us, itself a residue of the punitive agency of our childhood." (p. 243) And Freud tells us exactly why he thinks his conscience rebelled against him on the way to the Acropolis: it objected to the reality that he'd traveled so far beyond his father, both literally and figuratively. Freud labels himself "wrecked by success" (Freud 1936, p. 242), as he'd once put it in another paper entitled "Some Character-Types Met with in Psycho-Analytic Work." (Freud 1916) Here is Freud explaining in further detail in his paper on the Acropolis:

It seems as though the essence of success was to have got further than one's father, and as though to excel one's father was still something forbidden. As an addition to this generally valid motive there was a special factor present in our particular case. The very theme of Athens and the Acropolis in

75

itself contained evidence of the son's superiority. Our father had been in business, he had had no secondary education, and Athens could not have meant much to him. Thus what interfered with our enjoyment of the journey to Athens was a feeling of *filial piety*. (Freud 1936, pp. 247-248)

Here, Freud testifies directly to the costs of winning "the knowledge contest with Jacob Freud," as I put it in the last subtitle of this chapter on Freud's curiosity and ambition: victory over his father in the realm of knowledge provoked guilt and inhibition. Once his aspirations were realized in his great scientific discoveries, it would appear he felt a conflicting urge to retreat from that triumphant reality, as he says he did on the Acropolis in 1904, when traveling so much farther than his father ever did seemed "too good to be true." (p. 242)

Did Freud's aversion to proving his discoveries help him effect a retreat from the realization of his ambitions? Instead of pushing his scientific work to completion through proof and confirmation, did he feel the need to leave this last step in the work unfinished? Perhaps he could thereby imagine he'd returned some of the intellectual territory he'd conquered back to his humble, uneducated, penniless father. It seems obvious that despair over the fate of his grand creation, psychoanalysis, was a construct, a debt he believed he owed to his father, and underneath this constructed sense of "fate" was undoubtedly a sense of fulfilled destiny and greatness, which Freud must have secretly enjoyed.

Even in the dark days of World War I, when Freud foresaw doom for psychoanalysis, he must have known on some level that there's no such thing as "inevitable fate." It's only an invention of the psyche, and as such it can be analyzed and understood.

6. The Role of Anti-Semitism in Proof Aversion

Peter Gay describes it as a "notorious fact": The first psychoanalysts were all Jewish. (Gay 1988, p. 603) Arnold Richards develops the point in detail:

> For four full years—from 1898 to 1902—while Freud was challenging the place of race in the prevailing psychiatric paradigm, all of his lectures on his nascent science were delivered to the members of B'nai B'rith. Except for his friend Wilhelm Fliess, they were Freud's only auditors until he convened the Wednesday Night Discussion Group in October 1902.... Further, the first nineteen members of the Wednesday night group were Jews—heirs to and replacements for the brothers at the lodge. (Richards 2014, pp. 996-997)

It's a fact that the early analysts were Jews, and perhaps there's something "notorious" about it, too, as Peter Gay says—but what? And notorious to whom? In this chapter, I will explore the way anti-Semitism affected the birth of psychoanalysis and, more specifically, how it created another source of emotional interference in Freud's public attempts to demonstrate and disseminate his ideas, an emotional interference that amplified and dovetailed with his aversion to proof.

Frederick Crews's latest salvo against Freud accuses the founder of psychoanalysis of exaggerating the extent of anti-Semitism in Austria.[24] The Holocaust would suggest that Freud's perceptions of European anti-Semitism had a strong basis in reality—to say

---

24 https://www.nytimes.com/2017/08/14/books/review/freud-biography-frederick-crews.html, accessed December 18, 2017.

nothing of the fact that on March 22, 1938 the Gestapo literally arrested his daughter Anna. (Gay 1988, p. 625) But perhaps it's after all useful to demonstrate explicitly and specifically the hatred Freud countenanced in Vienna, and the psychological pressure it created for Vienna's Jews. To do so, I will cite some examples of the virulent anti-Semitism on display in Vienna while Freud lived there. I will also discuss the anti-Semitic stereotype of Jews' moral and sexual depravity, which is of special significance in understanding how anti-Semitism affected psychoanalysis and Freud's aversion to proof. Given the strength and particular character of Austrian and German bigotry in Freud's lifetime, I conclude that anti-Semitism was a significant source of anxiety, shame, and indignation for Freud, that it strengthened Freud's defenses against public demonstration of psychoanalysis, and that it further distorted his approach to public relations.

6.1. The Character of Viennese Anti-Semitism

The demonization of Jews is as old as Christianity. The Christian gospels first characterized the "Jew" as the enemy of God, "a mythic projection of perennial Christian anxiety," as James Carroll has put it. (Carroll 2001, p. 76) Elaine Pagels elaborates in her book *The Origin of Satan*:

> The New Testament gospels almost never identify Satan with the Romans, but they consistently associate him with Jesus' Jewish enemies, primarily Judas Iscariot and the chief priests and scribes. By placing the story of Jesus in the context of cosmic war, the gospel writers expressed, in varying ways, their identification with the embattled minority of Jews who believed in Jesus, and their distress at what they saw as the apostasy of the majority of their fellow Jews in

Jesus' time, as well as in their own. As we shall see, Jesus' followers did not *invent* the practice of demonizing enemies within their own group, although Christians (and Muslims after them) carried this practice further than their Jewish predecessors had taken it, and with enormous consequences. (Pagels 1995, pp. 13-14)

[A]s the Christian movement became increasingly Gentile during the second century and later, the identification of Satan primarily with the Jewish enemies of Jesus, borne along in Christian tradition over the centuries, would fuel the fires of anti-Semitism. (p. 34)

Christianity began as a rebel movement against the Jewish priests of its time, and its liturgy in a way projects that rebellion onto the Jewish priests, so that the priests are the ones who seem to have rebelled against Jesus, not just with patricide but deicide. Matthew 27:25: "Then answered all the people and said, His blood be on us, and on our children." It's a formidable curse to have uttered against a living people and all their descendants.

When Christianity spread across Europe, far from the world of ancient Judea, Jews remained symbols of evil, the "quintessential 'other' for Western culture" (Frosh 2005, p. 204), and as such repositories for projection of the inadmissible contents of the unconscious mind. Jews were for instance falsely accused of killing Christian children at Easter. (Levy 1991, p. 36) Until 1962, when the Second Vatican Council formally rectified relations between Christians and Jews, Catholic ritual openly depicted Jews as the enemy of God.

In Freud's day the anti-Semitism of the Christian Gospels and of Catholic rituals had an overt influence on Austrian and German culture. One of Grimm's fairy tales tells a "blood libel" myth of Jews sacrificing a Christian child named Anderl von Rinn on a stone—the "Judenstein"—due to their hatred of Jesus Christ. The Catholic Church beatified von Rinn in the 18ᵗʰ century and Kirche Judenstein, a church in western Austria, displayed the stone on which the sacrifice was supposed to have occurred. Its blood libel imagery remained in place until the 1990s.[25] Freud himself had the opportunity to hear about the so-called demonic Jew directly from the pulpit when he was a small child. His Czech nanny took him along to church in Freiberg often enough, Jones tells us, that Freud would come back home and pretend to preach his own sermons. (Jones 1953, p. 6)

The Enlightenment of the 18ᵗʰ century curbed some of this religious magic, but pogroms continued in eastern Europe and even modern Christians in the West continued projecting onto Jews. 19ᵗʰ-century French scholars, for example, dismayed by the sex, aggression, and bathroom humor of the Old French *fabliaux*, concocted a baseless theory that medieval Jews had imported the obscene tales from the Orient. One scholar proposed that they came from the Talmud. (Bloch 2013, pp. xv-xvi) They do not. But the scholars clearly preferred to imagine that the dirty stories were not French in origin; to admit that the sex and aggression in such tales are human—not Jewish—would of course be to admit some of "the unwelcome truths of analysis." (Freud 1914, p. 48)

Having been liberated from the shtetls by the progressive movement, Jews both celebrated and represented modernity in a way that unsettled the working class and the guardians of tradition. (Levy 1991, p. 17) The Panic of 1873, which began in Vienna and created financial stress around the world, caused many to look with jealousy on the newly emancipated Jews. "I see modern Jewry as a great

---

25 https://sourcebooks.fordham.edu/source/rinn.asp, accessed July 6, 2018.

danger to German national life," Lutheran bishop Adolf Stoecker said in a speech to the Christian Social Workers' Party in Berlin in 1879. (p. 60) Freud was at the time in medical school. With jealousy and suspicion toward Jews so prevalent, it's perhaps no surprise that the University of Vienna delayed academic promotions for able Jewish doctors. (Gay 1988, pp. 138-139)

By the time Freud published *The Interpretation of Dreams* and *The Psychopathology of Everyday Life*, anti-Semitic rhetoric in Germany and Austria had moved beyond xenophobia into open expressions of hatred and intimations of violence. The demagogue Karl Lueger, mayor of Vienna from 1897 to 1910, encouraged hate speech against Jews, hosted anti-Semites at his political rallies, and provided anti-Semitism with a mainstream respectability that would ultimately inspire an unstable young citizen of Vienna named Adolf Hitler. On December 10, 1902, for example, Lueger invited an anti-Jewish hatemonger to address the Vienna city council and incite the crowd against the Social Democrats. The speaker, Hermann Bielohlawek, attacked the Social Democrats for indifference to working-class Catholics and predicted that Jews on the city council would cry foul at his biases against Jews. Bielohlawek countered that at least he and the Christian Socials were honest about their hatred of Jews. "The difference, however," Bielohlawek said, "is that we speak the truth! Yes, we want to annihilate the Jews. We are not ashamed to say the Jew must be driven from society." (Levy 1991, p. 117)

In 1925, when Freud published *An Autobiographical Study*, Adolf Hitler published *Mein Kampf*. In it, Hitler cites Karl Lueger as the man who converted him to anti-Semitism. "Today I see the man," Hitler wrote, "even more than before, as the greatest German mayor of all times. How much of my basic outlook was changed by this altered position toward the Christian Social movement!" (p. 207) Hitler goes

81

on to describe public displays of lewd behavior in the Jewish quarter of Vienna:

> The relationship of Jewry to prostitution and still more to the white-slave traffic could be especially well studied in Vienna as in no other city of Western Europe, with the possible exception of the ports of southern France. Walking of a night the streets and alleys of Leopoldstadt, you witness everywhere, whether you want to or not, encounters that remained hidden from the greatest part of the German people until the war presented soldiers on the eastern front occasion to see similar things, or, more aptly put, forced them to see such. (p. 210)

In his account of Leopoldstadt, the Jewish ghetto where Freud grew up, Hitler makes the Jews responsible for all that is dirty and sexual, for bringing into the open that which ought to stay hidden. One can't help wondering what Hitler himself was doing in the red light district at night; the Nazi mind, perhaps, cannot tolerate sexuality and other human weaknesses, and so it projects these unwanted contents of the human psyche onto the Jews, where they can then be destroyed.[26]

This is the Vienna of Freud's adult life: a city in which there were 200,000 Jews, "newly 'emancipated' and able to claim influential positions, yet still victims of social exclusion, anti-Semitic populism and new forms of 'racial' anti-Semitism that were gradually replacing the old Christian anti-Judaism." (Frosh 2005, p. 1) Upwardly mobile Vienna Jews like the Freuds were still only one or two generations

---

26 Leopoldstadt's demographics today represent a ghastly controlled experiment which proves Hitler's hateful accusations exactly wrong: the Jews are gone and the prostitutes remain. Q.E.D. Sexuality is human, not Jewish. https://www.upi.com/Archives/1985/01/13/Viennas-vanished-Jewish-quarter/4132474440400/, accessed December 18, 2017. http://www.viennareview.net/news/front-page/women-of-the-shadows, accessed December 21, 2017.

removed from the shtetls and lived in a Jewish ghetto, Leopoldstadt (nicknamed Die Mazzesinsel, or "Matzah Island"). The neighborhood was named for the Holy Roman Emperor Leopold who in 1670 expelled all the Jews and turned their synagogue into a church. All this is to say, in other words, that Freud was a Jew with Yiddish-speaking parents in a city that had cast out all its Jews before and seemed intent on doing so once again. As such, Freud had ample reason to feel alien and paranoid.

In 1883, Freud wrote a letter to his fiancée Martha that demonstrates his fear of being perceived according to the old Christian idea of Jews as godless, immoral demons. In it, he describes the funeral of Nathan Weiss, a young Jewish neurologist of Freud's acquaintance who had committed suicide not long after his wedding. Weiss's father was, according to Freud, a brilliant rabbinic scholar and a "very hard, bad, brutal man." (E. Freud 1961, p. 60) At the funeral, another rabbinic scholar, "a relation and colleague of his old father," marshaled all his scriptural authority as he blamed the family of Weiss's widow for the young man's suicide. Freud writes:

And now in clear words he began to accuse the other family of having dealt the fatal blow. And all this he spoke with the powerful voice of the fanatic, with the ardor of the savage, merciless Jew.

We were all petrified with horror and shame in the presence of the Christians who were among us. It seemed as though we had given them reason to believe that we worship the God of Revenge, not the God of Love. Pfungen's[27] thin voice was lost in the reverberation of the wild accusation of the Jew. (p. 65)

---

27 See Freud's letter from earlier in 1883: Ernst Freud notes that Robert Pfungen was an "assistant in Meynert's Clinic." (E. Freud 1961, p. 43n)

The colleague of Nathan Weiss's father sounds in Freud's description like a Pharisee from the pages of the Christian gospels, a pitiless Shylock devoted to the letter of the law but possessing no human decency.

Freud began his career with ambitions to leave this backward Jewish character behind, become a citizen of the world, and make his mark on high German culture. At the time of Weiss's funeral he was headed in that direction. He'd already surpassed his father's station in life, but still he clearly feared that others would see in him some connection to the depraved Jew of Christian mythology.

And then he invented psychoanalysis.

6.2. Psychoanalysis as "Jewish Depravity"

Anti-Semitic Reactions to Psychoanalysis

Reactionaries like Stoecker and Hitler feared the godless modernity and supposed moral depravity of emancipated urban Jews. Psychoanalysis was vulnerable to the same attacks: it was practiced predominantly by Jewish physicians, it was urban, secular, modern, and to the narrow-minded it sounded depraved with its talk of infantile sexuality, and murderous, incestuous wishes. It's understandable, therefore, that Freud anticipated anti-Semitism in the public response to psychoanalysis. For Freud, critics of psychoanalysis and anti-Semites were one enemy, the Opposition, as he called it, a "social conservatism compounded by bigotry." (Gay 1988, p. 603)

Opponents of psychoanalysis did little to assuage Freud's fears. As soon as psychoanalytic theories traveled abroad, foreign psychiatrists began trying to explain away Freud's observations according to the peculiarities of his patients' geographical and cultural background. In his 1911 review of objections to psychoanalysis, Frankfurt neurologist and Freud-critic Adolf Friedländer[28] mentions Löwenfeld's belief that "the population of Vienna is particularly inclined to sexual matters." (Friedländer 1911, p. 310) Freud says Janet, too, made use of this argument in order to deny the general applicability of psychoanalytic claims:

As recently as in 1913 Janet was not ashamed to use this argument, although he himself is no doubt proud of being a Parisian, and Paris can scarcely claim to be a city of stricter morals than Vienna. The suggestion is that psycho-analysis, and in particular its assertion that the neuroses are traceable to disturbances in sexual life, could only have originated in a town like Vienna—in an atmosphere of sensuality and immorality foreign to other cities—and that it is simply a reflection, a projection into theory, as it were, of these peculiar Viennese conditions. Now I am certainly no local patriot; but this theory about psycho-analysis always seems to me quite exceptionally senseless—so senseless, in fact, that I have sometimes been inclined to suppose that the reproach of being a citizen of Vienna is only a euphemistic substitute for another reproach which no one would care to put forward openly. (Freud 1914, pp. 39-40)

The other reproach that Freud clearly had in mind was his own "Jewish origin," as the *Standard Edition* editors note, and the Jewish background of his patients and fellow analysts.

Alfred Hoche, a German psychiatrist and fierce opponent of psychoanalysis, may or may not have been an anti-Semite[29], but

---

28 Friedländer was himself Jewish. See http://www.juedische-pflegegeschichte.de/jewish-hospitals-in-frankfurt-am-main-1829-1942/, accessed December 22, 2017.

29 Hoche was married to a Jewish woman. See the Biographical Archive of Psychiatry, https://biapsy.de/index.php/en/9-biographien-a-z/80-hoche-alfred-erich-e, accessed December 17, 2017.

in his attacks on psychoanalysis he employed rhetoric often used by anti-Semites. Hoche vilified the new field as a religion that had infected psychiatry like a "psychical epidemic" (Freud 1914, p. 27) just as anti-Semites often compared Jews to vermin. And regardless of his intentions towards Jews, Hoche's intellectual kinship with his Nazi heirs has entangled his name with anti-Semitism and genocide for eternity. In 1920, he co-authored *Die Freigabe der Vernichtung lebensunwerten Lebens*, or "The Permission to Destroy Life Unworthy of Life," an essay which advocated euthanasia for severe mental disabilities. Hoche's essay became the position paper for the Nazi eugenics program (Lifton 1988, pp. 48-49), which began by murdering thousands of disabled and ended by murdering six million Jews. Freud had no need to weigh the terrible consequences of Hoche's rhetoric, however, to see him as a member of the anti-Semitic, socially conservative Opposition. The way Hoche talked about psychoanalysis alone was enough for Freud to nickname him *der böse Geist*, "the evil spirit." (Freud 1914, p. 45)

The trials of a young Jewish-Latvian tourist, Philipp Halsmann, in Innsbruck, Austria in 1928 and 1929 displayed in dramatic terms the anti-Semitic belief that only depraved Jews could feel Oedipal feelings, much less speak such obscenities in public. Halsmann was falsely accused of murdering his father while they traveled in the Alps, and the trials excited an anti-Semitic furor across Europe. The prosecution speculated on the peculiarities of Jewish psychology as it groped for a motive and finally landed on the Oedipus complex.[30] The defense asked Freud himself to comment and he wrote in the *Neue Freie Presse*, "Precisely because it is always present, the Oedipus complex is not suited to provide a decision on the question

---

30 Schriften der Österreichischen Liga für Menschenrechte (Austrian League for Human Rights). (1931). *Der Fall Halsmann*. Wien: Gilhofer and Ranschburg. p. 76.

of [forensic] guilt." (Freud 1931, p. 252) In a remarkable turn of events, Freud was thus literally called in to defend his theory against anti-Semitic prosecutors.

Since Freud's time, anti-Semitic reactions to psychoanalysis have persisted. As recently as 2006, Sheikh Nayef Rajoub of Hamas told David Remnick of *The New Yorker*, "Two hundred years ago in Europe, they were conservative people, but now the fashion world, the media—it's controlled by the Jews. And their people are sexually open. Freud, a Jew, was the one who destroyed morals, and Marx destroyed divine ideologies."[31]

Joseph Heller's famous line, "Just because you're paranoid doesn't mean they aren't after you," seems appropriate to Sigmund Freud's predicament in expounding the ideas of psychoanalysis just as two millennia of European anti-Semitism were building to a gruesome climax. Surely the confusion of anti-Semitism with resistance to psychoanalysis added intensity to Freud's experience of the resistant criticism. It must have been frightening and enraging to see the *Volk*'s pitchforks behind antipathy to psychoanalysis. And if Freud reacted to criticism of psychoanalysis with a fear and rage at its anti-Semitism, it follows that defense mechanisms might have corrupted those reactions in an attempt to contain the toxic feelings.

Projective Identification with the "Dirty Jew"

Freud's shame and anxiety about the sex and aggression he'd discovered in himself evidently caused him to project internal criticism onto his audience when demonstrating his theories to the public. Did Freud also feel ambivalent about his Jewish origins? Richards says so; Freud and other young Jewish intellectuals were inclined to feel "ashamed of the

---

31 https://www.newyorker.com/magazine/2006/02/27/the-democracy-game, accessed January 18, 2018.

provinciality of their parents." (Richards 2014, p. 990) Frosh agrees, and sees in Freud's reaction to the anti-Semite knocking off his father's cap Freud's "sense of his father as a failed hero, and of Jewish passivity in general as a sign of 'racial' disrepute." (Frosh 2005, p. 37) Richards further suggests that Freud's antipathy for religion masked an underlying shame about his Jewish origins. (Richards 2014, p. 1000) And if Freud felt a little ashamed of his Jewish origins, was that relevant to the psychodynamics of his public exposition of psychoanalysis? The answer seems self-evident: surely. But how, exactly?

Whereas the concept of projection of internal criticism seems sufficient to describe one of Freud's defenses against the shame and anxiety associated with his radical discoveries, Melanie Klein's concept of projective identification may be useful in understanding the machinations of Freud's Jewish self-hate. Early Christians projected their own sins onto the Jews in their gospels, as did later converts to the religion. When Freud reacts to the rabbinic scholar at Nathan Weiss's funeral with a Christian sense of horror at the "savage, merciless Jew," he engages in the same anti-Semitic, demonizing projection of sin onto "the Jew." But where Freud perhaps differs from other "self-hating Jews," is that he often acts as though he identifies with this projected demon and wishes to protect it from judgments, whether the judgments of bourgeois Christian society or those originating in his own conscience. Thus it is, perhaps, that at the opening of *The Interpretation of Dreams* Freud quotes Juno summoning up the Furies in Virgil's *Aeneid*: "If I cannot bend the Higher Powers, I will move the Infernal Regions." (Freud 1900, p. ix, p. 608n) Discovering the unconscious, infantile sexuality, and the Oedipus complex seems in Freud's eyes to have qualified him for the devil's company.

The Christian gospels, meanwhile, specifically characterize the kingdom of God in terms antithetical to the Oedipus complex: sons do not kill fathers, but rather God the Father sacrifices his Son; the Christian soul divests itself of patricidal wishes by projecting them out onto the demonic Jew where they become deicidal acts; Mother Mary is so virginal she's denied sexual intercourse even with the father of her baby. Freud's recognition that people want to kill their fathers and impregnate their mothers had no place in the Christian conscience. Accordingly, some Christian critics of psychoanalysis concluded that only a "dirty Jew" could feel and say such things. And according to Freud's willful defiance of the forces of repression, he was going to embrace being a "dirty Jew." "The more anti-Semitism he encountered," Richards writes, "the more openly and defiantly did Freud lay claim to his Jewishness." (Richards 2014, p. 998) This looks like a form of intrapsychic compromise in which he allows himself to hold onto his unholy discoveries, and even to sympathize with the devilish feelings, and at the same time avoids ostracism by retaining membership in a community of outcasts: the Jews.

Freud's 1926 letter to the Jewish fraternal society B'nai B'rith seems to support the idea that he sought membership among the outcasts specifically because he'd transgressed against the mores of polite Christian society. In the letter, he makes the familiar claim that being a diaspora Jew, and therefore a minority and an outsider, helped him to throw off conformity and make original discoveries: "Because I was a Jew I found myself free of many prejudices which restrict others in the use of the intellect: as a Jew I was prepared to be in the opposition and to renounce agreement with the 'compact majority.'"[32] (E. Freud 1961, p. 367) Freud used the same phrase the previous year

---

32 Ernst Freud draws our attention to the origin of the phrase "compact majority"—Henrik Ibsen's play, An Enemy of the People—and it's easy to see why Freud identified with Dr. Stockmann, Ibsen's hero from that play. Stockmann, the Medical Officer of the Municipal Baths, declares the baths unsanitary, and the townspeople rebel against him and try to prevent him from speaking out in order to protect their business interests. Dr. Stockmann dresses down the public assembly with the words: "The most dangerous enemy of truth and freedom amongst us is the compact majority." (Ibsen 1882, p. 189)

in *An Autobiographical Study*. (Freud 1925, p. 9) Belonging to an ethnic minority surely helped to shape Freud into the independent, intelligent man who created psychoanalysis, but that doesn't illuminate the psychology behind Freud's joining B'nai B'rith. In fact, Freud's attempt to credit his Judaism as a source of intellectual bravery distracts from deeper emotional meanings evident in the letter.

The letter actually devotes more space to the opposite relation between psychoanalysis and Jewishness; Freud says less about how being a Jew enabled him to discover the unconscious, and more about how discovering the dirty secrets of the unconscious drove him to join his fellow Jews at B'nai B'rith to protect himself from social isolation. That was when, in his words, "I became one of you":

> It happened that in the years after 1895 two strong impressions coincided to produce the same effect on me. On the one hand I had gained the first insight into the depths of human instinct, had seen many things which were sobering, at first even frightening; on the other hand the disclosure of my unpopular discoveries led to my losing most of my personal relationships at that time; I felt as though outlawed, shunned by all. This isolation aroused in me the longing for a circle of excellent men with high ideals who would accept me in friendship despite my temerity. Your Lodge was described to me as the place where I could find such men. (E. Freud 1961, p. 366)

There again is the social "void" that Freud perceived after he began to publish and lecture on his sexual theories, and Freud says it was this feeling of ostracism that drove him into the arms of his own people. They would not be so rejecting, Freud concludes, because they shared "the same psychological structure." He goes on in the

B'nai B'rith letter, "So I became one of you.... [A]t a time when no one in Europe would listen to me and I had no pupils in Vienna, you offered me your sympathetic attention. You were my first audience." (p. 367)

Freud hated religion and tribalism, and as Richards points out, founded a new psychology that emphasized experience and development over heredity (Richards 2014, p. 996), so it's remarkable that Freud expresses the belief that his fellow Jews share his "psychological structure." And yet he really did seem to believe that Jews could understand psychoanalysis more easily than Gentiles. In an attempt to forestall a dispute between Karl Abraham and Jung, Freud wrote the following to Abraham on May 3, 1908:

[D]o not forget that really it is easier for you to follow my thoughts than it is for Jung, since to begin with you are completely independent, and then you are closer to my intellectual constitution through racial kinship, while he as a Christian and a pastor's son finds his way to me only against great inner resistances. His association with us is therefore all the more valuable. I was almost going to say that it was only by his emergence on the scene that psychoanalysis was removed from the danger of becoming a Jewish national affair. (Falzeder 2002, p. 38)

Such projective identification with Jews' "racial" attributes reflects a certain clandestine Christianity and anti-Semitism in Freud's view of Jews. "Jews were stereotyped as less moral than the upright Germans, more governed by their passions," Richards writes. (Richards 2014, p. 989) And Jewish and Gentile physicians alike attributed to Jews "racial tendencies to 'nervousness.'" (p. 996)

Freud seems to buy into these canards in a way that reinforces his tendency towards splitting and avoidance: dirty Jews can understand psychoanalysis, but upright Gentiles can't; Gentiles are needed to help prove his dirty case to other Gentiles, while he remains silent. When Freud concludes "that the new movement's association with Vienna was no recommendation but rather a handicap to it" (Freud 1914, p. 42), and when he looks to Zurich Gentiles like Bleuler and Jung to defend psychoanalysis on his behalf, Freud implicitly accepts Janet's judgment that psychoanalysis is a product of Viennese-Jewish sexuality. Author of *The Ordeal of Civility* John Murray Cuddihy supposes, in Richards's words, "that in confronting Vienna with its unconscious, Freud demonstrated once and for all that Germans were just as *schmutzig* as the Jews." (Richards 2014, pp. 993-994) Freud demonstrated that, indeed, but he never fully believed it.

This pattern of keeping silent and asking help from Gentiles reappeared when, late in life, Freud was asked to speak up against anti-Semitism. In 1938, after Freud fled the Nazis for London, the British news magazine *Time and Tide* asked Freud to contribute to a special edition on anti-Semitism. Freud wrote back, "Don't you think you ought to reserve the columns of your special number for the utterances of non-Jewish people, less personally involved than myself?" And he added a French saying that concluded, "A Gentleman betrayed / Departs without a word." (Freud 1938, p. 301) The same sense of wounded Jewish pride seems to manifest itself in Freud's hunger for non-Jewish allies that could rescue psychoanalysis from the stigma of Jewish Vienna.

But more than encouraging splitting and avoidance, his feelings about anti-Semitism appear to have bolstered his pessimism about public demonstrations of psychoanalysis. When Freud expresses a feeling of futility in trying to prove the merits of psychoanalysis and underrates his own ability to win legitimacy for the field in the public eye, is he not perhaps expressing a darkness that originates with his feelings about anti-Semitism? When in the *Introductory Lectures* Freud despairs of changing resistant minds and states pessimistically, "Nothing can be done against prejudices" (Freud 1917, p. 462), is he partly thinking of Karl Lueger and Hermann Biehlolawek's evil intentions toward the Jews? Did Freud see a meaningful similarity between the fascist mind and the deeply repressed, resistant one? Both character types are perhaps so enslaved to an unexamined childlike conscience that they can't tolerate the unwanted parts of their home landscapes, whether mental or national, and seek to annihilate them.

The overlap between anti-Semitism and resistance to psychoanalysis imparts a frightening literality to the old wish of the Freud-haters, which has often been expressed in repressive style as though the wish were the fact: "Freud is dead." Freud took stock of such hatred a hundred years ago when he wrote, "At least a dozen times in recent years I have read that now psychoanalysis is dead, defeated and disposed of once and for all." (Freud 1914, p. 35) Cries of "Freud is dead" amidst cries of "annihilate the Jews" perhaps heightened Freud's rage at his critics and his sense of danger in connection with adversarial attempts at proof. Heightened rage and heightened danger would inevitably reinforce the strength of his defenses against proving. It would have been much harder for Freud to take a nuanced view of someone like Janet, and of how best to respond to him, when Janet's anti-Semitic taunts against Viennese sexuality sounded the same notes played by the mob of bloodthirsty Jew-haters. For Freud, such confrontations with critics were no mere instances of intellectual disagreement, but rather encounters with a dark fascist hatred that had real power to endanger his career and his family. Ultimately, that dark fascist hatred did endanger his career and his family. Peter Gay reports that in 1938 after the Nazi annexation of Austria, "The thought of suicide even invaded the Freud household." Anna asked her father, "Wouldn't it be better if we all killed ourselves?" Shortly after the *Anschluss*, 500 Austrian Jews actually did so. "Why?" Freud answered. "Because they would like us to?" (Gay 1988, pp. 621-622)

If premonitions of a Holocaust smoldered around anti-psychoanalytic criticism, Freud's reluctance to engage with critics once again seems understandable from a psychological point of view. From a rational point of view, however, did he do psychoanalysis a disservice by identifying with Janet's critique of Jewish Vienna, by consequently attempting to recuse himself from leadership of the movement, prematurely assigning leadership to Jung because he was Swiss and not a Jew? It's impossible not to sympathize with Freud's fear and outrage in the climate of anti-Semitism that surrounded him, and at the same time it's important to note how those feelings are likely to have skewed his thinking about proof and public vindication of psychoanalysis.

7. Freud's Authoritarianism as a Product of Proof Aversion

In *Discovering the Mind: Freud, Adler, and Jung*, Walter Kaufmann laments that Freud "is widely seen as a dogmatist who excommunicated disciples who dared to dissent." (Kaufmann 2017, p. 64) To be sure, critics frequently cite Freud's authoritarianism and dogmatism in order to discredit him. Perhaps that's why Freudians have for so long ignored the accusation; Robert Holt, who has brought a Freudian outlook to the analysis of Freud's authoritarianism, observes that "most writers who do not take a harshly critical approach to the founder of psychoanalysis hardly mention the issue of domination." (Holt 2015, p. 316) After all, Freud's domineering treatment of Jung no more discredits psychoanalysis than Thomas Edison's wars with George Westinghouse discredit the light bulb. But if Freud could be tyrannical towards colleagues and dogmatic in response to conflicting ideas, and if these patterns persist among latter-day psychoanalysts, then it's obviously an important problem to recognize, understand, and if possible correct. In this chapter, I will explore Freud's authoritarianism as another manifestation of his aversion to proof. My aim is to provide an explanation, but also a solution. Interpreting Freud and later psychoanalysts' authoritarianism in light of defense mechanisms entrained by the pursuit of psychoanalytic knowledge could, one hopes, help interrupt the syndrome of authoritarianism in the psychoanalytic community.

Many critics, dissidents, and Freudians have by now observed that in addition to Freud's many fine qualities as a person and a scientist, he could indeed be rigid and tyrannical, with profound consequences for the psychoanalytic movement. Arnold Richards writes, "For reasons perhaps more personal than scientific, Freud believed that psychoanalysis had to be protected from 'dissidents,' whom he relentlessly distanced, either by exclusion or by expulsion." (Richards 2015, p. 397) Holt says of Freud's biographers that "all of them agree: Whatever the nature of the critical dispute, Freud always took the uncompromising stance—my follower or my enemy." (Holt 2015, p. 339) Richards observes that the American Psychoanalytic Association continues to rule its constituents in an oligarchical, authoritarian manner, and both Richards and Holt aver that the psychoanalytic movement since Freud's death has continued to suppress dissent and banish dissenters.

Holt's study aims to describe Freud's authoritarianism more than to interpret it, but he does offer a compelling explanation for the problem of authoritarianism among psychoanalysts: "May it not be that at the heart of the dilemmas of psychoanalysis today is an unanalyzed and ultimately self-destructive pursuit of power?" (p. 342) Earlier in his paper, Holt notes that Freud "tended to play down not only aggression but competitiveness and power-hunger as psychopathologically unimportant motivations in his patients until after 1921 and the advent of the death instinct." Holt proposes that this was "in part because of his difficulty coming to terms with his own dominant, aggressive, competitive wishes." (p. 329) It's a cogent argument with far-reaching implications.

And yet it doesn't by itself explain the authoritarianism. Whereas unexamined rivalries and power hunger surely affect every human institution, psychoanalytic authoritarianism exhibits some unique characteristics. For one thing, there's a heavy proportion of existential anxiety in it. Whereas other scientists wrangle over prestige, credit, promotions, fiefdoms, publications, and the merit of various theories, Freud's battles with colleagues take place in a more existentially threatening sphere, which seems to necessitate Freud's invocation of emergency dictatorial powers. His disputes hinge upon the very definition of psychoanalysis. He doesn't quarrel with colleagues over which theories are correct, so much as over which theories are permissible and consistent with the continued survival of psychoanalysis. Newton and Liebniz, by contrast, didn't argue over the definition of calculus, nor over who would be allowed to practice it in future generations, but only over who deserved credit for its invention.

When Freud exercises despotic rule over the institution of psychoanalysis, it's usually in connection with the anxiety that psychoanalytic knowledge is especially vulnerable to corruption in the wrong hands. "I considered it necessary to form an official association," Freud writes in the *History*, "because I feared the abuses to which psycho-analysis would be subjected as soon as it became popular. There should be some headquarters whose business it would be to declare: 'All this nonsense is nothing to do with analysis; this is not psycho-analysis.' " (Freud 1914, p. 43) Freud's rationale for a strong central authority in control of psychoanalysis consistently points to the problem of psychological resistance to psychoanalytic knowledge: anyone who attempts to comprehend psychoanalysis, unlike physics, faces irrational, repressive emotional forces that are bound to distort rational thought. This is why Freud excommunicated Adler and Jung: he believed that they'd let their own emotional resistances distort their understanding of psychoanalysis.

According to Freud, both of them had suppressed the importance of sexuality in their thinking, and in so doing had become victims rather than students of repression. To allow them to continue to work under the banner of psychoanalysis and to influence others with their particular species of intellectual resistance, Freud implies, would be to endanger the hard-earned truths of psychoanalysis.

The view of life which is reflected in the Adlerian system is founded exclusively on the aggressive instinct; there is no room in it for love. We might feel surprise that such a cheerless *Weltanschauung* should have met with any attention at all; but we must not forget that human beings, weighed down by the burden of their sexual needs, are ready to accept any thing if only the 'overcoming of sexuality' is offered them as a bait.

> Adler's secession took place before the Weimar Congress in 1911; after that date the Swiss began theirs.... In 1912 Jung boasted, in a letter from America, that his modifications of psycho-analysis had overcome the resistances of many people who had hitherto refused to have anything to do with it. I replied that that was nothing to boast of, and that the more he sacrificed of the hard-won truths of psycho-analysis the more would he see resistances vanishing. This modification which the Swiss were so proud of introducing was again nothing else but a pushing into the background of the sexual factor in psycho-analytic theory. I confess that from the beginning I regarded this 'advance' as too far-reaching an adjustment to the demands of actuality. (p. 58)

Just as a fear of public resistance to psychoanalysis compelled Freud to avoid his critics outside the field, a fear of resistance to psychoanalysis from within the field compelled him to rule it with an iron hand.

The assumption seems to be that because resistance is irrational, it cannot be defeated by reason, but only by force. This is, of course, untrue. In *The Question of Lay Analysis*, Freud emphasizes the importance of tact in overcoming resistance. "You will be making a bad mistake if, in an effort, perhaps, at shortening the analysis, you throw your interpretations at the patient's head as soon as you have found them." (Freud 1926, p. 220) The only force that conquers irrational resistance in therapy is the force of reason, applied patiently, cautiously, tactfully, persistently, and compassionately. Freud's false belief that resistance among psychoanalysts demands tyranny in its institutions is only one indication that Freud himself was acting from emotion, not reason, when he embraced authoritarianism. Anxiety about the future of psychoanalysis had caused him to hand over the keys to the kingdom to Jung, and when Jung went astray, the same anxiety caused Freud to snatch the keys back.

The defense mechanisms that affect Freud's relations with critics outside the psychoanalytic movement naturally apply to his relations with dissidents too; dissidents are after all critics situated inside the psychoanalytic movement. Therefore, in trying to understand Freud's relationship to dissident criticism within the movement, I will appeal to the same analytic model for understanding his relationship to criticism: projection of his own internal criticism onto others; splitting of his audience into either friends or enemies, with avoidance of enemies; and reversals in which Freud gives his power away to his critics. I will then move on to two other pieces of analysis that are more specific and possibly more important to understanding Freud's authoritarian responses to dissidents: first, Freud's evident projection of his own impulse toward rebellion onto his followers along with his own attendant inner criticism; and second, the notion that dogmatism functions psychodynamically as a substitute for proof and a compensation for the doubts that conscience raises against psychoanalytic knowledge.

7.1. Defenses in the Context of Dissident Criticism

Projection of Inner Criticism onto Disciples

Much as Freud could sometimes imagine or exaggerate criticism from commentators outside the movement, he could sometimes imagine or exaggerate criticism from his followers. Freud's reactions to Jung's lectures at Fordham University in New York in late 1912 illustrate how

THE PSYCHOANALYST'S AVERSION TO PROOF

dramatically Freud could distort a dissident's views. When Freud agrees with Abraham that "Jung is in full retreat from psycho-analysis" (Freud 1914, p. 60), he misrepresents Jung's American lectures in the extreme. Gay evidently relies on Freud's account, as he too asserts that in the Fordham lectures "Jung had thrown overboard most of the psychoanalytic baggage—childhood sexuality, the sexual etiology of the neuroses, the Oedipus complex—and had openly redefined libido." (Gay 1988, p. 231) One need only read Jung's lectures, which were published in the first issue of *The Psychoanalytic Review* in 1913, to see that this is not accurate.

Jung's Fordham lectures, while inferior to Freud's own expositions of psychoanalysis both stylistically and theoretically, mostly read like a sincere effort to explain Freudian psychoanalysis, shocking facts and all, to the American doctors in the audience. The lectures take a somewhat different approach from Freud's but don't shy away from infantile sexuality, the Oedipus complex, or the unconscious. On the contrary, Jung makes innovative, cunning arguments on behalf of each of these core Freudian ideas. Admittedly, Jung probably spends too much time on his own minor questions, objections, and pet theories, and he makes some errors—for example, he seems not to grasp Freud's notion that the latent self-abnegating wishes of conscience manifest themselves in dreams as fears. But by raising his own questions about psychoanalysis, Jung also produces one felicitous rhetorical effect that generally eludes Freud—namely, a sense that psychoanalysis, like any other science, is an open field of inquiry and isn't yet in possession of all the final answers. His discussions of resistance, unlike Freud's, do not deny the audience the right to question. Jung asks his audience instead for scientific neutrality before observations of what is the case versus moral outrage over what ought to be the case. Jung's association experiments furthermore provided experimental proof of the validity of psychoanalytic ideas. Had Freud not curtly dismissed the possibility of experimental proof, Jung's approach might have helped to convince medical doctors in the long run. Jung says of unconscious thought processes in his first Fordham lecture:

> [I]t is possible to test the phenomena by experiment. The association-tests provide us with the necessary experiences. Here we find the extraordinary fact that associations pertaining to complexes saturated with emotion emerge with much greater difficulty into consciousness, and are much more easily forgotten.
>
> As my experiments on this subject were never reexamined, the conclusions were never adopted, until just lately, when Wilhelm Peters, a disciple of Kraepelin, proved in general my previous observation, namely, that painful events are very rarely correctly reproduced (*"die unlustbetonten Erlebnisse werden am seltensten richtig reproduciert"*). (Jung 1913, p. 8)[33]

Jung claimed he'd found novel ways of disarming audience resistance, but Freud interpreted these strategies as evidence of Jung's unconscious wishes to water down psychoanalysis—i.e., his resistance to psychoanalytic truths. (Freud 1914, p. 58)

Jung may have been destined to rebel against his mentor and take his own work in ever more mystical, unscientific, or puritanical

---

33 Jung's association experiments would certainly have been more comprehensible to my medical school classmates than the approach the lecturer took in the single lecture we received on psychoanalysis. The lecturer opened, in so many words, with the statement, "Put aside science for the moment and enter the world of dreams." I liked much of his lecture, but with his first three words, he'd lost even my close friends, to whom I'd been trying to explain what I knew about Freud for over a year.

directions. But his lectures at Fordham do not by themselves assure this outcome. Jung historian Sonu Shamdasani quotes James Jackson Putnam's 1912 letter to Ernest Jones in which Putnam says of Jung that he seemed "to be under the necessity of accentuating any peculiarity of his own position for his own personal satisfaction" but adds, "I cannot think that any serious breach would be occasioned by this present movement on his part." As an example of the minor sort of objection or modification to Freud's ideas that Jung proposed, Putnam cites Jung's attempt to distinguish an infant's pleasure in sucking at its mother's breast from explicitly sexual pleasure. (Shamdasani 2012, pp. 18-19) Later developments in psychoanalytic thinking would actually vindicate Jung to some degree in his belief that Freud had defined libido too narrowly. For example, Freud and many later analysts would increasingly think of libido as a composite of sexual and aggressive energy, not just sexual. (Brenner 1973, p. 30)

Right or wrong, Jung's complaints against a purely sexual definition of libido do not look radical or dangerous today except under the lens of a paranoia looking hard for resistances to the sexual candor of psychoanalysis. Shamdasani points out that Freud didn't even read Jung's New York lectures until early August 1913, after he'd already broken off personal relations with Jung. He then wrote to Sándor Ferenczi, "I have now read Jung's paper myself and find it good and innocuous, beyond my expectation.... On the whole, I have very much overestimated the danger from a distance." (Brabant et al. 1993, p. 505) Had Freud been able to assess the "danger" more objectively in the first place, he might have recognized it as a product of his own paranoia, from which no disciple was immune. Freud had even directed such paranoia at quintessential Freud loyalist Ernest Jones in 1909: "During the Worcester time Freud formed an exaggerated idea of my independence and feared, quite unwarrantably, that I might not become a close adherent." (Jones 1955, p. 58)

Just as Freud had overestimated the criticism forthcoming from Löwenfeld against his paper on the sexual etiology of neurosis, Freud overestimated the danger from Jones and Jung. And if Freud anticipated apostasy where it didn't really exist, he must have projected an expectation of it from inside his own conscience, just as he projected expectations of criticism onto his reviewers.

Splitting, Guilt by Association, and the Expulsion of Traitors

Once Jung became an enemy, Freud devalued everything he'd done. By virtue of such black-and-white division of psychoanalysts into loyal followers or apostate turncoats, Freud returned to his previous splitting practices with outsiders. "Once a break in a relationship came," Holt writes, "Freud was harsh, uncompromising, and unforgiving, no matter what the antecedent history of warmth and intimacy or the crushing effect on the rejected one." (Holt 2015, p. 328) Similarly: "He would scheme with his favorite followers to get rid of some others, whom he treated with contempt once they were out of his favor." (p. 341) Indeed, in response to the Adler and Jung "defections" and with Freud's encouragement, Jones famously organized a secret committee of Freud loyalists dedicated to reporting on colleagues who showed signs of resistance to core psychoanalytic tenets. (Gay 1988, pp. 229-230)

Freud practiced an almost McCarthy-like guilt by association, training extraordinary suspicion on those he deemed to have been intellectually contaminated by their contacts with an apostate. For example, Freud wrote to his first biographer Fritz Wittels in 1923, "unfortunately your relationship to Stekel rules out any further effort on my part toward a mutual understanding." (E. Freud 1961, p. 346) If Wittels still listened to Stekel, whom Freud had banished, then to Freud's mind there could be no middle ground of mutual understanding between Freud and Wittels—even though Wittels was himself a practicing psychoanalyst. Freud's authoritarianism toward Stekel and paranoia toward Wittels arguably had profound, unforeseen, and unfortunate consequences for the psychoanalytic movement, as I will later discuss.

In the case of American psychiatrists Smith Ely Jelliffe and William Alanson White, Freud displayed an even more irrational sort of McCarthyism. For years, he suspected them of being resistant to psychoanalysis because they knew Jung. In 1912, Jelliffe had invited Jung to Fordham and hosted Jung at his house. (Shamdasani 2012, p. 17) Jung performed his assigned duty of attempting to spread knowledge of psychoanalysis in America, giving his own introductory lectures on psychoanalysis and encouraging Jelliffe and White to start a psychoanalytic journal. They founded *The Psychoanalytic Review*, and in 1913 White invited Freud to submit a paper for its first issue. (Barnett 2013, pp. 13-14) Meanwhile A.A. Brill, who had founded the New York Psychoanalytic Society in 1911, seamlessly adopted Freud's practice of dividing the world into those for psychoanalysis and those against. He wrote to Freud in 1913, "The funny part of the whole thing is that Jelliffe is a very ardent worker for psychoanalysis, but of course he is thoroughly Jung...." (p. 15)

Knowing that Freud was paranoid about dissidence, Brill undercut Jelliffe despite having given Jelliffe more personal instruction in psychoanalysis than Jung ever had. Jung had given Jelliffe none aside from whatever he might have communicated to his host when he came to lecture at Fordham. Brill and Jelliffe, by contrast, had worked together at Columbia's Neurological Institute of New York. Jelliffe says, "After our clinics, three times a week Brill and I walked homewards together through the park and as formerly with Dr.

White we argued and argued and he persisted and thus I became a convinced Freudian." (Jelliffe 1933, p. 325)

In applying the epithet "thoroughly Jung" to Jelliffe, Brill looks deceitful and politically calculating. Instructed in Freud's McCarthyist ways, Brill, Jones, and others in turn encouraged Freud in his tendency to split his followers into good and bad, and with a clear ulterior motive: to preserve their own intimacy with Freud and deny their rivals the same privilege. What could "thoroughly Jung" really even mean, especially in 1913, when Jung still considered himself a Freudian? "Thoroughly Jung" sounds like a designation produced by the irrational defense mechanisms of splitting and avoidance: *You are contaminated with Jung and therefore I needn't bother with you.*

The truth was that neither Jelliffe nor White were even aware of the rift between Jung and Freud, nor had Jung given them any reason to believe that he represented a splinter movement, much less beckoned to them to join it. (Barnett 2013, p. 18; Jelliffe 1933, p. 326) Sabotaged by Brill, White received no reply from Freud and naïvely published Jung instead in his first issue. In 1914, ten months or so after White had invited Freud to contribute to his journal's first issue, White received a scolding letter from Freud. (Barnett 2013, pp. 16-17) In it, Freud accused White and Jelliffe—both of whom were famously altruistic physicians—of founding *The Psychoanalytic Review* for the "unseemly" motive of profit. Freud went on in a haughty tone:

> The cause would have been much better served if the psychoanalytic literature had been allowed to remain centralized for a good while yet, until experience had time to catch up with interest in America. This judgment of the *Review* is further supported by Jelliffe's intimacy with Jung, who in spite of his presidency has never lifted a finger for the

International Association or its organs, but only pursued his
own aggrandizement. (p. 17)

The letter distorted Jung's efforts on behalf of psychoanalysis,
exaggerated Jelliffe's "intimacy with Jung" in a markedly paranoid way,
and harshly rebuffed Jelliffe and White's interest in psychoanalysis.
It would have been no surprise if Jelliffe and White had become
enemies of psychoanalysis. But Jelliffe persisted in courting Freud's
favor and, to both Freud and Jelliffe's credit, they overcame their initial
misunderstanding and struck up an epistolary friendship that lasted
the rest of Freud's days.

When in 1929, however, Jelliffe again invited Freud to contribute
to *The Psychoanalytic Review*, Freud again refused, according to
an intractably paranoid ideation that White "feels a good deal of
resistance against Analysis." It was an extreme distortion. "[White]
outlines the principles of psychoanalysis everywhere," Jelliffe wrote
back, "and has done more for its extension over the USA than any one
other individual. I think you should know this." (p. 22)

Freud was content to accept Jelliffe and White's unrequited
devotion. He never contributed anything to their journal (though Brill's
English translation of the *History* did appear in the *Review* in 1916).
The entire North American continent would seem for Freud to have
been contaminated by apostasy. Even with loyalist A.A. Brill ruling
over it, Freud looked down on American psychoanalysis throughout
his life. (p. 17) He preferred that the Americans read a "centralized"
psychoanalytic journal under his authoritarian control so that he could
purify it of the traitors, enemies, and fools he imagined were ready to
attack or corrupt his theories.

The pattern of Freud's splitting and avoidance is so recurrent and
prominent a feature of his biography that it hardly seems necessary

to recount more instances of it. As Gay says, "This emotional trajectory raises the question of whether Freud somehow needed to make his friends into enemies. First Breuer, then Fliess, then Adler and Stekel, now Jung, with other ruptures to come." (Gay 1988, p. 242) As the case of William Alanson White suggests, there were not only ruptures to come, but relationships that ought to have been.

Reversal: Giving Power Away and Reclaiming It Through Tyranny

Does authoritarianism really derive from an unalloyed love of power, or is it a compensation for a feeling of powerlessness? Aren't dictators notoriously insecure? And if feelings of powerlessness and vulnerability contributed to Freud's authoritarianism, where did the feelings of powerlessness and vulnerability originate? Weren't they products of his own self-attack?

According to the theory of Freud's proof aversion, the bold, aggressive act of presenting his antisocial ideas to the public caused him shame and anxiety, which he relieved by defense mechanisms, including a reversal of this aggression so that he imagined the aggression echoing back at him in kind in the form of resistant criticism. He would then avoid the critics, deploy Gentile surrogates to defend psychoanalysis, silence himself, corrupt his own efforts at proof, or counterattack furiously against the bugbear of perceived resistance.

Freud seems to have imagined the same aggression rebounding back at him from dissidents inside his own movement, and his counterattack against dissidents' purported resistance to psychoanalysis in many ways looks similar to his counterattacks against his critics' resistance. Dissidents, however, were susceptible to his attacks in a way that critics outside the movement were not. For one thing, Freud could present his followers with analyses of their purported resistance. Sometimes this form of counterattack on dissident followers took the form of belittling interpretations. Thus, Freud sometimes ignored Jung's questions and theoretical objections and instead dismissed them as resistance. Shamdasani quotes a 1912 letter from Jung to Jones which describes Jung's helpless feeling before Freud's authoritarian technique. Freud overruled Jung's intellectual questions about psychoanalytic theory by psychoanalyzing them away and Jung had this to say:

> Freud is convinced that I am thinking under the domination of a father complex against him and then all is complex-nonsense.... Against this insinuation I am completely helpless.... If Freud understands each attempt to think in a new way about the problems of psychoanalysis as a personal resistance, things become impossible. (Shamdasani 2012, p. 21)

Once again, Freud substitutes a critique of enemy resistance for a substantive rational argument. Through a reversal of aggression, he seems to endow Jung with a partly imagined hostility to psychoanalysis that renders Jung deaf to proof and argument, though Jung was not.

Because Freud insisted on the unilateral authority to psychoanalyze away resistance among his followers, he could not allow Jung to use the same tactic against him. On December 3, 1912, Jung wrote to Freud to complain to him directly about this unequal state of affairs. Jung remembered how in 1909 he and Freud had analyzed each others' dreams aboard the S.S. George Washington en route to America (Gay 1988, p. 225), where Freud was to give his lectures at Clark University. "Our analysis, you may remember," Jung writes, "came to a stop with your remark that you 'could not submit to analysis *without losing your authority.*' These words are engraved on my memory as a symbol of everything to come." (McGuire 1988, p. 526)

If psychoanalyzing dissidents within the movement failed to arrest their drift away from Freudian dogma, Freud could get rid of dissent in a way he couldn't get rid of criticism outside the movement. He could kick dissidents out of their positions of power and exclude them from psychoanalytic societies and meetings. Through such authoritarian practices, Freud was perhaps only doing to his dissident followers what he would like to have done to his critics—eliminate them.

The aggression of such purges surely provoked in Freud still more anxiety and paranoia. His break with Fliess, for example, haunted him forever. On March 9, 1909, Freud expressed to Jung his anxiety about Jung's failing to write to him, and attributed it to his falling out with Fliess. It was as if Freud still expected to be abandoned just as he had abandoned Fliess:

Many thanks for your telegram and letter, which (the telegram in itself did the trick) put an end to my anxiety. I evidently still have a traumatic hyperaesthesia toward dwindling correspondence. I remember its genesis well (Fliess) and should not like to repeat such an experience unawares. (McGuire 1988, p. 209)

Presumably, excommunicating Jung caused Freud a similar anxiety and remorse. The relationship began with an unusual intensity, and when Freud met with Jung in Vienna at the end of March 1909 (p. 215), he pronounced Jung his adopted son and successor, despite misgivings about Jung's disconcerting interest in paranormal phenomena. (p. 218) Jung followed with a letter on April 2, 1909 in which he reacted to the father-son succession business in an incongruous way. He wrote,

"That last evening with you has, most happily, freed me inwardly from the oppressive sense of your paternal authority." (p. 217) Freud noted the incongruity in his letter of April 16:

> It is strange that on the very same evening when I formally adopted you as eldest son and anointed you—*in partibus infidelium* [in the lands of the unbelievers]—as my successor and crown prince, you should have divested me of my paternal dignity, which divesting seems to have given you as much pleasure as I, on the contrary, derived from the investiture of your person. Now I am afraid of falling back into the father role with you if I tell you how I feel about the poltergeist business.... I put my fatherly horned-rimmed spectacles on again and warn my dear son to keep a cool head.... (pp. 218-219)

After Abraham, Jones, and Ferenczi ganged up on Jung to get rid of Freud's misbegotten crown prince, and after Freud renounced his overly intimate relationship with Jung and threw him out of the movement, Freud refused to pay heed to the injury he'd caused Jung. Whatever remorse he felt, he covered it with a floodtide of authoritarian rage at Jung's apostasy.

In this way, perhaps, Freud's authoritarianism may have borrowed strength from an underlying guilt, in addition to underlying vulnerability. If so, it would be a case of what Freud called criminality from a sense of guilt (Freud 1916), a notion that could be summed up in Tacitus's observation *Proprium humani ingenii est odisse quem laeseris*, or "It is characteristic of human nature to hate the man you have wronged." More paranoia and more purges were bound to follow in a sort of vicious circle of aggression and guilt. The aggression towards dissidents necessitated a guilty feeling of vulnerability, and the vulnerability necessitated more aggression towards dissidents.

Freud's conviction that psychoanalysis was as vulnerable and despised as the Jews may have contributed to his authoritarianism in still other ways. It seems to have caused him to demand an unusual degree of professional consensus among its members—as if divisions within the movement would weaken it before the Huns encamped outside its gates. "I would not like any serious bad feeling to come between you," Freud wrote to Abraham in 1908, urging him to make peace with Jung. "We are still so few that disharmony, especially because of any personal 'complexes', should be out of the question among us." (Falzeder 2002, p. 38) The existential anxiety is palpable in "we are still so few" and the authoritarian note in "out of the question" unmistakable.

Perhaps it was also this feeling of vulnerability that made it hard for Freud to countenance fools, and brought out in him a reactionary violence. Freud makes an explicit connection between his hatred of fools and his "tendency toward tyranny" in his letter of August 22, 1883 to Martha Bernays:

> During these past few days I have been having some serious differences of opinion with Pfungen,[34] and I have treated him too harshly, which was very unfair of me. I am afraid I do have a tendency toward tyranny, as someone recently told me.... I also have the capacity, in other respects praiseworthy, of hating someone on intellectual grounds, just because he is a fool, and this is what the otherwise excellent man unfortunately is. He is quite *meschugge* and all his thoughts are crazy. But I must alter my attitude toward him, for he is really a very decent man. (E. Freud 1961, p. 43)

---

34 See also E. Freud 1961, p. 65.

Perhaps Freud's hatred of fools who ought to know better goes all the way back to his father Jacob, whose intellectual weakness caused Freud feelings of pride but also guilt. Having long ago vanquished his own father intellectually, Freud may have found in such fools a trace of the fallen Saul, and a corresponding instigation to Davidic guilt. Perhaps on some level he regretted trouncing fools in intellectual competition and empathically identified with them. Perhaps by identifying with fools, his conscience left him feeling unfairly diminished. Then, turning criminal from a sense of guilt, he may have sought to re-establish his intellectual superiority by rising up and utterly destroying the fools who had tormented his conscience.

7.2. Projection of Rebellion and Its Attendant Inner Criticism

As Freud saw it, his revolutionary discoveries put him into constant opposition with the "compact majority." (Freud 1925, p. 9) Once he'd founded psychoanalysis, however, he became famously intolerant of dissidence and rebellion within his own movement. The ironic career twist demands our attention as analysts of Freud and raises the question: Did rebellious dissidents remind Freud of himself? And was his hatred for dissidents a form of self-hatred? It's been observed that when children direct hatred toward younger playmates or siblings who are in earlier stages of development, they do so not because they hate the younger child but because the regressive tug of the earlier stage embarrasses the older child. Did something similar affect Freud, who had graduated from rebellion to authority?

Charles Brenner has observed that rebels have an unconscious Oedipal wish to usurp tyrannical power:

> Yesterday's foe of tyranny becomes today's tyrant.... [R]evolutionaries ... are motivated by an *unconscious* wish

to become like the very rulers they detest, to occupy the same position, to exercise the same prerogatives, the same power, and to enjoy the same authority.... [R]ebels unconsciously identify more or less strongly with their rulers, as do rebellious children with their parents. We can safely assume that this psychological fact plays an important part in revolutions. Thus, the French revolution produced an emperor, Napoleon, and a new aristocracy." (Brenner 1973, pp. 225-227)

Was Freud another revolutionary who secretly wished to become a tyrant? Was that why he swatted down his challengers with such fury?

Perhaps this is part of the explanation, but as I've tried to show, Freud's reactions to dissidence contained a significant proportion of anxiety and paranoia. Paranoia, in turn, according to the Freudian view, is an inversion of unconscious aggression, a turning against the self. One wonders, therefore, if Freud's hatred of rebels in his own movement was in part a result of paranoid projection of the self-judgment that he felt in connection with his own intellectual rebellion. If he hated authority, surely some countervailing, moralistic force inside of him hated rebellion too. Perhaps he unconsciously identified with authority when he put down insurrection, not only because it was pleasurable to wield that power over his subjects, but because he was wracked by guilt and fear at the sight of a revolution like his own, and had to banish it from before his eyes.

Kenneth Eisold makes a similar interpretation of Fritz Wittels, who began as a rebel and ended up an authoritarian. Wittels's *curriculum vitae* as a rebel included defending Stekel against Freud (Gay 1988, pp. 214n, 232), emigrating to America, and publishing a Freud biography against Freud's wishes. Then it was Wittels who threw Karen Horney out of the New York Psychoanalytic Society: "[I]t should be no surprise that it was Wittels who led the attack in New York because he ... was an early rebel himself.... Now, he disowned his own deviancy in standing up so vehemently for the authority of 'the Professor'." (Eisold 1998, p. 878)

Countless times in his writings, Freud expresses his contempt for authority. Men of lesser genius but greater authority than Freud himself are the great antagonists of his life story. From the *Autobiographical Study*: "The impression that the high authorities had rejected my innovations remained unshaken.... I found myself forced into the Opposition." (Freud 1925, pp. 15-16) Freud discovers a motto for scientific genius in Leonardo Da Vinci's "teaching that authority should be looked down on and that imitation of the 'ancients' should be repudiated," and traces this repudiation of authority back to the great scientist's childhood: "the 'ancients' and authority simply correspond to his father...." (Freud 1910, p. 122) From the shabby authority figure of Jacob Freud, a father who couldn't explain babies, to the puffed-up neurologists who couldn't explain hysteria, to the carping, resistant critics of Freud's brilliant published theories, the authorities constitute the lifelong enemies of psychoanalytic research and knowledge. They are the enforcers of that propriety which resists the unwelcome, unholy truths of psychoanalytic discovery.

On the other hand, as I've already said, Freud's knowledge-hungry filial rebellion against authority put him in an uncomfortable position. Having dared to pursue sexual knowledge with Oedipal audacity, he forced on himself the self-image of a pariah, an incestuous father-killer, a demonic Jew. "In most other human beings—no less to-day than in primaeval times," Freud writes, "the need for support from an authority of some sort is so compelling that their world begins to totter if that authority is threatened." (pp. 122-123) And what forces rock the world when human beings dispose of authority? Guilt, anxiety, and shame. Freud's rebellion against authority and modesty rocked his own world with guilt, anxiety, and shame and called out corresponding defense mechanisms. How could it have been otherwise?

To that list of defense mechanisms his conscience called upon to relieve the tension of psychoanalytic research and publication, should we add another? And should we call it the projection of rebellion? Did Freud's paranoia about betrayal among his followers reflect his own predilection towards betrayal of authority? Having rebelled against authority in a way that was sure to outrage his conscience, perhaps he projected that rebellion outward onto dissidents, where it could be destroyed. In that case, the tidy, surgical fury with which he destroyed Adler and Jung must have originated in a reservoir of moralistic, anti-rebel feeling first aimed at himself by his own conscience. Having punished himself for hunting after sexual knowledge and killing off his intellectual fathers, perhaps he expected dissidents to pay a similarly high price for their rebellion.

In the *History* Freud almost admits outright that he saw an image of himself in Adler and in other dissidents. He invites comparison between himself and Adler by applying his treasured nickname for psychoanalysis, "the Opposition," to Adler's incipient rebel movement:

One outcome of the Nuremberg Congress was the founding of the *Zentralblatt für Psychoanalyse* [*Central Journal for Psycho-Analysis*], for which purpose Adler and Stekel joined forces. It was obviously intended originally to represent the Opposition: it was meant to win back for Vienna the hegemony threatened by the election of Jung. (Freud 1914, pp. 44-45)

Just as the Christians projected the anxiety of their rebellion against the Temple fathers onto the Jews, making them into perpetrators of deicide in the Gospels, human psychology perhaps obligated Freud's rebel movement to invent its own rebel angels, and cast them out. And if Adler and Jung saved Freud the trouble of inventing rebels, then so much the better from the standpoint of his conscience. Freud seems to have rebuked them in the same harsh manner that his own conscience, piqued by his rebellion against his father, rebuked him.

7.3. Dogmatism as an Antidote to Doubt

"[T]his tradition of expulsion and suppression has been going on for a long time," Richards writes. "[I]t has managed to perpetuate itself consistently from generation to generation. How does it maintain such strength?" (Richards 2015, p. 397) Richards points to the authoritarian bureaucracy that Freud left behind in order to suppress dissidence and expel its perpetrators. Freud created that oligarchical bureaucracy in the hope that it would prevent intellectual resistance from swallowing psychoanalysis back into the repressed oblivion from which it had come.

I would like to add, however, that psychoanalytic authoritarianism is not just a system of governance, but also a dogmatic style of thought—and not a cultural style but a psychodynamic one, forged under emotional pressures that arise specifically in connection with the study of unconscious feelings. I believe this to be nearer to the heart of Freud's authoritarianism than anything: dogmatism in psychoanalysis, and a related insistence on omniscience, compensates for the doubt psychoanalysts feel about psychoanalysis—a doubt created by their own unconscious resistance to uncomfortable psychoanalytic knowledge. Providing justifications for psychoanalytic theories, I believe, feels to some analysts too much like catering to neurotic doubts about psychoanalytic insights. Therefore analysts pronounce psychoanalytic knowledge by edict, with disregard for those skeptical demands for proof that originate in the conscience.

Consider the following concrete example. In my psychoanalytic studies, I met an analyst who would raise his voice slightly when he came to a subject he thought would arouse his audience's resistance. Sometimes he raised his voice around the usual sources of public discomfort—infantile sexuality, the Oedipus complex, etc.—but also in response to student mistakes and questions. If a student used the term *subconscious*, say, the teacher would explain at a slightly elevated volume that *subconscious* was an equivocation, an attempt to deny or soften the reality of totally *unconscious* thought processes. If a student questioned Freud's assertion that certain symbols in dreams have more or less universal meanings—questioned Freud's assertion, for example, that in all dreams "*Shoes* and *slippers* are female genitals" (Freud 1916-1917, p. 158)—the teacher would raise his voice against the history of resistance to universal dream symbolism.

The volume of the teacher's voice did not have its intended effect—on the contrary, it invited skepticism—but then I'm not sure the teacher was aware of his habit. It seemed to me that at such moments he spoke not to his audience but to himself. It was as though he were saying in effect, *I will not let this student's resistance tempt me to regress and to forget the profound insights of psychoanalysis. I will speak louder so that I don't allow my own conscience to become emboldened by skepticism and to repress my psychoanalytic knowledge by doubting it away.* Raising his voice, in other words, seemed to be his unconscious solution to the problem of doubt.

Similarly, Freud's writing acquires a certain stridency in the face of doubts and objections. The teacher who raised his voice in defense of universal dream symbolism followed Freud's strident example in the same context. Freud describes such symbolism in Lecture X in the

Introductory Lectures: "In this way we obtain constant translations for a number of dream-elements—just as popular 'dream-books' provide them for *everything* that appears in dreams." (p. 150) At the end of this lecture, Freud asks how universal dream symbolism "can meet with such violent resistance in educated people when the wide diffusion of symbolism in myths, religion, art and language is so unquestionable. May it not be that what is responsible is once again its connection with sexuality?" (p. 169) 15 years later, in the *New Introductory Lectures*, he professes to remain dumbfounded that people object to this part of the theory of dreams. "One person will take objection to sexuality, another to the unconscious; what seems particularly unpopular is the fact of symbolism." (Freud 1933, p. 138)

It's a case of prolonged obstinacy, even for Freud. This part of his dream theory was introduced a decade after the publication of *The Interpretation of Dreams*, in 1911, when Stekel published *Die Sprache des Traumes (The Language of Dreams)*. A universal dream language was Stekel's idea, and it evidently caused Freud to regress against his own revolutionary advances in the understanding of dreams. The idea of a universal dream language doesn't even sound Freudian, it sounds Jungian, and before Freud gave his support to the idea, he wrote against it: "My procedure is not so convenient as the popular decoding method which translates any given piece of a dream's content by a fixed key. I, on the contrary, am prepared to find that the same piece of content may conceal a different meaning when it occurs in various people or in various contexts." (Freud 1900, p. 105) In later editions of *The Interpretation of Dreams* Freud qualified Stekel's idea of universal dream language with more circumspection. (p. 357)

And yet Freud still insisted on presenting the Stekelian symbolism theory in its somewhat cavalier, dogmatic form in the 1916 *Introductory*

Lectures and even in the *New Introductory Lectures* of 1933, as though daring his audience to object. Having thrown down the Stekelian gauntlet in a manner he knows is provocative and overreaching, he then denies rational objections with the iron insistence that Jones describes when he writes of Freud: "In his old age he would repeat the words '*nein, nein, nein,*' to the accompaniment of a vigorous shaking of the head...." (Jones 1955, p. 428)

Communicating in private in 1908 with a trusted ally, sheltered from public resistance and focused on the practical demands of psychotherapy, Freud was less doctrinaire. Compare his public account of *flying* in dreams in Lecture X of the *Introductory Lectures* to his discussion of the same subject in correspondence with Karl Abraham. Here he is in the *Lectures*, overruling objections to a rigidly sexual interpretation of flying dreams: "Do not take it to heart if dreams of flying, so familiar and often so delightful, have to be interpreted as dreams of general sexual excitement, as erection-dreams." (Freud 1916-1917, p. 155) And here is the much more nuanced, much less doctrinaire back-and-forth between Abraham and Freud on the same subject. On January 8, 1908 Abraham writes:

You see, I am just reading the *Interpretation of Dreams* once again and find that I have all kinds of questions to ask. I will confine myself today to the *flying dreams*. The infantile source seems clear to me, but I believe I have found an actual one as well, occasioned by the following dream of an acquaintance. The lady dreams that she is floating in the sky as a small pink cloud. Then a large hand appears, follows her, comes nearer and nearer, and finally grasps her. I find the following interpretation for this aesthetically very beautiful dream. Two sisters of the dreamer have been married for some considerable time. A third became engaged shortly before the dream. She alone is left, is no longer young, has been getting very stout for some time, and is obviously afraid of being left on the shelf. In the dream she is as light as air instead of plump, and a male hand finds her desirable. Might not the flying in the dream, for others too, mean: I should like to be lighter? Perhaps you have had some experience with regard to this. (Falzeder 2002, p. 19)

The next day Freud replies, "The actual meanings of flying dreams are of course very varied. Yours is a very fine case, I should like it for the second edition [of *The Interpretation of Dreams*]. But other things can equally well be made of the material, as I shall show from examples." (p. 21) Freud interprets flying in dreams in dozens of ways in *The Interpretation of Dreams*.

Freud would not back down against resistance, however, even when the resistance directed reasonable skepticism at the excesses of Stekelian dream symbolism, which Freud himself found cause to hold at arm's length. It would seem that in public, or before the uninitiated, admitting mistakes or uncertainty felt to Freud like kindling flames under the entirety of psychoanalysis. If so, a distortion appears to have entered into his thinking on public demonstration once again. Instead of seeing resistance as friction generated by his powerful theory, he seems to see resistance as a wildfire ready to consume all the fields and cities of psychoanalytic thought. It looks like another instance of reversal in which Freud has donated his power of proof to critics, dissidents, and skeptics—another case therefore of an internal conflict with his own guilt, shame, anxiety, and resistance to psychoanalytic knowledge. When Freud fights off the audience's doubts about Stekelian dream symbolism instead of acknowledging the merits of the audience's questions, is he in fact warding off his own doubt, which threatens to spread like obsessional wildfire? Was the aforementioned instructor in psychoanalysis doing the same?

In many different discussions, whether of dream interpretation or of the treatment of obsessional neurosis, Freud speaks of doubt as one of the primary instruments of conscience, deployed with special craftiness in its war of resistance against psychoanalytic insight. Patients doubt the significance of their own dreams and of their own free associations on the couch. In therapy they mire themselves in the public controversies over the validity of psychoanalysis in order to deny themselves the private benefits of psychoanalytic insight. They even surrender the gains they've made in analysis.

Eugene Mahon has described "the defiant, transgressive nature of insight" itself (Mahon 2015, p. 169) and the consequent tendency of insights to flee as soon as they're secured. Patients sometimes dismiss an insight just after seeing it "[a]s though to undo the power and pleasure of the insight." (p. 173) Or they forget the insights and have to work them out again. That is to say, psychoanalytic knowledge is hard to acquire but also hard to hold onto. The power and pleasure of insight perhaps redoubles the shame, guilt, or anxiety that repressed the knowledge in the first place.

If doubt so often lurks in the vicinity of psychoanalytic knowledge, ready to degrade and destroy it, does doubt in general exert a special influence on the shape of psychoanalytic discourse? Freud and later psychoanalysts who take on the burden of safeguarding and transmitting this vulnerable knowledge must pilot their patients, their students, and themselves through the chaos of doubts and distortions and forgetting. Evidently, they sometimes lean on authoritarian faith and perhaps even megalomaniacal fantasies of omniscience to keep the doubt at bay. Nathan Kravis speaks to this phenomenon when he observes that psychoanalysts' feeling of conviction sometimes masks underlying uncertainty: "In educational settings, fiercely held conviction about the potency and efficacy of psychoanalysis often masks and defends against the shame collectively felt about the dearth of empirical evidence supporting the recommendation of psychoanalysis as the treatment of choice for specific patients." (Kravis 2013, p. 105) But even if there were a mountain of empirical evidence supporting psychoanalytic theory and treatment—some would argue that there is—the psychodynamics of self-knowledge would surely threaten psychoanalytic ideas with doubt and call out a compensatory conviction and dogmatism.

If so, authoritarianism isn't just a personality trait of Freud's. It's a hostility to questioning that's endemic to the transmission of psychoanalytic knowledge. It's a rebellion against the obscuring force of doubt whose consequence is not traditional scientific efforts at proof but rather a system that supports truths by decree. Seekers after psychoanalytic knowledge may unconsciously need these decrees from their mentors. They may in fact wish for the authority of father-figures like Freud to relieve their own doubts, their own shame or anxiety or guilt about psychoanalytic knowledge, to help them to see and hold onto truths they're too afraid, guilty, and defensive to see by themselves. Ralph Greenson alluded to psychoanalysts' need for authority when he wrote:

The very need to belong to a school, the need to be 'in', seems to me to indicate a need for protection or a need to obey the dictates of a leader, or of an 'ideal analyst'. In my opinion, the concept of the 'ideal analyst' or the belief in a perfect or complete system, excludes doubt, criticism, and rejects new and different ideas. This is incompatible with a scientific approach.... (Greenson 1969, p. 512)

We *need* to believe in everything Freud said—and perhaps, so did he—because without that rigid system of belief, doubt cripples the ability to see beyond defenses, and we collapse once again into tormenting darkness.

8. Case Study Conclusion

In summary, though Freud made one of the great contributions to human knowledge, a lacuna runs through his work from end to end: an irrational, emotional interference in his efforts to prove his theories. The interference manifests itself in expressions of pessimism about proof, spurious arguments about proof, ambivalence about proof, and in authoritarian, dogmatic attitudes that conflict with scientific method. Freud was evidently at pains to hide this emotional interference from himself and from others, and Freud's followers have for many years been willing participants in his secrecy. Many have felt the same pessimism or discomfort about proof, or have considered it dangerous to question Freud, lest doubts begin to eat at the infrastructure of psychoanalytic knowledge. For these reasons, I think, Freud's errors on the subjects of proof and public resistance have escaped detection and been perpetuated.

Once observed, however, the fact of emotional interference in the effort to validate psychoanalysis looks both obvious and ubiquitous. In this respect, the idea of proof aversion resembles many other significant Freudian insights: it's hard to see at first, but looks inevitable in retrospect. Once you see it, as Freud said, "[It] calls for real ingenuity not to see all this or to see it differently." (Freud 1917, p. 316)

The most satisfactory explanation I've found for this distorted thinking and behavior around proof is that public presentations of charged psychological data caused Freud shame, anxiety, and guilt, which his ego sought to delimit through defense mechanisms. The defense mechanisms in evidence in his work and correspondence include: projection of internal criticism; avoidance of proof and disputation; and a doubt-ridden reversal in which Freud surrenders his own power of proof to his critics. He turns it into their power of doubt and resistance, which he then inflates into an impassable obstacle.

While these defensive distortions of thought "can be confirmed by any observer who cares to see them" (p. 325) in Freud's writings, the deepest determining layers underneath these defenses must remain more obscure. Nevertheless, Freud gives us enough information about his childhood to enable us to make some reasonable conjectures about the early origins of his aversion to proof. Freud's shame, anxiety, and guilt about sexual knowledge and its public demonstration appear to be intimately connected with his own infantile sexual researches and his competition in the realm of knowledge with his unlearned father—that is to say, with infantile conflicts around his curiosity and his ambition.

Anti-Semitism shapes the historical background for this drama, but also plays a role in it. It goaded Freud to rebel against the establishment but also amplified his anxieties about displaying sexual knowledge and about staging an intellectual revolution, and aggravated the defenses I've described. Freud's complex relationship to his Jewish ethnicity sheds additional light on the psychology of sexuality and rebellion.

Those aspects of Freud's aversion to proof rooted in his specific infantile history and his specific historical context do not, however, suggest to me that Freud alone suffered an aversion to proof. The continuing ambivalence about scientific proof in the psychoanalytic community indicates that many other psychoanalysts share the same aversion. Surely, latter-day psychoanalysts have been influenced by Freud's authoritarian ban on experimental research and public disputation. But how could anyone publicly demonstrate psychoanalytic ideas without facing some of the internal conflicts that Freud did?

Try this thought experiment: put yourself in front of an audience full of critics of psychoanalysis and explain repression and the Oedipus complex. Now ask yourself whether you feel comfortable with the task before you. Ask yourself whether it might be less stressful not to explain psychoanalysis to its critics, and to support that choice with one of the following arguments: psychoanalysis cannot prove its theories because of the resistance that's plain to see among those critics; psychoanalysis cannot prove its theories because proof can only take place in the consulting room, where the analyst can dismantle the patient's resistance; psychoanalysis cannot prove its theories because psychoanalysis treats the mind and soul, to which proof does not apply; etc.

If such counterarguments against proof continue to seduce you, try another thought experiment: pick a controversial political topic like gun control or climate change and put yourself in front of an audience full of adversaries. Prepare to express your political beliefs to that critical audience and ask yourself whether or not you feel at all stressed. Of course, you do. Ask yourself whether that stress justifies your silence on the important political matter. Of course, it doesn't! Now imagine that the audience contains close family members who oppose your political views. Expositors of psychoanalysis face exactly that sort of tension, since psychoanalytic knowledge pits the knower against forces of conscience that develop in the context of familial relationships in childhood, and since exposition of psychoanalytic ideas may be particularly susceptible to transference. The tension of public exposition and disputation may be high, but the ideas are too important not to uphold them, even before critics.

In the next chapters, I will explore aversions to proof in the psychoanalytic community after Freud, and aversions to proof in the larger culture. The idea of proof aversion excites me precisely because of its generality and its consequent relevance to solving chronic problems besetting psychoanalysis, such as internecine warfare and troubled public relations. The purpose of beginning this book with a case study of Freud himself was therefore not to examine Freud's idiosyncrasies or to heap more doubt upon his beleaguered theories, but rather to ground the general study of psychoanalytic aversion to proof in specifics, and to proceed as much as possible from available evidence.

III. THE LEGACY OF FREUD'S AVERSION TO PROOF

1. A Brief History of Proof Aversion after Freud

In general, psychoanalysts after Freud have recited his arguments against proof with liturgical fidelity. If Freud's arguments were more affective than rational, it raises the question: why have so many later analysts accepted those arguments? Orthodox devotion to Freud's word surely has something to do it. But is that the whole explanation? Do analysts perhaps hasten to accept Freud's anti-proof arguments because proof troubles them with the same anxieties that proof triggered in Freud? Do the same arguments against proof, in other words, defend later analysts from the same unwanted feelings of tension that arise in connection with the task of public proof?

Section III, chapter 1 begins with a brief examination of evidence of proof aversion in other analysts in Freud's lifetime and continues with an examination of the proof aversion manifest in the four horsemen of the mid-century American heyday: Rangell, Brenner, Arlow, and Greenson. Rangell and Brenner treat Freud's proof-averse rhetoric as accepted dogma. Arlow and Greenson sense that psychoanalysts' methods of creating and transmitting knowledge have somehow gone awry, but they both walk on eggshells when it comes to proof and public validation and leave psychoanalysis much as they found it: proof-averse and ill-equipped to hold onto its preeminent position in American psychiatry. I conclude chapter 1 by looking at proof aversion in the fifty-year period from 1968 to 2018, a period in which psychoanalysis underwent a steep decline in stature.

I will leave aside the topic of relational psychoanalysis until section IV, when I will consider in depth the proof-averse attitudes of the so-called "relational turn." Relational proof aversion finds expression in the postmodern thesis that scientific truth is not a valid aim. This postmodern philosophy of doubt has become its own gospel truth for relational psychoanalysts, and as I'll attempt to show in section IV, postmodern attitudes to proof and knowledge bristle with defensive affects.

The second chapter of section III is divided into four parts, each of which details a distinct way that psychoanalytic proof aversion has provoked criticism of psychoanalysis. Proof aversion has invited criticism of psychoanalysis as unscientific for the following reasons:

1. It has inhibited research and dialogue with other sciences.
2. It has promoted faith-based rhetoric that persists in practice to this day.
3. It has promoted psychoanalytic authoritarianism and dogmatism that persists today.
4. It has promoted contempt towards critics of psychoanalysis, which in turn has made new enemies and hardened old opposition to psychoanalysis.

In a "self-fulfilling prophecy," proof aversion has realized the fears of criticism that instigated the aversion in the first place. While exploring these unintended consequences of proof aversion, chapter 2 also supplies additional evidence of proof aversion among Freud's peers.

In the past, psychoanalysts have interpreted attacks on their scientific credentials as manifestations of public resistance. I believe such attacks ought to be reinterpreted as unintended consequences of proof aversion. Public resistance to psychoanalysis surely plays a role in these criticisms of psychoanalysis, but in the end I conclude that psychoanalysts' proof aversion explains the controversy over psychoanalytic validity better than Freud's theory of public resistance to psychoanalysis.

1.1. Freud's Era: Ernest Jones

The famous Johns Hopkins psychiatrist Adolf Meyer, a contemporary of Freud's who was friendly to psychoanalysis, knew how wary psychoanalysts could be when it came to criticism of their work. According to Leon Hoffman, Meyer understood this wariness of criticism to be the reason that Freudians didn't mix with other psychiatrists, and didn't present their findings to non-analysts. Hoffman cites Meyer to explain that "analysts needed a family milieu 'where fundamentals need not always be questioned' and where they would 'not face continual ridicule and skepticism'." Hoffman says that this avoidance of public criticism led to the isolation of the field, which in turn led to "a lack of scientific rigour" among psychoanalysts, "since basic concepts did not need to be independently verified." (Hoffman 2010, p. 463) In this way, Hoffman traces the marginalization of psychoanalysis not just to external pressure from Freud's enemies but to internal pressure from Freud's siege mentality. It was not simply that critics unjustly labeled psychoanalysis unscientific. Out of fear of criticism, Freud cloistered psychoanalysis in a way that caused it to adopt closed, unscientific habits.

Psychoanalysts like Ernest Jones swallowed Freud's proof-averse doctrines and regurgitated them whole. In the first issue of the *International Journal of Psychoanalysis*, Jones cites Freud's party line that "human nature" rebels against the "disagreeable truths" of psychoanalysis and so declares them false. (Jones 1920, p. 4) And when critics ask for proof, Jones does not provide it but instead offers counterattacks on critics' resistance, just as Freud did. In reviewing a 1920 book that inveighed against psychoanalysis, for example, Jones eviscerates the author for his ignorance of psychoanalysis, his narrow understanding of scientific method, and for denying the existence of unconscious processes despite "an enormous mass of published material, the observation of which can be repeated and verified by anyone who takes the trouble." (Jones 1922, p. 391) Jones, like Freud, recognizes resistance when he sees it, and its unfair character compels him to reduce the professor's arguments to rubble. But it also distracts him from answering the professor's question: *how do you know?* Jones does not cite or otherwise direct his readers to any of the "enormous mass of published material" to which he alludes. He either emulates or shares in Freud's defensive splitting and avoidance when it comes to relations with the larger scientific community.

1.2. The Postwar American Heyday: Leo Rangell, Charles Brenner, Jacob Arlow, and Ralph Greenson

The theory of universal, unrelenting public resistance to psychoanalysis does not reconcile easily with the following historical fact: psychoanalysis enjoyed decades of dominance in psychiatry and popular culture in the mid-20th century. The wide and unsolicited acceptance of psychoanalysis proved Freud wrong in his moments of pessimism over the fate of psychoanalysis.

Leading psychoanalysts of this era witnessed the success, but clung to the old public-resistance arguments. This was a habit and a conviction rooted in emotion, not rational thought. Here is Leo Rangell in 1985 reciting the outdated Freudian shibboleths about public resistance as though the public successes of psychoanalysis in the 1940s, 1950s, and 1960s had never happened:

> The small number of people who received [psychoanalytic ideas] positively must be regarded as heroic in their intellectual receptivity almost on a par with Freud's feat in his self-analysis.
>
> An unprepared subject [the public] reacted as a group, as would now be expected by the theory of psychoanalysis, with defense and negative affect to each interpretation offered without the resistances having been removed. (Rangell 1985, p. 62)

But Rangell himself had witnessed historical facts that undermined his severe Freudian account of public resistance; in actual fact, it had not been a small number of people who received psychoanalysis positively. If Rangell distorted the facts, he must have done so, like Freud, according to an emotional need.

In Charles Brenner's presidential address to the American Psychoanalytic Association in 1968, Brenner rejected criticism of psychoanalysis from the ranks of philosophers of science, confident that psychoanalysis would continue to grow. (Brenner 1968) The success psychoanalysts enjoyed at the time seems to have emboldened him to indulge his proof aversion; he declared that psychoanalysts needn't integrate themselves further into medical science nor improve the scientific standing of the field: "[Psychoanalysts] are scientists in their professional work every day of their lives. They don't have to *become* scientists; they *are* scientists already." (p. 685) If the critics ignored the fundamentally empirical nature of psychoanalysis and its valuable insights, of course Brenner was obliged to call the critics on their error and defend the good clinical work that psychoanalysts were doing. But he might also have taken seriously their request for further justification of psychoanalytic beliefs. Like Jones, he chose not to.

The psychoanalytic leadership of the era ignored calls for research even when they originated from inside the psychoanalytic community. British psychoanalyst Edward Glover warned in 1952 that the field was neglecting research, with the result that "a great deal of what passes as attested theory is little more than speculation, varying widely in plausibility." (Glover 1952, p. 403) At the same time that Brenner was dismissing the need for extra-clinical research in the late 1960s, Merton Gill and others were lamenting that calls for psychoanalytic research like Glover's "have evoked little response." (Gill et al. 1968, p. 232) Gill et al. rejected the predominant, Brennerian view among analysts that "every analysis is a piece of research and hence, presumably, every psychoanalyst is a research investigator." (p. 233) Meanwhile, psychoanalytic researchers like Hartvig Dahl did not share Brenner's optimism and rang alarm bells that got little response. Dahl wrote, "All current signs [in the field of psychoanalysis] point to a steady decline in creative innovation and fresh clinical insights." (1972, p. 237) History affirmed Glover, Gill, and Dahl, but Brenner's views clearly won the day.

Brenner's classic *Elementary Textbook of Psychoanalysis* never cites specific evidence for psychoanalytic theories. Instead it alludes to three general sources of proof of psychoanalytic ideas: the direct observation of children, analyses of children, and analyses of adults. (1973, pp. 22-23) Brenner notes, "It is truly remarkable how obvious are the evidences of sexual desires and behavior in small children," but, like Jones, he doesn't point the reader to this evidence so that he or she can see it for himself or herself. Psychoanalysts of Brenner's era did not think it feasible, appropriate, or necessary to compile this sort of research in a format suitable for persuading a skeptic. In order to make such observations one had to be a psychoanalyst oneself and conduct psychotherapy with small children, or one had to wade through psychoanalytic case studies like those in the *Hampstead Index* (Sandler 1962), which assume a prerequisite acceptance and understanding of psychoanalysis.

In the introduction to his 1982 book *The Mind in Conflict*, Brenner adopts Freud's conviction that psychoanalytic research can only occur inside the consulting room: "No one will speak to a stranger without consciously editing his or her thoughts.... It is [therefore] not possible to divorce a psychoanalyst's therapeutic activities from his or her scientific, investigative activities." (pp. 3-4) In addition, he makes the sweeping generalization that academic psychology can never address the elusive, complex phenomena studied by psychoanalysis. He dismisses academic psychology's work as altogether "of minor importance." (p. 3) Brenner thereby splits the study of the mind into inviolable, exclusive camps just as Freud did—psychoanalysis and everything of importance on one hand, academic psychology and nothing of importance on the other. Like Freud, he seems to rationalize his wish not to have to justify psychoanalytic ideas. More than unscientific, this is emotionally anti-scientific.

The landmark 1968 Shevrin-Fritzler study on the unconscious attests that Brenner's rigid, polarized account of psychological research distorted the more complex reality. Within months of Brenner's address, Howard Shevrin, a psychoanalyst and neuroscientist, and psychologist Dean Fritzler published a study in *Science* entitled, "Visual Evoked Response Correlates of Unconscious Mental Processes." (Shevrin and Fritzler 1968) Using electroencephalography and word association tests, their experiment demonstrated cortical excitation and associative thinking in response to subliminal visual stimuli of which the study subjects were unaware.

Brenner might have trumpeted these results from the hilltops, but he made no mention of them, as though they did not exist or made no difference. Brenner's 1973 revision of *An Elementary Textbook of Psychoanalysis* states humbly, "The fact is that we have as yet no method which permits us to observe unconscious mental processes directly." (Brenner 1973, p. 4) The text makes no mention of neuroscientific evidence of the unconscious. It would seem that emotion, not fact, elicited his conviction that extra-clinical proof was impossible.

Similarly, Brenner and others might have built upon—or at least acknowledged—the smart psychoanalytic validity research being conducted by Hartvig Dahl, Lester Luborsky, and the other brave souls who pursued it despite little institutional support. The psychoanalytic community of that era, however, not only ignored confirmatory research, but actually opposed it. Opponents of research in the psychoanalytic community considered would-be researchers dissidents who would undermine faith in psychoanalytic ideas. Jacob Arlow noticed this irrationality, and was concerned by it, but submitted only a very mild objection:

[A]s a practitioner I have been interested in the issue of validation of interpretation and of the basic concepts of psychoanalysis. This interest, I am certain, I share with many colleagues who would welcome empirically founded, scientifically secure validation of fundamental psychoanalytic propositions as well as of technical procedures.

To be sure, not a few analysts look askance at research of this kind. Many regard such concerns as evidence of persistent doubt concerning the "truth" of psychoanalytic findings, and they feel that interest in such research represents an effort on the part of the researchers to repudiate some unacceptable knowledge about their own motivation, conscious or unconscious. (Arlow 1993, p. 143)

Arlow made significant contributions to psychoanalytic research; for example, he supervised Hartvig Dahl in making the seminal first audio recording of an entire psychoanalysis. (Schachter and Kächele 2017, p. 74; Dahl 1972, 1974) But institutional proof aversion—and perhaps his own—seems to have constrained Arlow from vociferous advocacy of research. Hoffman says Arlow's statement is "notable" in that "at the end of the twentieth century, an eminent leader in psychoanalysis espoused an 'interest' in systematic methods of validation rather than championing its cause to be indispensable to the advancement of the field." (Hoffman 2010, p. 464)

Ralph Greenson (1969) expressed concern that the dogmatism of the psychoanalytic "schools" was unscientific and had stunted the growth of new ideas among psychoanalysts, but he didn't suggest a more scientific style of education or research. The usual Freudian shibboleths about public resistance to disagreeable truths, to which he refers in the beginning of his article, seem to prohibit such a recommendation.

Postwar Psychoanalysis and Communism

According to Arnold Richards, Rangell, Brenner, Arlow, and Greenson were members of the American Communist Party. (Richards 2016, p. 116) Greenson's critique of psychoanalytic dogmatism is therefore somewhat ironic; one wonders to what extent the communist outlook hardened these psychoanalysts' tendencies toward dogmatism, authoritarianism, paranoia, and the polarization of the public into friends and enemies, with nobody in between.

Freud and the later analysts thought psychoanalysis to be irreconcilable with public mores, but sociological factors surely inflamed that point of view. Just as anti-Semitism stoked Freud's paranoia about public antipathy, J. Edgar Hoover's persecution of communists may have stoked the postwar analysts' paranoia and their pessimism about public acceptance of psychoanalysis. "Otto Fenichel, Martin Grotjahn, Erich Fromm, and Wilhelm Reich were only a few of the analysts whom we know were tracked by the FBI," Richards writes. "Joseph Wortis's passport was revoked because he was or had been a member of the [Communist Party USA]." (p. 118)

When my grandmother Eleanor Weisberger, the child psychoanalyst, was in college in Ohio, she identified as a communist, in part because the communists were fighting the spread of fascism in Europe. She was later disillusioned by Stalinism, as were many young communists, but the FBI kept a file on her that later stalled her husband's promotion in the department of medicine at Case Western Reserve University. Throughout the history of psychoanalysis, such political realities have reinforced the psychical paranoia that attends the public presentation of psychoanalytic ideas.

1.3. The Fifty-Year Decline: 1968 to 2018

Joseph Masling and Robert Bornstein's series *Empirical Studies of Psychoanalytic Theories*, which published its tenth and final volume in 2002, reviews the considerable body of research in support of Freudian theories. Such credible research, for example on the dynamic unconscious, has made a real impact on cognitive scientists outside the psychoanalytic community:

> The impact of Jakoby's and Merikle's studies—as well as those of Greenwald (*e.g.*, Greenwald, Klinger, and Liu, 1989), Reber (1989), Schachter (1987), and others (*e.g.*, Kunst-Wilson & Zajonc, 1980)—cannot be overstated. Consider the following:

> During the 1980s, there were dozens of papers published questioning the existence of unconscious perception and memory. Since 1990, there has not been a single article in a mainstream psychology journal challenging the existence of these phenomena. (Bornstein and Masling 1998, p. xviii)

Yet evidence of the validity of psychoanalytic ideas has failed to impress the public at large, Masling argues, not only because of critics' distaste for psychoanalysis, but also because of psychoanalysts' distaste for proof.

> Even when it would be in the interests of organized psychoanalysis to cite favorable empirical evidence, it has failed to do so. I do not recall one instance when a critic like Crews has been answered by referring to empirical data. The Freud exhibit in the Library of Congress had many interesting displays, but not one showing the extent to which there is scientific support for psychoanalytic ideas…. [A] sizeable number of studies based on psychoanalytic ideas have been published. The psychoanalytic establishment deals with this fact by ignoring it. Critics like Crews deal with this fact by denying it. (Masling 1999)

Hoffman concurs: "Until the last two decades, systematic empirical research findings have been almost universally ignored in psychoanalytic clinical education. By eschewing the value for clinical work of systematic research, psychoanalysis has insulated itself from the rest of the scientific world." (Hoffman 2010, p. 455)

Howard Shevrin in 1998 described psychoanalysts as thoroughly uninterested in the neuroscience of consciousness:

What has largely disappeared in psychoanalysis, however, is a serious theoretical and conceptual consideration of the nature and function of consciousness, both as a general condition of mind and as a specific factor in psychopathology and treatment. Most recent thinking in psychoanalysis has been preoccupied with the *content* of the mind rather than with its various forms. What is generally taken for granted is the way in which consciousness and the unconscious, each with its own distinctive properties, affect the particular content. As a result critical questions remain infrequently addressed: What are the means through which something unconscious becomes conscious? Conversely, what are the means through which something conscious becomes unconscious? How and why does one become aware at all? And what is awareness as such? (Shevrin 1998, pp. 45-46)

Robert Holt has spent much of his career studying unconscious thought through the use of Rorschach tests and innovative psychometric techniques of analyzing data. (Holt 2002) Though he's obtained and published results that support Freud's theories, he too perceives the psychoanalytic community as generally uninterested in this sort of work. (Holt 2015, p. 342)

Psychoanalysts writing in the *Archives of General Psychiatry* in 2002 called for more studies to help validate their belief in the curative power of psychoanalysis, and they too noted that they faced indifference and opposition: "Research continues to play an insignificant part in the training of psychoanalysts. Only a minority of the training institutes in the United States include research as part of their curriculum, and many analysts are explicitly hostile to research beyond traditional case reports." (Gabbard et al. 2002, p. 508) Eight years later, Hoffman comments, "The attitude towards systematic investigations has come very far since Freud's dismissive letter in 1934 to the experimentalist Saul Rosenzweig." (Hoffman 2010, p. 465) But significant, paralyzing ambivalence about scientific research remains.

1.4. The Psychoanalytic Community Today

The 21st century could be a good one for psychoanalysis. The April 2014 cover story in *Discover* magazine heralded neuroscientists' recent successes in verifying Freudian hypotheses under the headline "The Second Coming of Sigmund Freud." (McGowan 2014) Such research, appearing in influential journals like *Science*,[35] has provided significant new evidence for the dynamic unconscious. Psychoanalyst Mark Solms grasped the extended hand of neuroscience in 1999 by founding the interdisciplinary journal *Neuropsychoanalysis*, which attempts to integrate psychoanalysis and neuroscience. (Solms and Turnbull 2011, p. 133) Efficacy researchers have at the same time finally begun to publish results that support psychodynamic treatments.[36] As more evidence of this kind emerges in mainstream journals, psychoanalysts have the opportunity to reverse the downward trend in the public perception of their field.

Meanwhile, doubts about the long-term effectiveness of cognitive-behavioral therapy are gathering force. Efficacy researcher Bruce Wampold recently surveyed three meta-analyses and concluded that evidence for the superiority of CBT over other forms of therapy is "nonexistent or weak." (Wampold et al. 2017, p. 14) A 2016 article in *The Guardian* noted the backlash against

---

35 See for example: "Prefrontal Regions Orchestrate Suppression of Emotional Memories via a Two-Phase Process" (Depue et al. 2007) and "The Unconscious Will: How the Pursuit of Goals Operates Outside of Conscious Awareness." (Custers and Aarts 2010)

36 See for example: Leichsenring and Rabung 2008 and 2011; Shedler 2010; Fonagy et al. 2015; and Gibbons et al. 2016.

THE PSYCHOANALYST'S AVERSION TO PROOF

CBT among psychologists, in public opinion, and among policy-makers.[37] The front page of the *New York Times* "Style" section on February 18, 2018 declared, "Freud is still dead, but psychoanalysis may be experiencing a rebirth."[38] The tide may be turning once again in favor of psychodynamic psychology.

That said, the psychoanalytic community today remains more than a little ambivalent about the pursuit of scientific proof, just as Freud was, and so it remains unclear to what extent psychoanalysis will exploit and pursue new research findings in order to resurrect itself. The *Times* article makes no mention of research in connection with the purported "rebirth" of psychoanalysis. If psychoanalysts are thriving, according to the article, they're thriving in a quirky, heterogeneous way, outside of the academy, and farther than ever before from core Freudian tenets like repression. The picture of psychoanalysis in the article is closer to alternative medicine than to medical science.

Jonathan Shedler is another psychoanalytic researcher who has attempted to bridge the "unbridgeable gulf between psychoanalysts and academic researchers." (Shedler 2002, p. 429) He has tried to do so, like Enrico Jones[39] before him, by developing creative research methods that reliably operationalize complex clinical psychoanalytic judgments. And he has had to fight to do so against psychoanalysts' objections. "Analytic objections to research," Shedler writes, "appear

---

37 https://www.theguardian.com/science/2016/jan/07/therapy-wars-revenge-of-freud-cognitive-behavioural-therapy, accessed January 7, 2018.

38 https://www.nytimes.com/2018/02/17/style/american-psychoanalytic-association-donald-trump.html?rref=collection%2Fsectioncollection%2Ffashion&action=click&contentCollection=fashion&region=rank&module=package&version=highlights&contentPlacement=3&pgtype=sectionfront, accessed February 18, 2018.

39 Among Jones's innovations was his application of the Q-sort technique to psychoanalytic research. See "The Psychoanalytic Case Study: Toward a Method for Systematic Inquiry" (Jones and Windholz 1990) and "The Legacy of Enrico Jones" (Hauser 2005).

to fall into three categories: it is impossible, it is unnecessary, and it is irrelevant." (p. 430) He might have added another: it's anxiety-provoking and even humiliating to present evidence of repressed feelings in public.

While the American Psychoanalytic Association research fund did support neuropsychoanalytic research with $40,000 in grants in 2016,[40] very few American psychoanalysts today participate directly in research outside their own clinical practice. Schachter and Kächele estimate that under 5% of APsaA members do any extra-clinical research. (2017, p. 247) The 2014 *Discover* article notes that even as neuroscientists provide new evidence for the validity of psychoanalytic theories, psychoanalysts themselves remain "hostile to the idea of testing hypotheses through experiments." (McGowan 2014, p. 56) Falk Leichsenring, a German psychoanalyst and efficacy researcher, reported in 2015: "Efficacy research has been neglected in PDT [psychodynamic therapy] for a long time." (Leichsenring et al. 2015, p. 648) Because psychoanalysts are disengaged from research, they generally do not look to new empirical evidence to drive "changes in psychoanalytic theory and practice." When those changes occur, psychoanalyst Morris Eagle observes, they instead reflect "shifts in cultural, philosophical, and social-economic conditions." (Eagle 2007, p. 11)

The American Psychological Association's push for evidence-based practices (APA 2006) has further alienated psychoanalysts who still "see no way to quantify important psychoanalytic constructs without trivializing and distorting them" and those analysts who believe "the analytic method can answer all relevant questions [without appeal to extra-clinical evidence]." (Shedler 2002, p. 430)

---

40 https://npsa-association.org/news/research-neuropsychoanalytic-researchers/, accessed January 5, 2018.

Jones's and Shedler's success developing reliable psychometric language for complex psychoanalytic observations contradicts the first objection to research—namely, that it's impossible. But all the psychoanalytic objections to research are, in Shedler's words, "mistaken." (p. 440) They're also irrational and, if my hypothesis is correct, emotional in nature.

Relational psychoanalysts have reacted to the APA's evidence-based practice terminology with abhorrence, but not just because evidence-based medicine neglects the individual or overestimates the value of randomized controlled trials. They have recoiled from the very notions of evidence and empiricism, as though they came from another planet:

> Practice guidelines for psychotherapy? Empirically supported psychotherapeutic treatments? Evidence-based practice? Treatment manuals? These words and ideas are generally unfamiliar to and seem foreign and perhaps even threatening to most psychoanalysts. They may be particularly grating to those of us who are immersed in the specific subculture known as relational psychoanalysis—those of us who feel at home here in the pages of *Psychoanalytic Dialogues*. (Safran and Aron 2001, p. 573)

Relational psychoanalysts concur with all those critics from Hoche to Grünbaum to today who say that psychoanalysis is untestable or untested; but, unlike the critics, they revel in untestability and disdain tests. I'll speak more on this in section IV; for now I'll merely say that the relationalists and the critics are wrong on both counts: psychoanalysis is testable and has in fact been tested, if in a piecemeal fashion.

2. Self-Fulfilling Prophecy: Proof Aversion as a Stimulus to Criticism of Psychoanalysis

I've suggested that the critique of public resistance plays a major role in psychoanalysts' defenses against proving. I've also suggested that the actual history of psychoanalysis does not support the rigid idea of unwavering, universal public resistance to psychoanalytic ideas. I would now like to suggest that aversion to proof not only explains psychoanalysts' defensive approach to public presentation, it also explains the most common criticism directed at psychoanalysis over the last hundred years: the notion that psychoanalysts refuse to test and prove their theories.

That is to say, critics call psychoanalysis unscientific not only because of these critics' own emotional resistance but because psychoanalysts really have presented themselves unscientifically; this is, as I see it, an unintended consequence of psychoanalysts' aversion to proof. Defensive attitudes to proof and public presentation may have in this sense created a "self-fulfilling prophecy." In this chapter I will consider various ways in which Freud's and other psychoanalysts' aversion to proof may have instigated and exacerbated resistance to psychoanalysis.

2.1. Neglecting Research and Losing Academic Status

Brenner's 1968 predictions of untrammeled growth were not borne out over the next decades. In fact, as psychoanalysts ignored calls for more evidentiary support from within academia, the academic status of psychoanalysis steadily deteriorated. When Joseph Masling presented a paper to the Rapaport-Klein Study Group in 1999, he reported declines in psychologists' and psychiatrists' citations of psychoanalytic literature, in the number of practitioners of psychodynamic therapy, and in the number of psychoanalytic patients. (Masling 1999) Leon Hoffman chronicles psychoanalysts' fall from grace in the steady decline of their academic appointments:

> In the middle of the twentieth century, many chairs of psychiatry in the USA were psychoanalysts: 40—at a third of all medical schools—in the 1960s. By 1984 the number of psychoanalysts who were chairs declined to 21 and by 2004 to 12. So in a mere 40 years the number of psychoanalysts in key academic psychiatric positions declined by almost four-fold. (Hoffman 2010, p. 460)

Opponents of psychoanalysis will be encouraged to hear that as of 2018 psychoanalysts occupy zero psychiatry chairs at the nation's top medical schools.[41] Whatever happened to Freudian curiosity and ambition? Just as Freud's curiosity and ambition halted before the thin red line of proof, so too, it would seem, has the curiosity and ambition of the psychoanalytic community at large.

This failure of curiosity and ambition has had measurable consequences not only in psychiatry but in academic psychology. In a study of "150 highly ranked colleges and universities," investigators found that less than 15% of psychology departments include Freud or psychoanalysis in their course descriptions. (Redmond and Shulman 2008, p. 398) For an explanation, *The New York Times* consulted Alice Eagly, then chair of Northwestern's psychology department:

---

41 According to a January 30, 2018 web search of the psychiatry departments at medical schools ranked in the top 25 in *U.S. News and World Report*'s 2017 rankings. Of note, psychoanalyst Elizabeth Auchincloss is one of two Vice Chairs of Psychiatry at Cornell.

The primary reason [psychoanalysis] became marginalized, Ms. Eagly said, is that while most disciplines in psychology began putting greater emphasis on testing the validity of their approaches scientifically, "psychoanalysts haven't developed the same evidence-based grounding." As a result, most psychology departments don't pay as much attention to psychoanalysis.[42]

And as a result, accrediting bodies have shifted support and recognition away from psychoanalysis and toward forms of psychotherapy whose practitioners argue their case with proof. Of 80 empirically supported treatments listed by the Society of Clinical Psychology (Division 12 of the APA), only 2 are clearly psychodynamic: "Psychoanalytic Therapy for Panic Disorder" and "Short-Term Psychodynamic Psychotherapy for Depression."[43] The Society recommends the former with the following caveat: "[A]lthough psychoanalytic psychotherapy appears to work, it is not yet clear that the treatment works via the reduction of unconscious conflicts—the proposed mechanisms of change."[44]

That doesn't sound like a statement of wholesale resistance to psychoanalysis. It sounds more like a statement of the same fact Howard Shevrin, Falk Leichsenring, and many others have observed: psychoanalysts in general have not pursued evidentiary support for their theories and practices. Consequently, that support is lacking.

---

42 http://www.nytimes.com/2007/11/25/weekinreview/25cohen.html?action=click&content Collection=Style&module=RelatedCoverage&region=EndOfArticle&pgtype=article, accessed February 19, 2018.

43 https://www.div12.org/psychological-treatments/treatments/, accessed February 16, 2018. "Transference-Focused Therapy for Borderline Personality Disorder" clearly draws on the psychoanalytic idea of transference, but its description does not allude to other aspects of psychoanalysis. No other treatments make discernible reference to psychoanalytic ideas.

44 https://www.div12.org/psychological-treatments/treatments/psychoanalytic-treatment-for-panic-disorder/, accessed February 16, 2018.

And consequently, psychoanalysts have not persuaded policy-makers to sign off on psychoanalytic treatments and have allowed rival disciplines like cognitive-behavioral therapy to dominate APA and psychiatric practice guidelines.

Here at last is the fallout from Freud's aversion to proof as he articulated it in the *Introductory Lectures*: "Friends of analysis have advised us to meet the threatened publication of our failures with statistics of our successes drawn up by ourselves. I did not agree to this." (Freud 1917, p. 461) 85 years later, Jonathan Shedler identified the exact same aversion to outcome studies as the reason CBT has outstripped psychoanalysis: "[P]sychoanalysts have rarely published empirical outcome studies. Most published studies have been conducted by cognitive-behavioral and other nonanalytic investigators, who understandably wish to demonstrate the advantages of their own approaches." (Shedler 2002, p. 441n) The final and most harmful consequence of all this, of course, is that patients seeking help for problems that are actually caused by defense mechanisms do not get help understanding and disarming their defense mechanisms.

2.2. Faith-Based Psychoanalytic Rhetoric

Anyone who reads deeply in Freud's works, and is not too angry with him to appreciate some of his insights, can see that he derived his ideas from sincere observation and deduction, not from faith. But he did ask others to accept his ideas on faith—specifically, their faith in him. By neglecting public demonstration of the validity of psychoanalysis, psychoanalysts continue to ask the public to accept psychoanalysis on faith. For this reason, it's readily apparent to me why some people call psychoanalysis a religion. Those critics may prefer to call it a religion, of course, to protect themselves from its offensive and threatening ideas. But it's not clear to me that their resistance plays a bigger role than Freud's rhetoric. His obsession with public resistance to psychoanalysis often leads him to ask his audience for their faith in a way that sounds vaguely religious.

Consider, for example, Freud's summary of the problem of public resistance in "A Difficulty in the Path of Psycho-Analysis": "Where sympathy is lacking, understanding will not come very easily." (Freud 1917, p. 137) Herein he expresses his belief that resistance causes hostility to psychoanalysis and hostility causes misunderstandings of psychoanalysis; therefore he must ask for faith in psychoanalysis before he presents proof or justification. Scientific explanation typically works the other way around. The speaker justifies his or her ideas so that the audience understands and trusts them. Religion, by contrast, asks for faith at the outset, and advocates faith as an instrument of understanding.

When Freud makes the argument that he has to break through resistance to his ideas *before* he presents them, he's saying, in so many words, *My theory will elicit doubt, but doubt is only resistance, which my theory will explain, and therefore it constitutes evidence of my theory. So I must ask you to check your doubt at the door.* The rhetorical structure of this argument resembles a religious statement like this one: *If you doubt Jesus is your Savior, that's just the Devil whispering in your ear.* Critics of psychoanalysis then opine that a Freudian "can say, with Saint Anselm, that one believes in order to understand and understands in order to believe." (McHugh and Slavney 1986, p. 20) Such critics may be resistant, but surely they're also responding to Freud's idiosyncratically religious-sounding rhetoric.

When Freud asserts in the *Introductory Lectures* that the best way to learn psychoanalysis is to undergo a psychoanalysis, he adopts the same rhetorical structure. Who undergoes an analysis unless he or she first trusts in the merits of analysis? Freud does not use explicitly religious language, but he does engage in the St. Anselm-like tautology that implicitly demands trust at the outset: *sympathy first, understanding later*. Auchincloss and Kravis write:

> Despite being a dazzling lecturer and a masterful rhetorician whose published lectures were (and still are) widely read, Freud doubted the possibility that a real understanding of psychoanalysis could be transmitted via purely intellectual means. On several occasions, Freud maintained that only those who have opened themselves to the experience of undergoing and practicing psychoanalysis can understand its principles well enough to judge them. These assertions (and their echoes in contemporary discourse) have long riled critics of psychoanalysis within the university, many of whom argue with some justification that analysts are 'true believers' and therefore among the least capable of a critical assessment of psychoanalytic ideas. (Auchincloss and Kravis 2000, p. 753)

Here is Freud making the faith-based *sympathy first, understand later* argument in the *Introductory Lectures*. He begins with the faulty assumption that "there is no objective verification of psycho-analysis":

> But you will have a right to ask another question. If there is no objective verification of psycho-analysis, and no possibility of demonstrating it, how can one learn psycho-analysis at all, and convince oneself of the truth of its assertions?

"No possibility of demonstrating it" is an exaggeration, probably an expression of Freud's own doubt at that moment, and certainly an invitation to suspicion. He goes on:

It is true that psycho-analysis cannot easily be learnt and there are not many people who have learnt it properly. But of course there is a practicable method none the less. One learns psycho-analysis on oneself, by studying one's own personality....

So far, so good. And then:

Nevertheless, there are definite limits to progress by this method. One advances much further if one is analysed oneself by a practised analyst and experiences the effects of analysis on one's own self, making use of the opportunity of picking up the subtler technique of the process from one's analyst. This excellent method is, of course, applicable only to a single person and never to a whole lecture-room of students together. (Freud 1916-1917, p. 19)

What he says makes good sense, but if I try to put myself in the shoes of a skeptic of psychoanalysis, I could imagine that person hearing: *These mystical truths are impossible to describe, so you must come inside the circus tent and pay your fee, and then I'll show them to you.*

It seems to me that Freud could avoid this effect if he were less anxious about his audience's resistance. What if, instead of accentuating the difficulties of demonstration, he minimized the differences between psychoanalysis and other sciences—or better yet, just got on with the demonstrations? After all, he *does* provide persuasive, if anecdotal, evidentiary support for psychoanalytic principles in public lectures without subjecting each individual to an analysis. Freud's Clark lectures in America were a dramatic success.

They earned the admiration of two of the most influential psychiatrists and neurologists in the United States: Adolf Meyer of Johns Hopkins and James Jackson Putnam of Harvard. Putnam had been a critic of psychoanalysis, but Ernest Jones opened his mind to the merits of psychoanalysis (Jones 1955, p. 58), and Freud's lectures finally converted him into a stalwart supporter. A few years later he became the first president of the American Psychoanalytic Association (Hoffman 2010, p. 461) and, in Freud's words, "the chief pillar of the psycho-analytic movement in his native land." (Freud 1914, pp. 31-32)

Similarly, Smith Ely Jelliffe and William Alanson White were converted by Jung's lectures, Freud's writings, and Brill's disputation—not by undergoing psychoanalysis—and they became important contributors to the field.

The principle that psychoanalysts-in-training must undergo psychoanalysis perhaps creates the same appearance of tautology and invites a similar suspicion. It may look to critics like another instance of *believe in order to understand.* Of course a thorough training in psychoanalysis requires a personal analysis—but consider once again how Freud's rhetoric might sound to a skeptical outsider. In "Recommendations to Physicians Practising Psycho-Analysis" Freud writes, "It may be insisted, rather, that [a psychoanalyst] should have undergone a psycho-analytic purification and have become aware of those complexes of his own which would be apt to interfere with his grasp of what the patient tells him." (Freud 1912, p. 116) The choice of the word *purification,* or *Purifizierung* in the original, has religious overtones. It creates a false impression that acolytes are initiated into psychoanalytic knowledge not through education but through a secret rite.

If a Scientologist said to me, *The best way to understand Scientology is to become a Scientologist,* I would of course be suspicious. Once again, it seems to me that if Freud were less afraid of resistance, he would have no need to use a word with overtones of religious extremism like *purification*. And perhaps if he were less anxious about resistance he could be a little more trusting of "unpurified" but nevertheless valuable allies like Smith Ely Jelliffe and William Alanson White, who had studied his writings in depth, and received informal education in psychoanalysis from analysts like Jung and Brill, but had not undergone a formal psychoanalysis.

Freud's advice for how to begin a treatment suffers from a bit of the same faith-based rhetoric, and such rhetoric is moreover still being used by psychoanalysts in practice today. In "On the Beginning of Treatment," Freud advocates withholding as much information as possible about psychoanalysis so as not to inflame immediate resistance in the new patient. If the patient voices skepticism, Freud advocates welcoming the skepticism, but then suggests psychoanalysts dismiss it as a symptom of resistance:

> To the sceptic we say that the analysis requires no faith, that he may be as critical and suspicious as he pleases and that we do not regard his attitude as the effect of his judgement at all, for he is not in a position to form a reliable judgement on these matters; his distrust is only a symptom like his other symptoms and it will not be an interference, provided he conscientiously carries out what the rule of the treatment requires of him. (Freud 1913, p. 126)

It makes sense to advise a fellow psychoanalyst that "the analysis requires no faith" on the part of the patient. As a communication from Freud to other psychoanalysts, it simply means that a patient's skepticism will not adversely affect the outcome of the analysis. But

Freud advocates saying this to the patient before the psychoanalyst has earned the patient's trust. The patient has said, *I don't know if I believe that psychoanalysis works.* And Freud has said back, *Don't worry, your beliefs have no bearing on the success of the treatment.* Faith is precisely what he's demanding of the patient.

To explore the effect Freud's reply might have on a skeptical mind, consider an analogy: A first-time skydiver is about to jump out of a plane. He says to his instructor, *I'm afraid this parachute might have a hole in it.* The instructor replies, *Don't worry, the parachute's performance does not depend in any way on your confidence in its integrity.* The skydiver laughs, assuming this is a joke, and clarifies, *But I'm not asking if my fear has any effect on the parachute. I'm asking, is there a hole?* The instructor, confident that the parachute has no hole and that the man has imagined the hole because he is afraid to jump out of the plane, says, *Your fear cannot damage the parachute.*

The instructor has provided the first-time skydiver with psychotherapy, but at the wrong moment. Does the skydiver jump out of the plane? Maybe not, if only because the instructor seems to misunderstand or trivialize his question. *Your fear cannot damage the parachute* could be a very useful thing to say to dispel fear on the tenth jump, say, when the skydiver has learned to recognize his fear of a hole as a product of psychic reality, not practical reality. But if, on the skydiver's first jump, the skydiving instructor seems to consider the actual presence or absence of a hole in the parachute irrelevant, that could be positively terrifying.

Psychoanalysts expect patients to invest large sums of time and money in their treatment, and patients do so because they're suffering and afraid. But as they stand on the threshold of a psychoanalysis, they really are in a sense about to jump out of an airplane. It seems only fair at the beginning to try to show them that the parachute's parts are in order and to explain how the parachute works. Granted, a patient's resistance may cause him or her to fixate on the inspection of the parachute and prevent the skydiving. In that case the analyst may have to leave parachute questions behind and give the skydiver a choice: to jump or not to jump. But to thoroughly ignore the patient's skeptical questions at the beginning is paternalistic and quasi-religious. In a *Guardian* article on the potential rebirth of psychoanalysis, Oliver Burkeman displays the requisite "sympathy" and respect for Freudian ideas before conceding the following to critics of psychoanalysis: "The practice of charging clients steep fees to ponder their childhoods for years—while characterising any objections to this process as 'resistance,' demanding further psychoanalysis—looks to many like a scam."[45]

In each of the above examples of faith-based rhetoric, Freud comes across as obstinate in regard to proof, and each example in some way, large or small, encourages the view that psychoanalysis is a closed system of thought like a religion. What's also evident in these examples is Freud's fear of public resistance, and his feeling of helplessness before it. To eliminate faith-based rhetoric from psychoanalytic vocabulary, psychoanalysts might remind themselves that the helplessness before public resistance derives in part from the analyst's own shame and anxiety. The helplessness before the task of proof is itself a defensive distortion. Proof is possible. Whatever crisis now besets psychoanalysis, its history shows that public acceptance is possible. Doom is a construct.

And if the field of psychoanalysis can use proof to restore the public's trust, then the public standing of psychoanalysis would confer more authority on individual practitioners. With increased

---

45 https://www.theguardian.com/science/2016/jan/07/therapy-wars-revenge-of-freud-cognitive-behavioural-therapy, accessed January 7, 2018.

THE PSYCHOANALYST'S AVERSION TO PROOF

authority in the eyes of patients, practitioners could more easily address their patients' skepticism and would have less need to ask for patients' faith. The reduction in faith-based rhetoric would in turn reduce suspicion towards psychoanalysis. What I'm envisioning is the opposite of a vicious circle—what in economics is sometimes called a "virtuous circle."

2.3. Authoritarianism: An Unintended Consequence with Unintended Consequences

Conscience sets the dogs of doubt barking, chasing after psychoanalytic knowledge, corralling it back under cover of repression. As I've already suggested, authoritarianism and dogmatism among psychoanalysts may derive from a fierce overcompensation against these dogs of doubt. But psychoanalysts' ambivalence about scientific proof makes authoritarianism all but inevitable in still another way.

Consider once again Freud's disputes with Adler and Jung. Because Freud had long felt so much ambivalence about testing psychoanalytic claims and codifying psychoanalytic research methods, he had no way to adjudicate controversies. If he said, *repression of sexual urges is in general more important to the etiology of neurosis*, and Adler said, *no, aggression is more important than sexuality*, there was no established criterion and no method to help decide between the theories. Without the instruments of public proof, Freud had to settle controversies by authoritarianism and dogmatism. In 1968, Merton Gill and his co-authors warned that psychoanalysis had to embrace research for precisely this reason: "The need within any scientific body for resolution of disagreements and additions to knowledge provides steady pressure for the development of improved research methods. The alternatives—and there are instructive examples in the history of science—are decline or hardening into dogma." (p. 231)

Psychoanalytic authoritarianism and dogmatism in turn reinforce the perception inside and outside the field that psychoanalysis is a closed ideology refractory to proof, not a science. When Jung wanted to broaden the definition of libido—a modification later adopted, more or less, by Freud and other psychoanalysts (Auchincloss and Samberg 2012; Brenner 1973, p. 30)—Freud refused to consider Jung's arguments on their own merits, and in place of scientific debate he substituted authoritative interpretations of Jung's neurosis. Jung was not allowed the authority to interpret him in the same way, as the incident on the ocean liner to America shows. Jung was surely not alone in the sentiment he expressed a few years later in a letter to Freud on December 18, 1912, "I would, however, point out that your technique of treating your pupils like patients is a *blunder*. In that way you produce either slavish sons or impudent puppies...." (McGuire 1988, p. 534) It was a prescient remark.

The resolution of old critical disputes by authoritarian means has left scars on modern-day psychoanalytic organization and practice. The secret committee established to prevent more Jungs and Adlers gave way to the Board of Professional Standards, which is still prosecuting old grudges:

The old us-versus-them proponents established themselves on these shores almost as soon as psychoanalysis did. The rules were different here, but the method was the same: circling the wagons to keep interlopers away from the campfire. After some early skirmishes, many of them around the subject of nonmedical analysis, Freud's technique of control by exclusion was institutionalized in the reorganization of 1946, when the Board of Professional Standards (BoPS) was established as APsaA's central educational committee and keeper of the flame, a dual mission it has pursued so assiduously that it is only now, after almost seventy years, that the William Alanson White institute has been invited into the fold. (Richards 2015, p. 399)

The William Alanson White Institute, like the American Institute of Psychoanalysis, is a descendant of the American Association for the Advancement of Psychoanalysis, formed by Karen Horney and other "dissidents" after their expulsion from the New York Psychoanalytic Society.

What happened to Karen Horney illustrates vividly the ugliness and lasting influence of psychoanalytic authoritarianism. Horney was an M.D., trained and analyzed by Karl Abraham, and a founder of the Berlin Psychoanalytic Institute. She openly challenged Freud on the male bias of psychoanalytic theories like penis envy, whose existence she didn't deny, but she did reinterpret. Instead of regarding it as a universal component of female psychology, she regarded it as a defense mechanism against the Oedipus complex. (Gay 1988, pp. 520-521) She was right and Freud was wrong, as Auchincloss and Samberg tell us in their psychoanalytic glossary:

Penis envy is no longer considered to be fundamental to feminine development or to be the "bedrock" of female psychology, as Freud had thought.... Horney quickly challenged Freud's argument that penis envy lies at the center of the female psyche, asserting views that have formed the foundation for current psychoanalytic theories of female psychology. Horney also argued that the masculinity complex observable in adult women is a regressive neurotic position, a "flight from womanhood" in the face of oedipal anxieties, guilt, and disappointment.

Freud remained unmoved either by Horney's arguments or by the objections of others in his circle. However, over time, Freud's theory has been revised in the light of material drawn from both the psychoanalyses of women and direct child observation. (Auchincloss and Samberg 2012)

For her dissident views, Horney was on April 29, 1941 formally voted out of the New York Psychoanalytic Society by a vote of "24 for disqualifying, 7 against, with 29 abstentions." (Eisold 1998, pp. 871-872) Fritz Wittels, the dissident-turned-authoritarian, led the charge. His orthodoxy punished Horney for speaking truth, suppressed innovation, and cut off several generations of Freudians from access to "the campfire," to borrow Richards's metaphor. Horney's creation, the American Institute for Psychoanalysis, was only granted membership in the American Psychoanalytic Association in 2016.[46]

Members of the outsider movements descended from Horney's expulsion would ultimately go much farther in rejecting Freud than Horney ever did, and would furthermore acquire more serious power over the field of psychoanalysis than any dissidents ever have. Wittels emulated Freud by expelling Horney; Horney formed her own institutions, which were excluded from mainstream psychoanalysis for decades; Horney's outsider movement produced the William Alanson White Institute, where Jay Greenberg and Stephen Mitchell trained. They in turn rebelled against Freudian psychoanalysis, using postmodern ideologies to throw doubt on it and to replace it with relational psychoanalysis. Now Greenberg is no longer an outsider. He occupies a position of power in the psychoanalytic mainstream as editor of The Psychoanalytic

---

46 http://aipnyc.org/about-aip/our-history-and-mission/, accessed January 8, 2018.

Quarterly, and he denies peer review to submitted papers if he deems them insensitive to relational analysis.[47]

Mitchell likewise embraced this new postmodern dogmatism when he rejected the inclusive or "evolutionary" view of psychoanalysis. He had no interest in views descended from Freudian psychoanalysis because, to his mind, they belonged to an old paradigm. And paradigms, according to Mitchell, are a matter of culture and taste, not truth: "With theoretical perspectives, as with meals, taste is important. It is not possible to decide which is better on purely rational grounds (this does not mean that the theories themselves are irrational). A great deal depends on whether the theory speaks to you." (Mitchell 1993, p. 469) If taste is the arbiter of truth, however, then power is the only method available to decide controversies.

Freud's neglect of proof led to his authoritarianism under conditions of controversy, and postmodernists' neglect of proof has led to theirs. Greenberg's unwillingness to permit a scientific discussion of proof typifies the problem. By denying peer review to those who disagree with him, he is perhaps doing to others exactly what was done to him. In reflecting on the years since he and Mitchell published their 1983 relationalist manifesto *Object Relations in Psychoanalytic Theory*, Greenberg recalls with an evident mixture of pride and contempt how a critic once disdained to debate with him, preferring instead to disqualify his argument: " 'The question about this book is not whether it is well done, it certainly is, the question is whether it should have been done at all,' " Greenberg says the critic told him. "And his answer, as you can imagine, was in the negative...."

---

47 When I submitted a paper on proof aversion to *The Psychoanalytic Quarterly*, Greenberg held onto the paper for seven months and then rejected it without peer review. His reason: my paper assumed proof was a valid construct without paying due respect to postmodern skepticism.

(Greenberg 2013, p. 12) Now Greenberg decides who's permitted to question according to radical skeptic tastes that are, to his opponents, indistinguishable from authoritarian whims.

Infighting, authoritarianism, dogmatism, and censorship breed more of the same. Even when Freudian orthodoxies have defended truth, has authoritarianism really availed psychoanalysis anything? Psychoanalysis is more marginalized than it was 50 years ago when Brenner gave his presidential address, and the relational turn that predominates in much contemporary psychoanalysis departs from Freud's orthodoxies even more than Adler or Jung did, let alone Horney. In addition to suppressing good ideas and excluding worthy contributions and contributors, psychoanalytic authoritarianism has arguably provoked more resistance, both inside and outside the movement.

Kenneth Eisold defines authoritarianism and its dangers like this:

Excessive authority—or authoritarianism, that is authority beyond what is required for the work of an organisation—leads to inhibition and covert forms of rebellion. Eventually, as in the example before us [of Karen Horney and Sándor Rado], it can lead to open revolt…. (p. 873)

Eisold goes on to trace the authoritarianism in psychoanalytic institutions to psychoanalysts' concerns with bolstering their authority "in their own consulting rooms," an authority which depends on the credibility of institutional standards of professional training and competence.

To create the professional authority of psychoanalysis, [the American analysts of the 1930s] wove two strands together from two very different—and, in the end, two essentially incompatible—sources: on the one hand, they took the professional authority of medicine, based on experimental investigation and strict standards of training and certification; on the other, they took the charismatic authority of Freud as the founder and decisive thinker of the psychoanalytic movement. (p. 874)

What if, as Merton Gill and many others have suggested (Gill et al. 1968), psychoanalysis were to cultivate another, more scientific means of adjudicating disputes and establishing authority? What if its authority derived neither from a superficial affiliation with medicine nor from the charisma and dogmatism of Freud, but rather from scientific proof of its ideas? The interference of resistance surely complicates public proof of psychoanalytic ideas. But is a complicated and imperfect scientific process really a worse alternative than an authoritarian style of governance? As Winston Churchill said: "Many forms of Government have been tried, and will be tried in this world of sin and woe. No one pretends that democracy is perfect or all-wise. Indeed it has been said that democracy is the worst form of Government except for all those other forms that have been tried from time to time...."[48]

Jon Mills describes recent developments in relational psychoanalysis as "mainly a response to—if not a revolt against—constricting prescriptive technique foisted upon us by previous generations." (Mills 2012, p. xiii) Daniel Kriegman makes the similar point that relational psychoanalysis has rejected science in order to correct psychoanalysts' history of abusing their patients with

---

48 https://www.winstonchurchill.org/resources/quotes/the-worst-form-of-government/, accessed December 28, 2017.

dogmatic interpretations. (Kriegman 1998, p. 200) Because relational psychoanalysis justifies itself with radical, postmodern skepticism, it's unlikely that a relational analyst could see science as democratic or liberating. Postmodernism seeks liberation through doubt of scientific authority. In so doing, however, postmodernists create their own inexorable march to dogmatism and tyranny, albeit dogmatism and tyranny of a different kind.

Indeed, I would regard the incursion of postmodern schools of thought into psychoanalysis as still another troubling sequel of Freudian dogmatism and Freudian aversion to proof. Relationalists have tried admirably to rid psychoanalysis of authoritarianism, but have done so untenably, by ridding psychoanalysis of rationality and scientific progress. This does not achieve the aim. Without reason and science there is nothing left *but* authoritarianism.

2.4. Treating Critics with Contempt

In his 18th-century autobiography Giacomo Casanova wrote, "one runs a mighty risk in this world if one seeks to disillusion the self-deceived." (Casanova 2011, p. 10) He meant it's dangerous to speak honestly of others' passions and flaws, for these are what people deceive themselves about. He meant one runs a risk by speaking truth—specifically, speaking Freudian truth. Anyone who values Freudian truth has been taken aback by the myriad forms of irrational hatred it provokes.

Freud in turn hated his irrational critics, and he sometimes treated them with contempt, which was itself an expression of irrational, if understandable, feeling. I'd like to consider the complaints of two critics of psychoanalysis who felt mistreated by Freudians. One is German neurologist Adolf Friedländer, a contemporary of Freud's whom I cited briefly in my discussion of anti-Semitism, and the other is Paul McHugh, who was head of psychiatry at Johns Hopkins Medical School when I attended. Both critics could justifiably be called emotionally resistant to psychoanalysis, and yet both of them have rational complaints against the field as well. Their examples illuminate some of the consequences of psychoanalysts' dogmatism and of psychoanalysts' contemptuous treatment of their critics.

Adolf Friedländer

The first cadre of psychoanalysts took wicked satisfaction in making fun of Friedländer, both in their correspondence and to his face, and they did so with Freud's active encouragement and participation. Friedländer was an easy target. He doubted most of the findings of psychoanalysis as unscientific and meanwhile supported the quack Weimar fad of "diagnoscopy," which Cornelius Borck describes as "personality profiling by electric phrenology." (Borck 2001, pp. 565-566) The presentation Friedländer gave in Brussels in 1910 does not do him credit as a forward-thinker on psychiatry:

> Psychical treatment, as it is practiced by those who do not belong to Freud's school, accomplishes as much as sexual psychoanalysis, but it must be aided according to the particular case by general therapeutic measures applicable to functional neuroses and psychoses. (Training in work, hydro and electro therapy, dietetics, etc., and under certain conditions hypnosis.) (Friedländer 1911, p. 319)

He only approved of psychoanalysis inasmuch as he thought it aimed "to train the patient in self-control, to suppress the emotions and to train the patient in diverting work" (p. 305)—i.e., the exact opposite of everything psychoanalysis actually aims to accomplish with its patients. When he encountered psychoanalysts, he would obsequiously ask for instruction in psychoanalysis and for dialogue, but because he published articles criticizing psychoanalysis, Jung and Freud found his requests disingenuous.

Karl Abraham had a slightly more sanguine view of Friedländer's interest in psychoanalysis. Abraham wrote Freud on February 23, 1908, "At least the time of killing us through silence [*Totschweigen*] is at an end. However full of misunderstanding Friedländer's collective review in the *Journal für Psychologie und Neurologie* may be, it does show that the ideas are being discussed." (Falzeder 2002, p. 29) Even though Friedländer had criticisms of psychoanalysis and did not particularly understand it, he was taking it seriously and he wanted the psychoanalysts to take him seriously too.

But they found him stupid and irritating and made a policy of ignoring him. Jung wrote to Freud on October 14, 1909:

Have you seen the new article by Friedländer? ... Imagine, Friedländer was with me yesterday, sweet as sugar and wagging his tail. He would like to be answered *à tout prix*, you were absolutely right. Unless the fellow has taken it into his head to convert me, I simply don't know what his real purpose was in coming. He told me he would be delighted to have more contacts with us so as to learn something from our work. (A damned sight too many patients seem to be demanding psychoanalytical treatment, don't you think?) He must have a mighty big bee in his bonnet that leaves him no peace. From all this I gather that our opponents are inconsolable because of our inviolate silence. He tried to work up my enthusiasm for a public appearance, so naturally I put on an unenthusiastic air. I distrust the fellow, especially as I cannot believe that he has any real scientific interests. He must be pursuing a quite different purpose which is still opaque to me. He wants to come again tomorrow, to sit in at a conference with my students. I almost hope these people will remain our opponents for a long time to come. (McGuire 1988, pp. 250-251)

Jung evidently wanted to show Freud that he'd mastered the Professor's time-honored method for dealing with critics: "inviolate silence." Freud replied with more petty contempt for Friedländer:

I hope and trust Friedländer hasn't got anything out of you. He is an unsavoury individual, even in his private affairs; he left his country because of some crooked business, he owes his clinic to his marriage to a woman he has since then divorced, and is now operating it for his former father-in-law, etc. All he wanted of us, it seems to me, was a kind of rehabilitation through our hostility. Now he is inconsolable because we have shown by our silence that we regarded him as unfit to duel with, so to speak. Either he has some specially beastly plan in visiting you, or he is stupid as well; can he think that we don't notice the contrast between the sweets he is dispensing and his public statements? In private the fellow deserves to be treated with all possible rudeness, in our literature we must simply ignore him; he is plain riffraff. (p. 253)

A month later Jung wrote Freud to inform him of another visit from Friedländer:

I treated him in the "grand" or haughty manner and received him in the circle of my 4 foreigners. They started talking in English, and it turned out afterwards that he doesn't understand a word. Yet he acted so sagely that I never noticed it. Otherwise I was polite, keeping my distance. Pfister also suffered a visitation from him, likewise Foerster. (pp. 256-257)

Indeed, Friedländer became so desperate for Freud to acknowledge him that he resorted to the childish stunt of calling up Freud under a fake name so he could get an audience with him. Despite Friedländer's obvious psychological vulnerabilities—or perhaps because those vulnerabilities disqualified him in Freud's eyes as a credible rival—Freud showed him no mercy and would not give him what he wanted. Jones describes the affair as follows:

Although all [Friedländer's] publications were extremely adverse to psycho-analysis it seemed to have some peculiar fascination for him. He would visit Jung, be sugary sweet to him and express the hope they would come to an understanding. What pained him most was that none of us would reply to his writings. Knowing this craving of his for acknowledgement we decided to ignore him entirely, and he found that very distressing. In a paper he gave at Budapest he complained bitterly about the way he was neglected. 'My review of the Freudian theory was announced several months ago, so why does not Freud, who did not mind travelling to America, give himself the trouble of coming to Budapest to refute me? Why does he dispose of his opponents in only a footnote?'

Friedländer was a curious man, a doubtful personality with a shady past, of which Freud was informed. When I was with Freud in Holland in the Summer of 1910 he told me the following story. One Saturday, May 28, 1910, the telephone rang and Professor Schottländer, a psychiatrist, asked for an interview. Freud said he might call that evening, but he was extremely puzzled since he knew the names of all the German psychiatrists and could not recollect this one. At nine o'clock Professor Friedländer appeared and assured Freud he had misheard his name on the telephone. Talk proceeded and soon came on to the topic of the Dora Analysis, which Friedländer referred to under the name of the Anna analysis. Freud pricked up his ears, leaned forward and said: 'If you please, Herr Professor, we are not on the telephone now. I suggest that we analyse this slip of the tongue.' From there on he did not spare the visitor and he kept him on the rack until one in the morning. He admitted to us that he had given him a hard time—he had a good deal to work off and it was a rare opportunity—and his final summing up was that Friedländer was 'a liar, a rascal and an ignoramus'.

Freud could not keep his opinion to himself, and Friedländer, hearing of a remark he had dropped in Switzerland a few years later, threatened to bring an action for slander against Freud. Nothing, however, came of it. (Jones 1955, p. 117)

It's possible that Freud's technique of inviolate silence was shrewd public relations. It may have created more intrigue and excitement around psychoanalysis than it hardened his enemies' resistance. And maybe after all a man like Friedländer is a lost cause, though Freud's account of him seems untrustworthy. The ethos of psychoanalysis as practiced by Karl Abraham, furthermore, rates no man a lost cause. When Abraham put a positive spin on Friedländer discussing Freudian ideas, Abraham then went on to say:

> I find from conversations with my colleagues that indifference is increasingly giving way to enmity. This enmity, however, does not always mean a poor prognosis. I have brought two of my colleagues to the point where I can debate with them, and one of them already gets me to interpret his dreams. I hope that the establishment of a Freudian Society, like those in Vienna and Zurich, is not too far off. (Falzeder 2002, p. 29)

Abraham seems to have applied psychotherapeutic calm and understanding to his colleagues in order to help them overcome their doubts and resistance—a more productive use of psychotherapy outside the consulting room than Freud practiced when he used interpretation to establish his authority over Jung.

If Freud were less sensitive to criticism and less averse to argument and demonstration, could he have engaged Friedländer and other critics in a profitable discussion along the lines Abraham pursued? Smith Ely Jelliffe says that he only learned about psychoanalysis because William Alanson White and then A.A. Brill had the patience to argue with him. At first, he says:

> I was mulish and would not understand. Our argumentation then was vociferous and protracted and if [Dr. White] had not been the tactful and indulgent friend then as ever, he would long ago have consigned me to where I undoubtedly then belonged and possibly still would be welcomed. (Jelliffe 1933, p. 322)

In 1910, Brill took over as Jelliffe's informal psychoanalytic instructor. They argued about psychoanalysis three times a week after their clinics were done and Brill persisted and won him over. (p. 325)

Admittedly, Friedländer was no Smith Ely Jelliffe. But if Freud had recognized that behind his critics' judgments lay real fear and vulnerability, could he have reached out to that fear to dispel it with his enormous powers of empathy and psychological insight? If Freud had been able to arrest his paranoid conviction that critics had the power to destroy him, could he have used his enormous powers of persuasion to engage their innate curiosity? Friedländer nakedly displayed his own psychological needs and Freud saw them quite clearly, but took them as affronts rather than opportunities. He also neglected to make use of Friedländer's reactions as information— about the effect his inviolate silence and indiscriminate insults could have on doctors who were skeptical about psychoanalysis.

Friedländer's remarks on psychoanalysis at the medical congress in Brussels in 1910 give a somewhat different impression of him than the one that Freud and Jones paint. The speech begins by expressing that he feels offended. He quotes Freud insulting certain critics "who lack discernment and who are malicious." We know the reason Freud insulted his foes—he felt attacked—but the insults he hurled made Friedländer feel equally abused. Friedländer writes, "Such strong attacks call forth equally strong defences." (Friedländer 1911, p. 297) Freudians with a penchant for revolutionary rhetoric, like Otto Gross, proclaimed that old ways of treating mental illness were now irrelevant, and Friedländer clearly felt threatened and defensive: "All those neurologists, therefore, who treat their patients by other methods must necessarily appear as ignorant." (p. 298)

Friedländer was not alone in his belittlement by Freudians. Sándor Ferenczi put experimental psychologist Géza Révész on the defensive in the exact same way when Ferenczi lectured on psychoanalysis in Budapest in 1909. In a letter to Freud, Ferenczi gloats about his arrogant, unfriendly behavior towards Révész:

I didn't spare psychophysics and the experimental psychologists; I was even rather aggressive in regard to them.—After the end of the lecture, the *Privatdozent* in psychology, Dr. Révész, gets up (a rather capable experimental psychologist, who has worked a lot in Göttingen and now has a large following among the students). He must—he said—defend himself against the charge that experimental psychologists are not scientists, that those who are concerned with it are handymen and machinists, as I (Dr. F.) characterized them. He spoke about the accomplishments of their methods, etc. He seems to have been particularly pained by the accusation that everything that they do is sterile, because, instead of first studying the macroscopic anatomy of the mind, psychoanalysis, they work prematurely with their "microscopic" instruments and they don't want to give that up even *now*; I dismissed all their results as worthless because a pure psychology of consciousness [that neglects the unconscious] can only yield partial, or even false, results. (Brabant, E. et al. 1993, p. 92)

Ferenczi adds with pride, "I held true to my convictions." Ferenczi wishes to display his own mental health to Freud in the letter, and he clearly interprets his aggression towards Révész as a sign that he's conquered his own inhibitions.

Is the scene Ferenczi describes in fact a picture of rosy mental health? Or is it evidence of the speaker's inhibitions about speaking publicly on psychoanalytic ideas, and his aggressive overcompensation for those inhibitions? Ferenczi seems to have wavered internally, then celebrated the victory of his aggression, even though his victory has not taken very good account of the reality of his audience's feelings.

Meanwhile, if Friedländer really subscribed to silly fads like "diagnoscopy," maybe he really was foolish—but was it necessarily productive to call him out on his ignorance and embarrass him for his conservatism? Foolish or not, he was a neurologist who published in mainstream journals and presented at conferences. He expressed cautious interest in learning more about psychoanalysis. Perhaps it was an insincere gesture, but it was interest nonetheless. Why upset him?

I have tried to show that Freud anticipated criticism due to pressure originating in his own conscience, and that the pressure could set him on the offensive, as it appears to have done to Ferenczi in Budapest. If Freud had more completely analyzed his shame about sexual research and his anxiety about intellectual revolution, might he have felt less besieged by his conscience and might he have hurled fewer provocations at his critics? And might this have made fewer enemies in the first place? Friedländer quotes psychoanalyst Isidor Sadger as toeing Freud's party line that all criticism of psychoanalysis is just prudery in disguise; perhaps if Freud himself felt less prude and uncomfortable with sexual research, he would have felt less need to call his critics prudes.

But Friedländer objected to the personal insults especially because they ignored his questions. He had some valid questions for Freud, questions that were not wholly conceived in ignorance and deserved answers. "Freud and his disciples have laid themselves open to the charge that instead of argumentation and proof they have substituted personalities and dogma," Friedländer writes. (Friedländer 1911, p. 297) This wasn't an outright dismissal of all Freudian claims—Friedländer in fact says he considers Freud's work on hysteria credible and important. Rather, it was an objection to the problematic manner in which later claims were made. Of Isidor Sadger, Friedländer writes:

His work, on the other hand, is not lacking in such dogmatic assertions as "Every man is from his very beginning bisexual." "To the youth, woman is always either a goddess or a wench." "As we learn from psychoanalysis all boys have the fancy of putting themselves in their fathers' places and impregnat[ing] their mothers." To establish such statements, which are denied by many observers or regarded as erroneously interpreted experiences—to establish these as a *science* obtained from psychoanalysis is indeed going too far. *It is orthodoxy free from all timidity....* [T]hese unproved theories have been treated with the greatest publicity as firmly established facts.... All those who dared to have other views have been branded as ignorant. (p. 299)

It's hard to argue that Friedländer didn't at least try to consider Freud's work with objectivity. He says that *Studies in Hysteria* "surely belongs to the best work on hysteria, and indeed is the best of Freud's work." Friedländer concurs with Bleuler's view that the work is so seminal it should now be "part of a general medical education." But Friedländer denies "the all-powerful sexual factor" as the cause of every neurosis. (pp. 301-302)

He was in a sense in agreement with Jung at the time, who sought to broaden the definition of libido so that it was not exclusively sexual, but could describe other needs, like hunger. And Friedländer was in agreement with later psychoanalysts, who have emphasized that neurotic conflicts arise not only when conscience frustrates sexual needs, but also when conscience frustrates needs for love or the expression of anger. As Robert Holt has said, Freud really did exaggerate the role of sexuality in his theorizing until late in his career. By then the dissident criticisms won out and got him to pay more attention to aggression. Furthermore, even before he theorized the death instinct, Freud was in practice less doctrinaire about sexual etiologies for neurosis than he was in his theoretical formulations. Look at his 1909 case study of the Rat Man: it includes much analysis of Rat Man's sexual feelings, but just as much of Rat Man's troubles consciously processing his own aggression—and the analysis of the latter would seem more important to the cure. In other words, Friedländer was not only raising a valid question, his critique was also more or less correct.

Freud and his followers really did tend toward reductive insistence on "the all-powerful sexual factor" in their public presentations, and my studies of Freud's thinking on public presentation suggest he had psychodynamic motives for doing so. He was attempting to get rid of his own shame by externalizing an inner conflict over sexual research. He identified with forbidden sexual research, projected the prude criticism of his own conscience onto external critics, and then avoided or dismissed those critics.

In some cases, his critics were undoubtedly as prudish and outrageous as his conscience expected them to be. Hoche comes to mind. Friedländer and Révész, however, seem more outraged by Freud's abstention from scientific debate, an abstention created by Freud's own psychodynamic, projective drama. Friedländer says quite explicitly that skeptics are not prudes, but scientists who object to dogmatic assertions that psychoanalysis is the best therapy in the absence of proof:

Almost all writers recognize the value of Freud's and Jung's psychologic work.... Surely [these critics doubt the efficacy of psychoanalysis as a therapy] not on account of prudery or on the grounds assigned by Sadger (see above), but because they regard the theories upon which this therapeutic procedure is founded as false, or because they can achieve their ends by other means. That the latter is the case has been sufficiently proven. The ignoring by Freud's school of these proofs, and their attitude that before their time there existed no psychotherapy, that no hysteria or fear neuroses were cured—this is in my judgment the greatest mistake of such authors as Gross and Stekel. This is not a matter of error in judgment, it is unscientific. I am personally acquainted with the success which such authors as Binswanger, Vogt, and Boardmann had in the treatment of hysteria. (pp. 314-315)

Friedländer praises Jung's association experiments because they offer proof, and he laments that the Freudians will not listen to requests for proof and that they decline invitations to debate their critics. Friedländer quotes Wilhelm Weygandt's view that a critic "has no hope of obtaining a hearing from Freud's followers, who have fortified themselves against all criticism." (pp. 311-312)

Freud won his battle with these critics in the sense that his theories have made a bigger impact on psychology than anything Friedländer or Weygandt or Révész did. Yet Friedländer's criticisms have not gone away either, and the heirs to his views today occupy more positions of authority in psychiatry than psychoanalysts do. Freud and his followers really had fortified themselves against all criticism—most especially those criticisms arising in their own superegos.

Paul McHugh

I never met Adolf Friedländer but I did meet Paul McHugh. He was a well-meaning man of passionate ideals and sometimes iconoclastic convictions. He once told *The New York Times*, "My record is a record of confronting power."[49] When speaking of depression in his thick Boston accent, and sometimes when speaking to a depressed patient, he used to say, "Thaaaaat's grim." He came of age when the culture took a secular turn and Freud was in fashion, but he held fast to his Catholicism and rejected psychoanalysis. Like many other critics before him, he believed that Freudian psychiatrists had invented the dynamic unconscious and elicited evidence for it from their impressionable patients by tendentious hints and suggestions.

McHugh himself had a tendency to pronounce what he wished were the case as if it were fact. In his 1992 essay "Psychotherapy Awry," he writes, "Among psychiatrists, a long, growling dispute—about twenty years in duration—has been fought and is now ending between romanticists and the empiricists, who insist that all the practices of psychiatry be based upon observation and methodical study of patients." (McHugh 2006, p. 18) He thought of Freud as a romantic, not an empiricist. By saying the dispute "is now ending," he meant that *Freud is dead* and he had been among the assassins. Since that is not true, I would further translate his statement to mean, *I wish Freud's ideas were finally discredited and that I had been the one to discredit him.*

Stating wishes as facts was in many ways the essential doctrine of his psychiatry. "One learns early that teaching psychiatry resembles practicing it," he writes. "You must knock bad ideas out of heads before you can start putting good ones in. You also learn—from both experiences—that bad ideas have a strong grip on people." (p. 1) Whether through drugs, electroconvulsive therapy, cognitive-behavioral psychology, anti-Freudian propaganda that revised optative into indicative declarations, or through the authority of his chair at the preeminent Johns Hopkins Hospital, he was determined

---

49 http://www.nytimes.com/2002/08/05/us/psychiatrist-says-he-was-surprised-by-furor-over-his-role-on-abuse-panel.html, accessed January 10, 2018.

to change students' and patients' behavior. He would do it like the prophets of the Bible, by making reality conform to his ideal. He was in his way kindly, relatable, interesting, but his bedside manner gave off an unintended whiff of Margaret Thatcher in the Falkland Islands.

McHugh credited Freud for discovering drives, but he saw the rest of psychoanalysis as vastly overreaching, and was so intent on correcting its course that hypothesis and theory had almost no place in his psychiatry at all. He viewed all talking psychotherapy not as a scientific pursuit of insights and answers inside the consulting room but rather as an amorphous form of empathic storytelling, no version of which differed substantially from any other, and all of which had one limited end, namely, to help in correcting the patient's behavior. He wanted psychiatry to emulate field biology—observing, describing, counting, and manipulating, but only with great caution venturing to explain its observations. While he believed he'd modernized psychiatry and while his pharmacological tools were better than Friedländer's, his vision of psychiatry closely resembled the one Friedländer outlined in his 1910 lecture in Brussels. Friedländer and McHugh both hoped to stop destructive behavior less by understanding it from within and more by applying pressure on it from the top down. I am tempted to say: "Thaaaaat's grim."

At the time my college and medical education took place, the public standing of psychoanalysis in general looked grim indeed. In 1991 my Intro to Psych professor had had to cut one lecture due to a scheduling conflict, and so he cut the one lecture he'd planned on Freud! My English professors had read some Freud, but they mainly looked to him for support for their deconstructionist literary theories. Students dismissed him as a quack or a misogynist and postmodernists dismissed his sincere attempts to describe human nature as outdated. And now here in medical school at a leading institution was well-meaning, grim Paul McHugh, sitting on Freud's mausoleum like a stone gargoyle with its talons closed around Freud's throat. Anny Katan's Hanna Perkins Center for Child Development, my psychoanalytic nursery school and kindergarten in Cleveland, felt far, far away.

McHugh's educational experiences were in many ways diametrically opposed to mine. When he was in college, the cultural *zeitgeist* was tuned to Freud. He tells this story about the first, disastrous time he came into contact with the idea of psychoanalysis. Like Friedländer, McHugh exhibits a certain vulnerability before Freud and his followers. Like some of the analysts in the Friedländer affair, the particular Freudian whom McHugh encountered as an undergraduate comes across as overzealous and bullying:

One bright day in the late 1940s, the poet John Ciardi substituted for our instructor, Mr. Ludwig, in English A, the freshman composition course at Harvard College required of those who had misspent their high school years and needed help learning to express themselves. Ciardi was not prepared to work on elementary matters that we, the backward freshmen, needed. He wished to show us the future as he saw it written out in Sigmund Freud's monograph on Leonardo da Vinci.

Ciardi enjoyed himself that day. He exuberantly explained how Leonardo's dream about a great bird beating its tail against his face when he was a baby was a prototypical Freudian dream. As Freud explained them, dreams hid from consciousness by representing in disguise an unconscious impulse—in this instance, Leonardo's homosexual urges. "That long tail, don't you know."

Ciardi believed that the Freudian "discoveries" of dream mechanisms and the dynamic unconscious unveiled hidden

motivations that lay at the heart of all human actions....
[He] became irritated when a couple of us—with little more
than an offhand reluctance to accept his point without more
evidence—challenged the argument....

Several days before, Mr. Ludwig had emphasized,
when teaching about figures of speech, that metaphorical
images used by writers revealed as much about the authors'
preoccupations as about the things they portrayed....

And that's what we said to Ciardi. Freud has extrapolated
a sexual image from a dream. That action, we suggested,
may tell more about Freud's mind than about Leonardo's. But
Ciardi had not come to listen to such talk. For him, Freud was
a wonder and source, not an author to be examined. "You
must have some unresolved sexual problem," he said to
me in particular and thus provided my first (and far from
last) exposure to the repression-resistance stratagem
psychiatric storytellers tend to use against their critics. The
class broke up into those persuaded by Ciardi's argument
and those unpersuaded, with me as a highly irritated member
of the latter....

[W]hy did this gifted man come to have such confidence in
Freud that he failed to work with what he knew from his own
profession? What prompted him to bully us, the strugglers
with language before him, rather than win us round with more
information? (pp. 36-37)

Perhaps McHugh could never have integrated psychoanalysis
into his worldview under any circumstances. If no one ever
rescued him from Catholicism, surely no one could rescue him from
resistance to Freud. But from what he says about the psychiatrists

who taught him while he was in medical school, they probably didn't help to open his mind much more than Ciardi had. They practiced closed thinking and interpretive dogmatism. For example, in his essay "What's the Story?" McHugh says that in medical school he presented a patient with anxiety about swallowing to an attending psychiatrist, Ives Hendrick, who interrupted him with the pronouncement, "as a case of globus hystericus, this patient's problem was obviously over oral sex.... His opinion was greeted with solemn noddings of heads by everyone in the room." (p. 41) Turned off by this arbitrary style of diagnosis, McHugh trained in neurology and returned to psychiatry in order to expel Hendrick and his like from the academy.

But it was Ciardi who had aimed a humiliating interpretation at McHugh himself, and so Ciardi leaves a bigger footprint in McHugh's memories of his development as a psychiatrist. Ciardi might have known better. Many of his poems comment indirectly on the dynamic unconscious, and on the hazards of looking into its depths. One such poem, "The Lungfish," says that in Africa the lungfish has another name.

...It is called

Kamongo there, but does not answer.
 If you cut its head off
(whether in fact or legend, and who
 knows which?) its jaws still snap

two days later. (Which
 we do know, all of us, about
what we cut off.)

Dr. Brown the ichthyologist takes a hibernating lungfish back to his lab, where Kamongo awakes and in his hunger spits stones against the glass walls of his tank, so hard that Dr. Brown fears the walls of the tank will break. He puts Kamongo back to sleep and builds a new tank with stronger walls:

> strong enough to hold both sleep
> and waking. If anything can be. If we
> can learn sleep whole and not choke
>
> on what we are while we learn it.
> (Ciardi 1978, pp. 269-270)

And then there is this doggerel poem from 1962, called "About the Teeth of Sharks."[50] It might as well have been called "How I Carelessly Created a Freud-Basher."

> The thing about a shark is—teeth,
> One row above, one row beneath.
>
> Now take a close look. Do you find
> It has another row behind?
>
> Still closer—here, I'll hold your hat:
> Has it a third row behind that?
>
> Now look in and...Look out! Oh my,
> I'll *never* know now! Well, goodbye.

---

50 https://www.poetryfoundation.org/poems/49771/about-the-teeth-of-sharks, accessed January 10, 2018.

3. Conclusion: A Critique of Pure Resistance

It's my hypothesis that psychoanalysts' anticipation of resistance and their consequent obstinacy regarding proof has created at least as many enemies of psychoanalysis as public resistance has. Going all the way back to the inception of psychoanalysis, complaints against unscientific rhetoric and method look far more numerous than expressions of moral outrage. As Robert Wallerstein observes, "[F]ew theoretical issues are more constantly and passionately argued ... than the standing of our discipline as a science." (Wallerstein 2006, p. 303) I would contend that Freud's aversion to proof explains Wallerstein's statement better than Freud's theory of public resistance to psychoanalysis.

Think of that crisis point at the very beginning of the fifty-year decline, 1968. That was when *Science*, the most mainstream, most highly cited journal in America, opened its arms to Howard Shevrin and published his proof of the unconscious—while Charles Brenner, the president of the American Psychoanalytic Association, completely ignored this study and expressed disdain and pessimism about proving the validity of psychoanalytic ideas. Which was more significant in 1968: public resistance to psychoanalysis or psychoanalytic proof aversion?

Before you scoff, consider the many weaknesses of Freud's theory of public resistance to psychoanalysis. Compare all the evidence and arguments you've heard on behalf of Freud's aversion to proof with the sparse details Freud supplied to his theory of public resistance to psychoanalytic ideas. Public resistance may be unique in Freud's writings on repression in that he never gives public resistance any context or specificity, never attempts to describe its variations, its inner complexity, or its relation to individual human beings. Freud intends the theory of public resistance to apply to anyone, anywhere who criticizes any one of the many different ideas in psychoanalysis, whether the dynamic unconscious, defense mechanisms, the importance of childhood, the importance of the nuclear family in child development, the phases of child development, childhood sexuality, the Oedipus complex, the role of instincts and guilt in provoking neurosis, talking therapy, free association, transference, the dream theory, the theory of jokes, parapraxes, libido theory, the tripartite organization of the personality, etc.

Mustn't various people in various contexts react in different ways to many different parts of psychoanalysis? Of course psychoanalytic theories are bound to trigger defenses, but not all theories will trigger defenses in all people. And if the theories trigger defenses, which defenses? Even the same basic defense mechanism varies in its particular expression from person to person. And what about the style of presentation of the theory? That too is bound to have an enormous impact on whether psychoanalysis provokes a defensive reaction and on what kind it is.

Now contrast Freud's generic discussions of public resistance with his more nuanced discussions of resistance to psychoanalysis in the consulting room. A patient's resistance is a highly personal phenomenon manifesting itself in the context of unconscious feelings transferred from the patient's past into his or her relationship with an analyst. When a patient resists an interpretation, it's not an interpretation of all humanity in the form of a psychoanalytic theory, it's an interpretation aimed directly at the patient's highly individual defenses, which have organized themselves according to the patient's highly individual history.

Yet Freud treats public resistance as though it were identical to patients' resistance: "I made a first application of psycho-analysis by explaining to myself that this behaviour of the crowd was a manifestation of the same resistance which I had to struggle against in individual patients." (Freud 1933, p. 138) How could the two forms of resistance in such different contexts possibly be identical? I am tempted to say that the specter of public resistance to psychoanalysis is so vague as to be almost chimerical—a half-factitious ideation produced by psychoanalysts' fear of criticism and doubts about psychoanalysis. And psychoanalysts' efforts to escape or preempt this specter have ironically caused skepticism towards psychoanalysis to hypertrophy into a monster worthy of their nightmares.

Those like Freud who have the courage to research into repressed feelings, and to present their research, have more to lose than the audience does. The psychoanalysts are the ones standing up and daring to talk about instincts and guilt and pain and the lies we tell ourselves, and sometimes the audience repays this bravery by branding analysts uncivil, touchy-feely, overly sexual, rebellious, disrespectful, weird, wildly speculative, unscientific, unfeeling or too full of feeling.... Members of the audience at a psychoanalytic presentation may have less insight into themselves than the expositor of psychoanalysis has, but the expositor of psychoanalysis faces much stronger psychodynamic pressures in the act of transmitting psychoanalytic knowledge. So we must have sympathy for John Ciardi and Ives Hendrick.

We must have sympathy for Freud himself, who faced more pressure than anyone else. And we must ask whether we want to emulate the way he acted when he was under pressure, insulting colleagues like Friedländer behind their backs and refusing to engage them face-to-face in rational dialogue, or whether we should emulate Freud at his most relaxed and confident. I propose the latter: we should emulate him as he was in writing his masterpiece *The Interpretation of Dreams*, or telling us Yiddish jokes, or in the middle of the *Introductory Lectures* talking sanity to a world entrenched in war and madness. Or best of all, perhaps, as he was in the privacy of his consulting room with a patient like Hilda Doolittle. She tells us he spoke to her "seriously yet kindly," his arm shooting forward "as it did on those occasions when he wished to stress a finding or focus my attention to some point in hand," treating her as "an intellectual equal" even as he offered "some rare discovery, some priceless finding," adding " 'Perhaps you may feel differently,' as if my feelings, my discoveries, were on a par with his own." (Doolittle 1974, pp. 85-86) We should emulate him when he and Hilda together would sometimes approach "the clearest fountain-head of highest truth, as in the luminous *real* dream of the Princess and the river...." (p. 92)

IV. THE POSTMODERN AVERSION TO PROOF

1. Introduction: Postmodernism and Current Events

Postmodern thinkers make a virtue of suspicion. They don't accept ideas at face value as truthful reflections of the world, but rather scrutinize ideas for hidden biases. This search for biases relies on the principle that ideas aren't just discovered and revealed, but created by human beings in a social, historical, and psychological context. While postmodernism is relatively new, its central principle is old; it certainly predates the 18th-century philosopher Giambattista Vico, who gave it the name *verum factum*, or "made truth."[51]

People rely on the principle of *verum factum* every day of their lives, whether they're aware of it or not. They use *verum factum* when assessing the reliability of an advertisement given the ad's vested interest in selling a product. They use *verum factum* when assessing gossip according to its sources and the sources' motives. Freud used *verum factum* when he supposed that thoughts could be influenced by defense mechanisms that do not honor truth but rather protect the thinker from it.

Postmodernists, however, apply *verum factum* in a more devout way. They apply it so assiduously, in fact, that they undermine

---

51 https://plato.stanford.edu/entries/vico/, accessed January 21, 2018.

their own confidence in any criteria of proof and fact whatsoever. If everything observed and thought is shaped by its context, they argue, then nothing is reliably true anymore. Postmodernists therefore won't talk about facts, but only about subjective narratives put forward by specific people in a specific context.

Postmodernism has had a significant impact on psychoanalysis both in theory and in practice. Some have called the influx of postmodern thought into psychoanalysis "the relational turn," others the "new view." Other names for the postmodern psychoanalytic movement include "intersubjectivity, dialectical constructivism, or two-person psychology." (Govrin 2006, p. 507) "The central philosophical position of new view theorists," according to Morris Eagle and his colleagues, "is that [the human mind] is in its entirety interpretively constructed in the context of interpersonal interaction." (Eagle et al. 2001, p. 459) This extreme dedication to *verum factum* "casts doubt on values such as objective knowledge, truth, and correspondence to reality" for those psychoanalysts who subscribe to it. (Govrin 2006, p. 507) And there are many who do. Jon Mills asserts that relational analysts have taken "center stage" while Freudians are now "a marginalized community" within psychoanalysis. (Mills 2012, p. x)

In section IV, "The Postmodern Aversion to Proof," I will critique postmodern epistemological ideas as they relate to contemporary psychoanalysis. I do so according to a decidedly Freudian-rationalist worldview. That does *not* mean I criticize or reject the use of *verum factum*, or "made truth," without which psychoanalysis could not begin to do its work of analyzing defenses and transferences. Nor does it mean that I criticize or reject all the work that's done under the banner of postmodernism or under the banner of relational psychoanalysis.

As Mills says, "I certainly do not want to categorize all relationalists by placing them in the same camp sharing unanimous convictions, nor do I wish to charge them all with denouncing Freud or casting aspersion toward classical psychoanalysis." (p. 65) It doesn't make sense, for example, to blur Jay Greenberg's work with Jacques Lacan's.[52] In comparison with Lacan, Greenberg's view of the postmodern questions facing psychoanalysis looks understated and practical. He writes the following in a *Psychoanalytic Quarterly* editor's introduction entitled "Is Truth Relevant?":

> **Freud left us with a paradox: psychoanalysis as a project is unimaginable unless we see it as the relentless pursuit—in the face of formidable resistance—of truths about ourselves. And yet we have no certainty about what "truth" means, or, more personally and more immediately, what it means to "know" that something is true. Over the last couple of decades, this paradox has burgeoned into a new conversation about the way that psychoanalysis is conceived and practiced. (Greenberg 2016, p. 271)**

Fair enough. Greenberg is no Lacan, whose prose could clog a kitchen disposal.

But Greenberg's mild-mannered statement does embed within it the radical skepticism characteristic of hardcore postmodernism—*we have no certainty about what "truth" means*. And, while Greenberg's revisions of psychoanalytic theories in many ways respond to his extensive clinical experience, his competing doubts about empiricism appear to play an equally significant role in his thinking. Relational revisions to psychoanalysis that undermine empiricism have important implications for the practice of psychoanalysis, for its dealings with the public and

---

52 Greenberg is one of the founding theorists of relational psychoanalysis. Lacan reconceived of psychoanalysis as a branch of literary deconstructionism.

with other disciplines, and for psychoanalysts' ability to address proof aversion. Radical doubt of scientific method won't help to assuage critics, for example, who complain that psychoanalysis is unscientific or assuage critics who ask for more proof. Such radical doubt won't help convince insurance companies to reimburse patients for psychoanalysis, either.

I'm a political liberal, but I'm not a postmodernist.[53] I don't need philosophies of radical doubt in order to question authority or uncover lies, since skepticism is in the first place one of the cardinal virtues of science. Furthermore, no postmodernist has ever been able to explain to me how it's even possible to doubt all thought-products of induction and deduction without first trusting and applying induction and deduction. In other words, how do you make a postmodern argument on behalf of radical doubt without using induction or deduction? Epigrams 115 and 354 of Ludwig Wittgenstein's *On Certainty* summarize this self-defeating attribute of radical doubt. 115: "If you tried to doubt everything you would not get as far as doubting anything. The game of doubting itself presupposes certainty." (Wittgenstein 1972, p. 18) 354: "Doubting and non-doubting behaviour. There is the first only if there is the second." (p. 46)[54] As I will later discuss, philosophical arguments for and against radical doubt have been vying for millennia, and our best thinkers, from Epicurus to Wittgenstein, have repeatedly settled them in favor of limited, scientific doubt, not radical doubt.

---

53 http://www.nytimes.com/2012/10/30/opinion/global/the-jews-of-cuyahoga-county.html. Accessed January 13, 2018. http://www.nytimes.com/2013/11/05/opinion/role-of-humanities-in-school-and-life.html. Accessed January 13, 2018.

54 Consider this argument on behalf of radical doubt: "I see an oasis in the desert, but when I come closer I see that the oasis was an illusion created by heat and where I thought there was water, there's really nothing but sand. I realize that my senses are fallible and I no longer trust them." It's a fallacious argument because I only learned to doubt the perception of the oasis when I looked closer and, under the particular conditions of looking closer, trusted my perceptions. There is no doubt without trust, no falsehood without truth.

I don't need postmodernism or a relational psychoanalytic perspective in order to criticize or revise Freud, either. As Eagle et al. put it, the "untenable" philosophical positions taken by postmodernists "are unnecessary to sustain the legitimate criticisms of psychoanalysis advanced by new view [relational] theorists." (Eagle et al. 2001, p. 461) My ideas about Freud's attitude to proof did not begin as a diagnosis according to any particular theoretical orientation, but merely as an observation that Freud's writings on proof and public demonstration were not consistently rational. My first work on the subject did not attempt to explain the phenomenon of Freud's irrationality about proof, but only to describe it. I had no explanation at first, and it took me many years to develop one that made sense. Ultimately, it was Freud's particular variety of *verum factum*—the analysis of defense mechanisms—that supplied the best explanation: that Freud had an aversion to proof of which he was not fully aware.

Relational psychoanalysis presents useful critiques of Freudian orthodoxies, as Eagle, Mills, and many other Freudians acknowledge, but so far it hasn't helped me explain the irrationality I've observed in Freud's writings on public proof. If a letter I received from Greenberg is any indication, relational psychoanalysis does not even permit such an inquiry to begin. He questioned my assumption that "proof" was a valid aim and furthermore expressed resentment at my attempt to diagnose emotional interferences around proof because he felt it was an *ad hominem* attack on those who do not accept "proof" as a valid notion. The entire formulation was for Greenberg "unacceptable in a scholarly publication." He would not publish my ideas in the streets of Askelon—nor even peer review them—lest the daughters of the Philistines rejoice.

If postmodernism can't help me explain Freud's irrationality about proof, however, the concept of proof aversion has helped me to understand postmodernism. An aversion to certainty—in other words, an aversion to proof—is in my view the *verum factum* at the heart of postmodernism. Postmodernism is a metastasis of the doubts that tripped up Freud in proving his case, and it's explicable according to the Freudian psychology of defenses. But whether you share my Freudian-rationalist worldview or you're ambivalent about science versus postmodernism, take a moment to consider the dangers of radical postmodernist doubt in light of current events.

President Donald Trump is a postmodernist. He doesn't question power, of course—he exploits it. But he's a postmodernist in the sense that he doesn't believe in truth. He believes in narrative. And his consequent abuses of truth, and of those who try to report it, starkly illustrate the problem with postmodernists' radical indifference to truth. How can postmodernists condemn Trump for lying when they don't believe in reliable, reality-based criteria by which to divine truth from falsehood?

Paul Ricoeur asked a similar question in his paper "The Question of Proof in Psychoanalytic Writings." (Ricoeur 1977) His question was, in so many words: if all psychoanalytic knowledge is purely linguistic, relative, context-dependent, uncertain, and socially constructed—and that is what Ricoeur believed—how can psychoanalysts establish criteria by which to judge theoretical accuracy or therapeutic success? The answer is: not very easily. At the end of a tortuous attempt to create epistemic criteria within a closed linguistic system that denies any correspondence with reality, Ricoeur concedes: "It may be granted that this apparatus [for determining what constitutes proof or fact in psychoanalysis] is extremely complex, very difficult to handle, and highly problematical." (p. 869)

The field of journalism has by comparison begun reckoning with radical doubt in a more practical way. On December 1, 2017 Brooke

Gladstone of WNYC's "On the Media"[55] eloquently characterized the problem of radical doubt created by Trump's assault on the news media:

> The president's most awe-inspiring accomplishments are trampling on the idea that reality matters—that in fact it has a material impact on the life of every citizen—and marketing the notion that the best of the American press, however imperfect it may be, is not a truth-seeker but just another special interest....

Is truth relevant? Yes, it is. Gladstone also provided a Freudian diagnosis of Trump's refusal to accept objective facts. She compared his refusal to that of war criminal Slobodan Praljak. When an international court rejected Praljak's appeal, he rejected the court's decision and committed suicide on live television. Both Trump and Praljak, according to Gladstone, represent extreme cases of denial.

> Trump of course is not alone in his intolerance of reality. On Wednesday at the Hague a convicted war criminal received the news that his twenty-year jail term would be upheld, declared that he wasn't a criminal, and took a swig of poison. He chose death over life in a world that saw the truth of him. Denial itself is a poison, and it's polluted America's ether. Call it special pleading if you will, but take heed when America's president works so tirelessly to sow distrust in our engines of accountability, our data collectors, our research institutions, our best media organizations, and emboldens others to do the same.

---

55 https://www.wnyc.org/story/on-the-media-2017-12-01, accessed January 27, 2018.

Washington Post columnist Margaret Sullivan then came on to give some suggestions as to how the "reality-based press" could defend its credibility when Trump and alt-right news outlets propose that any and every news story is "fake news." "I don't think that most people understand anonymous sourcing or the difference between an editorial and a news story," Sullivan said. She continued:

> So I think we need to explain ourselves better.... [That means] taking a paragraph early in an investigative story to say *here's how we did it*, it means telling people to the extent you can who your sources are, it means publishing your documentation when you can, it means telling people about your methodology, printing and publishing primary sources.... [W]hen I was the public editor at *The New York Times* I really campaigned against the overuse of anonymous sources. In investigative reporting, particularly in the national security area, you sometimes have to use them, there's no other way to get at this information, but the overuse of them begins to really eat away at credibility....

In other words, the solution to radical doubt is a recommitment to truth and to transparency in journalists' fact-finding methodology.

The problem of radical doubt of the press, as Gladstone and Sullivan characterize it, resembles the epistemic problems confronting psychoanalysis. The public and much of medical science doubt the veracity of Freudian claims, which can be hard to prove. Both psychoanalysis and national security journalism at times rely on confidential sources, which threatens public credibility. The solution, Sullivan says, is to rededicate ourselves to proving what is true. The solution, Gladstone says, is to point to radical doubt as a species of denial. The psychoanalytic community has done little of either, and the doubtful postmodern outlook within the field will make it much harder to counteract doubts outside of it.

Analysts who are hardcore postmodernists will probably reject my analogies. I am more than willing to continue discussion with them, but I confess I don't know how; it's difficult to argue with anyone who disavows rational argument itself according to the conviction that rationality is a cultural construct. As Sullivan said, you can't have the conversation about validity with readers who totally reject the possibility of truth:

> If they're now convinced that this is just a bunch of claims and counterclaims and in essence [they throw up their] hands and say, *It's all a bunch of lies*, I mean, there's really not much of a way to penetrate that. But for people who are truly interested in trying to figure out what's true and what isn't true then...

Then: there is constructive work to do. And we can only assume that those who aren't interested in what's true and what isn't true—those who in other words reject reality—will ultimately come around. Because reality meets no one halfway.

2. Postmodernism Is Narcissism

2.1. Disavowing Reality, Childhood, and Mortality

As unlikely as it seems for a mental health profession to hold reality at arm's length, some leading psychoanalysts were early adopters of postmodern and existentialist philosophies that shrug off objective knowledge. Thus psychoanalyst Roy Schafer could write in 1978, "Reality is not, as Freud usually assumed, a definite thing to be arrived at or a fixed and known criterion of objectivity." (Quoted in Hanly 1992, p. 9)

Charles Hanly describes the relational turn in psychoanalysis in his book *The Problem of Truth in Applied Psychoanalysis*. He conceptualizes the shift as a movement away from what philosophers call a "correspondence theory of truth"—the traditional scientific attitude, where knowledge reflects reality—towards a "coherence theory of truth," which promotes ideas according to their internal consistency or their consistency with other ideas. Scientists sometimes use coherence to choose or create their hypotheses but not to test them. If postmodernists accept any epistemic criteria at all, they apply the criterion of coherence and do so very intuitively and heterogeneously.

The shift from correspondence to coherence—or to incoherence, depending on your taste for writers like Lacan and Ricoeur—seems to have coincided with the outbreak of postmodernism in the humanities in general after 1968, and to have appealed especially to analysts in Heinz Kohut's self-psychology tradition. Like all postmodern schools of thought, postmodern psychoanalytic thought throws doubt on objective knowledge, but relational psychoanalysis quarries from that radical doubt advantages to human dignity in the practice of psychotherapy. The analyst no longer claims to know more than the patient, so postmodern analytic strategies theoretically accord the patient greater respect. Since postmodern philosophies see knowledge of reality as "constructed" by the human mind, the mind occupies a more important position in relational psychoanalysis than does material reality, and hence human thought acquires a certain kind of elevation in stature. It would seem that in the wake of Galileo and Darwin's scientific demolition of biblical Creation, postmodernism has attempted to rescue humanity from its peripheral position in the cosmos by secular means.

As I've already discussed, Freudian psychoanalysis and many other schools of thought apply the *verum factum* principle that the human mind can make knowledge, not just receive it. But radical postmodernism asserts that *all* knowledge is made by the human self, and nothing received from an objective source outside of it. According to postmodernism's radical doubt of objective reality, human existence can no longer be regarded as a remarkable feature of the universe; rather, perceptions of an external universe must be regarded as one of many remarkable features of the mind. Thus philosopher Jürgen Habermas asserts, in Hanly's words, "that human psychology, and with it psychoanalysis, 'escapes' or 'transcends' the ordinary world of other animate and inanimate things." (p. 6) Thus, psychoanalyst Donald Spence[56] claims that not only the patient but "the analyst functions more as a pattern-maker than a pattern-finder." (Quoted in Hanly, p. 6) And thus some analysts choose Jean Paul Sartre's free will over Freud's psychic determinism. Kohut's rhetoric echoes Sartre quite clearly when he declares he's moving on from Freud's psychic determinism (p. 8) and so does Schafer's rhetoric when he says "the concept of action requires us to regard each action as inherently spontaneous, starting from itself." (p. 9)

In adopting Sartre's idea of free will and rejecting Freud's psychic determinism, Spence and Schafer have thrown doubt upon a core psychoanalytic conviction—that childhood has lasting psychological importance. Hanly explains:

Spence's account agrees with the existentialist notion (Sartre 1943), repeated by May (1958), that a present intention or perception interprets the past—that there is no discrete,

---

56 I will later touch upon Spence's scientific work in psycholinguistics. His variegated thought, ranging from scientific to postmodern, once again shows that people cannot be sorted into rigid categories of "friend" versus "enemy" in the style of Freud's proof-averse defenses.

specific, particular past that continues to be what it was.... The idea that the meaning of a person's past, as well as its influence upon his present life, is determined by present choices is very different from the idea that contemporary affective experiences activate chains of associated memories leading back to infantile precursors. (p. 7)

And so, in disregarding objective reality, some postmodern psychoanalysts ultimately disregard childhood, which is rather shocking. As Govrin says, "if one wants to be called psychoanalytic, it is very hard to avoid the causality that exists between childhood and transference." (Govrin 2006, p. 527)

It's an even greater shock to learn the extent to which some practitioners allow themselves to doubt "the idea that reality matters, that in fact it has a material impact" on every person's life, as Brooke Gladstone puts it. That any psychoanalyst could suppose suffering and its relief take place in a world of pure semantics, where one story is as good as another, defies common sense. And it contradicts my most deeply felt personal experience.

If my personal, subjective experience means more to postmodernists than any "logocentric" rationalist argument, then I'd like to ask them: In my own personal history, was the reality of my father's premature death immaterial? Did it even happen? Does it matter to my past development and my psychology? Can I tell myself the story that he didn't die? That he's alive and I know him and we've had the opportunity to share all the things that fathers and sons are meant to share over the course of their lives?

I can't tell myself that story, because it's not true.

Should I instead tell myself the story that a psychoanalyst will be my father and give me all the love I didn't get from my biological father? To assign an analyst the duties of my father is only transference of my past onto my present. Surely, playing with that fantasy is useful both in understanding and in working through my feelings, but it's also a lie. Investing that lie with a validity equal to other "narratives" can't spare me my real feelings, because my analyst is not in fact my father, nor can he ever succeed at filling that hole in my heart. In fact, I've found a source of healing and empowerment in the insight that such transferences and their accompanying defense mechanisms distort my view of the present reality. With that insight, I am liberated from the past, I see the present as the present, and I reclaim some semblance of the free will I lost when my childhood dominated my thinking so obstreperously.

The fairy tale that my father is alive or has transubstantiated into the body of my analyst could never change my feelings in the slightest, because those feelings were annealed in the crucible of a scarring reality. My feelings correspond indelibly to the material fact of my father's death from cancer 11 days before my third birthday, a fact I cannot consciously remember, have many psychological incentives to forget, but nevertheless know to be true from indirect evidence inside and outside myself: my family knew him and speaks of him and has relayed to me the facts of his life and death; I remember him not being there all those years; there are photographs; I have a few of his belongings; I am told I walk like him, share aspects of his character, and my thumbnails have a wave in them like his. Most of all, I know he was real because his absence hurts. I feel so much about him whether or not I consciously remember him. Any therapy that denies the real, material impact of my childhood on my adult life has never been useful to me, and I'm not sure it ever could be useful to me. Is truth relevant to me as a former psychoanalytic patient? Yes, it is.

Whereas Freud's irrationality about proof subtly interfered with his larger scientific aims, postmodernists have founded their entire ideology on the central, defining characteristic of defense mechanisms: the denial of objective reality. And inside postmodernists' denial of objective reality there is clearly an infantile wish. It is an infantile wish that there were no cruel, unyielding reality, a reality that does whatever it likes despite the impotent protests of the tiny human will. It is an infantile wish that instead of reality there were only words, that instead of reality there were a "text," which is really a wish that instead of reality there were just the human self. It is the infantile wish that our minds were not brains destined to die, but immortal books instead. The repudiation of objective reality is childish megalomania as Freud describes it in his paper "On Narcissism":

[M]egalomania [*Größenwahn*]: [children's] over-estimation of the power of their wishes and mental acts, the 'omnipotence of thoughts' ['*Allmacht der Gedanken*'], a belief in the thaumaturgic force of words [*Zauberkraft der Worte*], and a technique for dealing with the external world—'magic'—which appears to be a logical application of these grandiose premisses. (Freud 1914, p. 75)

Postmodernism is narcissism.

Hanly puts it more delicately when he describes Ricoeur's ideas as "particularly naïve and unsatisfactory" and asserts that Ricoeur "makes nonsense of the clinical testing of [Freud's] ideas, which Freud advocated." (Hanly 1992, p. 8) But it's no exaggeration to say that Ricoeur, like so many other postmodernists, wrote a well-meaning paper full of grandiose witchcraft. The only sense in Ricoeur is the bleating of a child crying out, *I am immortal, I am not a body that dies, I am something*

more, I am a soul! O lords of chaos, hear my incantations, come ye
contradictions and watchwords of paradox, save me from my own reason,
which forces me to see the truth that I am a real living mortal thing with
lungs and a pumping heart and a childhood, full of air and blood and salt
and love and sorrow, not an everlasting book in dialogue with eternity.

Now, if a new generation of psychoanalysts has broken free of the
dogmatism of their forebears, I applaud them for that in all sincerity.
As Jon Mills says in his critique of relational psychoanalysis:

From the standpoint of redefining therapeutic intervention,
analytic posturing, and technical priority, relational analysis
is a breath of fresh air. Having questioned, disassembled,
and revamped the classical take on neutrality, anonymity,
and abstinence, analysts now behave in ways that are more
personable, authentic, humane, and reciprocal rather than
reserved, clinically detached, socially artificial, and stoically
withholding. (Mills 2012, p. 97)

If relational analysts have broadened Freud's concept of instinct to
include a wider range of interpersonal motives, that makes sense. If
they've refined or expanded the process of working through in the
transference, and have found more ways to help patients manage
their present lives, perhaps it's about time. If they've warmed up
relations between therapist and patient in a way that is in their clinical
experience better for patients, okay. If they think case studies are
enough and psych experiments superfluous, I don't blame them. If
they object to the nomenclature of "personality disorders" that's used
in psychological research because they find such labels reductive,
pejorative, and pathologizing of commonplace phenomena, I tend
to agree.

But how can they practice psychoanalysis without differentiating clearly and unequivocally between fantasy and reality? Rejecting the distinction between fantasy and reality amounts to more than the mere rejection of childhood; it's a rejection of the dynamic unconscious, repression, and the theory of defense mechanisms. I am taken aback by the repudiation of repression, not because it's a repudiation of Freudian dogma, but because psychoanalysis becomes incoherent and meaningless without the theory of repression and defense mechanisms.

When I was growing up, I told myself neurotic, depressing stories about myself, about my relationships, and about the world. These were ugly daydreams that hid even uglier feelings from myself. They were lies that could only be identified as lies by studying them in contrast with reality, a reality that I did not allow myself to see clearly for many years. One by one, again and again, through psychoanalysis, I replaced lies with truth. It was hard, because reality is hard. Hand over hand, I felt my way backwards from a lie to the real and palpable psychodynamic forces that had shaped the lie, to the real feelings and original situations that had triggered the distorting forces. Sometimes it hurt like surgery. And eventually the possession of the slippery truth became liberating, sometimes even uplifting. It became indispensable to me in living a decent life. I would probably be dead without psychoanalysis.

By giving up on truth, postmodernists seem to have given up their relation to reality, as Freud puts it. They've adopted the neurotic's narcissistic withdrawal from the world:

A patient suffering from hysteria or obsessional neurosis has also, as far as his illness extends, given up his relation to reality. But analysis shows that he has by no means broken off his erotic relations to people and things. He still retains them in phantasy; i.e. he has, on the one hand, substituted for real objects imaginary ones from his memory, or has mixed the latter with the former.... The libido that has been withdrawn from the external world has been directed to the ego and thus gives rise to an attitude which may be called narcissism. (Freud 1914, pp. 74-75)

To suppose that the mind can exist independent of reality and of historical truth, and that psychoanalysis need engage only with words but not with facts of real life, to suppose that the world is a text—what is that? Surely, this is no revolutionary philosophy. It is regressive, narcissistic withdrawal of the cathexes into the ego, so that the ego's thoughts replace reality, so that reality and fantasy are interchangeable, in accord with the pleasure principle. It is an infantile dismissal of the reality principle, which Lacan denigrates as "the expression of a scientific prejudice most hostile to the dialectic of knowledge." (Lacan 1966, p. 182) For Lacan, science itself is not the ideal of objectivity we strive towards in order to discover defensive prejudice, but is itself a form of prejudice against the idle pleasures of narcissistic philosophy. His statement is not even comprehensible except as an expression of a feeling: a neurotic wish to withdraw from reality.

2.2. Radical Doubt Is Obsessional Neurosis

If neurotics withdraw from reality into narcissism, doubt is their primary means of doing so. It has evidently not occurred to psychoanalytic postmodernists that the ideologies of radical doubt look a great deal like the symptomatic doubt Freud observes in obsessional neurotics. Freud observes in his patient the Rat Man a "capacity for being illogical which never fails to bewilder one in such highly intelligent people as obsessional neurotics" (Freud 1909, p. 48) and comments on obsessional neurotics' "characteristic liking for indeterminateness." (p. 58) The embrace of paradox and illogic on one hand and the love of uncertainty and indeterminateness on the other are the hallmarks both of postmodern style and of Rat Man's character. So many passages in Rat Man apply equally well to obsessional neurotics and to postmodernists:

> Another mental need which is shared by obsessional neurotics …. is the need for *uncertainty* in their life, or for *doubt*…. The creation of uncertainty is one of the methods employed by the neurosis for drawing the patient away from *reality* and isolating him from the world—which is among the objects of every psychoneurotic disorder. (p. 67)
>
> Our present patient had developed a peculiar talent for avoiding a knowledge of any facts which would have helped him in deciding his conflict. (pp. 67-68)
>
> The predilection felt by obsessional neurotics for uncertainty and doubt leads them to turn their thoughts by preference to those subjects upon which all mankind are uncertain and upon which our knowledge and judgments must necessarily remain open to doubt. (p. 68)
>
> In obsessional neuroses the uncertainty of memory is used to the fullest extent as a help in the formation of symptoms…. (p. 68)
>
> [Obsessional neurotics'] essential characteristic is that they are incapable of coming to a decision, especially in matters of love; they endeavor to postpone every decision, and, in their doubt which person they shall decide for or what

measures they shall take against a person, they are obliged to choose as their model the old German courts of justice [which were so slow, Freud implies, that nothing was ever decided]. (p. 71)

[A]nother means by which the obsession is protected against conscious attempts at solution ... is the choice of an indefinite or ambiguous wording. (p. 80)

Lacan and Ricoeur would seem to have adopted each of these symptoms as a strategy for writing a psychoanalytic paper. Presumably, they haven't noticed the blatant resemblances between their philosophical style and the style of obsessional neurosis because it would be uncomfortable to do so.

The *verum factum* idea that knowledge is constructed enthralls postmodernists, and yet they never consider the possibility that postmodernism itself is a psychological construct, not a valid philosophy. They exempt themselves from such considerations with the rationalization that there's no such thing as "valid" knowledge. In the words of Weygandt the Freud critic, they have "fortified themselves against all criticism." To do away with the anxiety-provoking reality, they have created a religion of doubt that permits questioning anything at all, except the religion of doubt itself.

Still another line from Rat Man could describe all of postmodernism: "he exploited the uncertainty of reason ... to the benefit of the religious attitude which he had outgrown [but still felt attached to]...." (p. 5) Perhaps that's why Jacques Derrida, the father of deconstructionism, at one point described his own work as a kind of "negative theology" (Derrida 1968, p. 388), which defines God according to what He is not. In the next chapter, I will examine in further detail the clandestine religious character of postmodernism.

3. Postmodernism Is a Recrudescence of Ancient Skepticism

The very name *postmodernism* calls out "avant-garde," but radical doubt is in fact older than Socrates. Postmodernism has introduced no arguments for doubt that weren't around 2500 years ago. Even the analysis of signification in language, which the postmodern movement claims to have originated, occurred among ancient philosophers, who used arguments nearly identical to those of postmodern linguistic analysis. The unchanging nature of these skeptical lines of thought points to their origins not in the evolution of philosophy but in the unchanging pressures of human psychology.

The early 5th-century BCE thinker Protagoras, for instance, whom Anthony Kenny describes as "the doyen of a new class of philosopher: the sophists," coined the saying *Man is the measure of all things*, one of the earliest mottoes of "relativist epistemology." (Kenny 2004, pp. 28-29) Kenny summarizes Protagoras's beliefs as they have come down to us in the reports and rebuttals of other philosophers and ancient commentators:

> Whatever appears true to a particular person *is* true for that person. All beliefs, therefore, are true: but they only have a relative truth. There is no such thing as the independent, objective truth that Democritus sought, and failed to find in sense-appearance…. Diogenes Laertius tells us that [Protagoras] said that there were two opposed accounts of every matter, and Seneca that [Protagoras] claimed that on every issue one could argue equally well on either side…. Protagoras is sometimes described as a sceptic…. [F]rom the point of view of someone like Democritus, the replacement of

a universal, objective concept of truth with a relative one is itself a very deep form of scepticism. (pp. 146-147)

Man is the measure of all things: a pithy way of saying what many postmodern psychoanalysts apparently believe—that human subjectivity is the only criterion of knowledge, that reality is measured relative to human perception, not the other way around.

Plato, who was born in the latter half of the 5th century BCE, dealt thoroughly with most of the arguments for skepticism found in postmodern writings. In *The Republic*'s Theory of Ideas alone, Plato touches on all of them—most especially the conundrum of the epistemic divide between symbol and object that preoccupies so many postmodernists. Elsewhere, for example in his dialogue *Theaetetus*, Plato deals with relativism and other epistemic problems directly and at length.

Then came the Ancient Skeptics, who based their entire philosophies on the same arguments as the postmodernists do: first, Pyrrho of Elis, who lived around the time of Aristotle, then Arcesilaus, who ran Plato's Academy in Athens in the late 3rd century BCE, and finally Carneades of the 2nd century BCE, also associated with Plato's Academy. All three so insisted on suspending judgment that they wrote little or nothing and left it to their pupils to convey their teachings. (Inwood and Gerson 1988, pp. 159-160, p. 181) Diogenes Laertius reports on Pyrrho, "[H]e said that nothing exists in truth but that men do everything on the basis of convention and custom; for each thing is no more this than that." (p. 173) Cicero spares Pyrrho his contempt only because he regards him as primitive and "*iam abiectos*"—"out of date" or "already rejected." (Cicero 1951, pp. 636-637) *A core tenet of postmodern philosophy out of date according to Cicero!*

Laertius also reports in his *Life of Pyrrho* on fives modes of Pyrrhonian doubt enumerated by the School of Agrippa. This is the Mode of Relativity: "The [mode] based on relativity says that nothing is understood just by itself, but always with something else; for which reason, things are unknowable." And this is the Mode of Infinite Regress: "The [mode] based on infinite regress forbids that that which has been sought has been firmly established because confidence in it is based on establishing something else which is in turn based on establishing something else, and so on to infinity." (Inwood and Gerson 1988, p. 178)

Laertius goes on: "[The skeptics] used to abolish all demonstration, criterion, sign, cause.... For every demonstration, they say, is constructed out of things [claimed to be] previously demonstrated or things not demonstrated [at all]." (p. 179) "[T]he criterion is unknowable, and because of this, so is the truth. Further, there is no sign." (p. 180) Elaborating on the skeptics' doubt of signs' meanings, Laertius reports: "the sign, being relative, must be grasped along with that of which it is a sign, whereas it is not in this case. Thus nothing non-evident could be grasped, because it is by means of signs that non-evident things are said to be grasped." (p. 180) What postmodernists call a *signifier*, ancient philosophers, according to Sextus Empiricus, designated a *lekton*, or "thing said." Some ancient philosophers propounded the uncertainty of all statements because all statements are composed of *lektons* which can only be defined by other *lektons*, which always stand at some remove from the actual thing spoken of. (p. 215)

Derrida seems to ignore this ancient tradition of doubt when he says that Swiss linguist Ferdinand de Saussure discovered the untrustworthy relationship between signs and signifiers. "It was Saussure who first of all set forth the arbitrariness of signs and the differential character of signs as principles of general semiology." (Derrida 1968, p. 392) But long before Saussure—long before Switzerland—the ancient skeptics had observed that nothing binds a sign irreversibly to the object it's supposed to represent, and so the meaning of a sign can always be doubted. The "differential character of signs" is furthermore only an argument for doubt of signs based on the Mode of Relativity and the Mode of Infinite Regress. If Saussure introduced innovations in the linguistic basis for doubt, they're hard to distinguish from arguments the skeptics made more than two millennia ago.

The ancient roots of radical skepticism undermine postmodern analysts in their claims that postmodern philosophy represents progress, a paradigm shift, and an update to classical psychoanalysis, and undermine them in their claims that critics of relational psychoanalysis only criticize because they're too old-fashioned or conservative to understand it.

3.1. Ancient Skepticism Was Impractical

The inability to produce new ideas would seem to be one of the major drawbacks of philosophies of radical doubt, both ancient and modern. Laertius:

> The skeptics, then, spent their time overturning all the dogmas of the schools, whereas they themselves make no dogmatic pronouncements, and while they presented and set out in detail the views of others, they themselves expressed no determinate opinions, not even this itself [that they had no determinate opinions]. (Inwood and Gerson 1988, p. 175)

Likewise, Aner Govrin writes:

> The postmodern paradigm in psychoanalysis ... does not strive to generate a "true" theory of mind that claims to fit

reality, nor does it claim to be another school of thought.... A shortage of analysts who "know the truth" today will make it extremely difficult for new schools of thought to arise in psychoanalysis, or for new and compelling theories and descriptions of the human psyche to be constructed. (Govrin 2006, p. 507)

Govrin later adds:

Postmodernists, especially the American relational group, retrieve what they see as valuable in existing theories, extricate it from its positivist moorings, and reposition it in an intersubjective and constructivist model.... The authors do not aim to generate novel ways of describing clinical phenomena, or even new techniques. (p. 520)

The radical skepticism of the ancients and of postmodern analysts shares another impractical feature as well: people may espouse radical skepticism as a philosophy, but it obligates them to hypocrisy because they can't live by it, nor reconcile it to their daily work. Cicero didn't believe that the ancient skeptics really lived in total doubt of all their senses (Inwood and Gerson 1988, p. 163), and Sextus Empiricus observes that of necessity "the sceptic does not live in accordance with a philosophical theory.... [H]e is able to choose some things and avoid others in accordance with unphilosophical observations." (pp. 238-239) Similarly, Govrin points out that when writing up case histories, even postmodern analysts who reject psychic determinism still look to their patients' childhoods as explanations of their adult emotional lives. (Govrin 2006, pp. 526-527) Relational analysts themselves concede that radical doubt cannot rule their consulting rooms or therapy could not occur: "[W]ith all the attention given to relativistic epistemologies and the postmodern sensibility with its glorification of uncertainty and fallibility, relational analysts are still clinicians and practitioners who are reminded daily of the pragmatic, goal-oriented, purposive nature of psychoanalysis." (Safran and Aron 2001, p. 574)

The impracticality of postmodern skepticism is no small problem for relational psychoanalysis. It was precisely Pyrrho's impracticality that caused Cicero to reject ancient skepticism as *"iam abiectos"* in the days of the Roman Republic. The shared impracticality of both ancient and postmodern skepticism underscores the deep logical flaws of postmodernism and, more than that, it underscores how fundamentally incompatible postmodernism is with the practical objectives of treating real mental suffering.

3.2. Skepticism Is a Defense Against the Anxiety of Influence

Analysts who in clinical practice surreptitiously rely on Freud while disavowing him in their theoretical discourse would seem to be avoiding acknowledgment of their debt to Freud. Is there an element of Harold Bloom's "anxiety of influence" in this? (Bloom 1973) Do postmodern psychoanalysts endeavor to escape Freud's shadow by doubting away the sun? By labeling Freud passé, diminishing him as a quaint Enlightenment figure, unhip to Saussure's signifiers, Michel Foucault's *déraison*, Derrida's *différance*, and Jacques Lacan's *manque-à-être*, do they express a feeling of rivalry with Freud? Lacan wished to reinvent psychoanalysis by translating it into Saussurean semiology (Lacan 1966, pp. 197-198), just as Derrida wished to reinterpret all thought according to Saussure. An anxiety of influence seems to corrupt Lacan and Derrida's work as they both seek to create the facade of a new philosophy from ancient, rudimentary ideas.

It's probably no coincidence that philosophies of radical doubt appear in history after explosions of knowledge and scientific progress. The ancient skeptics appeared in the generations after Plato who, like Freud, was a tough act to follow. For some philosophers in Plato's shadow, the only easy way forward was perhaps to tear down everything Plato said. In other words, if Arcesilaus couldn't find anything new to say when he took over Plato's Academy, maybe that's why he decided to doubt away the entire process of finding new things to say.

The history of postmodernism likewise dovetails intimately with individual careers distinguished by anxiety of influence. Edmund Husserl, for instance, whose philosophy was so important to subsequent postmodernists, was a peer of Freud's who began his career with an interest in psychology. Freud and Husserl both studied under Franz Brentano, author of *Psychology from an Empirical Standpoint*, and like Freud (Gay 1988, p. 29), Husserl was profoundly influenced by his teacher. Husserl started out in Brentano's direction by writing a psychological treatise on arithmetic, but shrank from the criticism he encountered. His professional anxieties soon afterward diverted him from Freud's scientific path onto a relativist philosophical one. He gave up psychology just as he gave up his Judaism by converting to Protestantism.[57]

Husserl's relativist critique of Brentano's scientific psychology began in earnest in the context of Husserl's struggles to establish himself as a philosopher:

Husserl underwent a crisis in the year 1906. He was then having doubts about his own philosophical importance. These

---

[57] https://plato.stanford.edu/entries/husserl/, accessed January 18, 2018.

doubts were compounded by his failure to be appointed full professor in Göttingen.... [T]hese five [Göttingen] lectures were the beginning of a new phase, the characteristically Husserlian phenomenology, a phase initiated by Husserl's determination to take stock of himself as a philosopher. (Nakhnikian 1970, p. xiii)

The new phase in Husserl's thinking meant turning away from scientific psychology and toward an intuitive, relativist, and more epistemologically unwieldy account of the mind: "*Natural thinking* in science and everyday life is untroubled by the difficulties concerning the possibility of cognition. *Philosophical thinking* is circumscribed by one's position toward the problems concerning the possibility of cognition." (Husserl 1970, p. 3) Husserl's most famous student was Martin Heidegger, who went even further in his repudiation of scientific psychology and thereby laid significant groundwork for the post-structuralists and postmodernists.[58] Derrida's career in radical doubt also begins with Husserl, on whom Derrida wrote his dissertation.[59] An anxiety-of-influence account of the birth of postmodernism might go: Husserl couldn't move psychology past Brentano, as Freud did, and chose instead to doubt scientific psychology away; Heidegger and Derrida came tumbling after.

In the field of postmodern imaginative literature, two central figures demonstrate overt anxiety of influence in formulating their

---

58 Here is Heidegger in *Being and Time* (1927): "When we have to do with anything, the mere seeing of the Things which are closest to us bears in itself the structure of Interpretation...." (quoted in Rivkin and Ryan 2000, p. 368) "When we merely stare at something, our just-having-it-before-us lies before us as a failure to understand it anymore." (p. 368) "[T]he interpretation has already decided for a definite way of conceiving it.... it is grounded in something we grasp in advance—in a fore-conception." (p. 369) "[W]hat 'stands there' in the first instance is nothing other than the obvious undiscussed assumption [*Vormeinung*] of the person who does the interpreting." (p. 369) All of this regurgitates the old radical *verum factum*, but disguised by translation into Husserl's "phenomenology" and re-translation into Heidegger's particular brand of bombastic sorcery.

59 https://plato.stanford.edu/entries/derrida/, accessed January 20, 2018.

nihilistic, skeptical literary styles: Samuel Beckett and Jorge Luis Borges. Borges was a major inspiration to the famous postmodernist Michel Foucault (Foucault 1966, p. 377) and Borges and Beckett each struggled mightily with the giants of modernism that preceded them.

Irishman Samuel Beckett began his career in awe of James Joyce. He trailed Joyce to Europe, hoping to make a name for himself, and in 1932 wrote an acrostic poem full of Joycean wordplay that spelled out Joyce's name, then his own. Two years later, a reviewer said of Beckett, "he knows his *Ulysses* as a Scotch Presbyterian knows his *Bible*." (Bair 1990, p. 179) But Beckett struggled to define himself in Joyce's wake, and he pivoted from Joyce's style of realism, maximalism, deep psychology, and wordplay to a style of austere minimalism, to themes of silence and nothingness, and postmodern tropes of mystic paradox and self-contradiction. Deirdre Bair explains: "Unconsciously at first, then with gradually dawning perception, [Beckett] watched his own writing become less and less like Joyce's as he concentrated for a single meaning, explicit, immediately apparent, in the most ordinary language possible...." (p. 329) *Waiting for Godot* would be written in Beckett's second language, French, which automatically confined him to minimalism. He became the Samuel Beckett we know, author of spare, satirical, self-contradictory, postmodern plays with titles like *I Not I*. Beckett chose the path of "working with impotence, ignorance" (Bloom 1994, p. 463) instead of challenging Joyce on the master's home turf: an art of teeming vocabulary and encyclopedic knowledge.

Jorge Luis Borges was so ambitious and yet so constipated with anxiety about writing in the wake of Kafka, to say nothing of Cervantes and Shakespeare, that he could hardly bring himself to say a single intelligible word. In stories and essays he frequently explored nightmarish fantasies that everything possible had already been written. For instance, "The Library of Babel" envisions a library where each book represents one random combination and permutation of the letters of the Roman alphabet. The library is nearly infinite in size so that it contains every book ever written and every book that could ever conceivably be written in the future hidden somewhere among its vast stores of gibberish. The clever idea implies that a writer's best work has already been written by somebody else, and equates literature with meaningless automatism.

"Pierre Menard, Author of the Quixote," describes an author who attempts to rewrite *Don Quixote* word-for-word, not by plagiarizing it, but instead by a deep identification with Cervantes. Like much of Borges's and Beckett's work, it's very funny and at the same time a harrowing bore. "Menard" is less story than witty and satirical faux-criticism. "Cervantes' text and Menard's are verbally identical," Borges writes, "but the second is almost infinitely richer. (More ambiguous, his detractors will say, but ambiguity is richness.)" (Borges 1964, p. 42) Borges goes on in the same story: "History, the *mother* of truth: the idea is astounding. Menard, a contemporary of William James, does not define history as an inquiry into reality but as its origin. Historical truth, for him, is not what happened; it is what we judge to have happened...." (p. 43) Far from "astounding," the idea is moldy *verum factum* tediously conscripted in the service of archaic radical skepticism. It's the same *verum factum* that Protagoras and other pre-Socratic philosophers first voiced, the same *verum factum* that's been expressed in so many different forms across the centuries— Hamlet: "there is nothing / either good or bad, but thinking makes it so." And it's the same *verum factum* that one postmodernist after another, convulsed with anxiety of influence, claims to have invented, again and again and again, ad nauseam. What is remarkable about deconstructionism and postmodernism in Borges's hands is not the ideas but the way he turns anxiety of influence into art, an art that's ingenious but constrained by anxiety to one narrow self-destructive gimmick. For this reason, Harold Bloom says:

> I recall the best sentence I have read about Borges, by Ana María Barrenechea: "Borges is an admirable writer pledged to destroy reality and convert man into a shadow." That breathtaking project, had Shakespeare pledged himself to it, would have been beyond even his resources. Borges can wound you, but always in the same way, so that one arrives at Borges' prime flaw: his best work lacks variety.... Perhaps sensing this, Borges attempted a movement back to naturalistic realism in the later 1960s.
>
> ... A comparison of his stories and parables to Kafka's, read side by side, is not at all flattering to him but seems inevitable.... (Bloom 1994, p. 438)

It's harder to attend to the complexity of reality than to destroy it with clever doubts and nihilism. And it's strenuous to challenge one's predecessors with aggressive, bold, new creations because of the Oedipal anxiety that ensues. It's so much easier to challenge artistic fathers by destroying their works with doubt—or even with a gum eraser, as Robert Rauschenberg did in his 1953 "Erased De Kooning Drawing."[60] Joyce, a master realist, and Kafka, a master expressionist, both ushered in literary postmodernism—not by writing it themselves but by provoking it in their belated, anxious, and overawed competitors. In the same way, Plato seems to have called Arcesilaus into being. In the same way, Freud helped to create Husserl, Derrida, and Lacan—not by providing the postmodernists with genuine

---

60 It sounds like something from a Borges story, but it's real: https://www.sfmoma.org/artwork/98.298, accessed January 19, 2018.

ideological support, but merely by overwhelming their ambition with his own daunting achievements.

Postmodern analysts must ask themselves whether or not they've fallen prey to anxiety of influence in embracing a "paradigm shift" that masquerades as something exciting and new when it's in fact archaic and empty. Any "paradigm shift" whose central principle is itself the relativist notion of "paradigm shift" warrants our suspicion. That's not how Einstein's theory of relativity updated Newtonian mechanics. You derive $E = mc^2$ from the Lorentz transformations and mathematical proof, not Kuhnian deconstructionism. Kuhnian deconstructionism *is* how Arcesilaus updated Plato and how Husserl updated Brentano. If this sort of anxiety of influence and imposture has affected relational psychoanalysis, relational analysts would be better off recognizing it and eliminating it in order to safeguard their genuine contributions to psychotherapy. Both relational and Freudian analysts would be better off recognizing and eliminating proof aversion in order to safeguard their contributions.

3.3. Knowledge and Doubt: Two Means of Relieving Anxiety

Pyrrhonian skepticism made no secret of it: the philosophy's primary aim was to relieve anxiety. Laertius writes, "The skeptics say the goal is suspension of judgement, upon which freedom from anxiety follows like a shadow...." (Inwood and Gerson 1988, p. 182) Sextus concurs in his summary of the reason behind skepticism: "the man who determines nothing in regard to things honourable or bad by nature does not flee or go after them excessively. For this reason he has a freedom from disturbance." (p. 189) Sextus's account of ancient skepticism in particular resembles an account of neurosis in that it describes not only the renunciation of reality but the renunciation of desire and the anxiety that attaches to it.

THE PSYCHOANALYST'S AVERSION TO PROOF

In pursuing freedom from anxiety, that state of tranquility the Greeks called *ataraxia*, the ancient skeptics shared the philosophical aim of their peer Epicurus, but the skeptics pursued *ataraxia* by different means than Epicurus did. Where they chose to relieve anxiety with radical doubt, Epicurus believed that knowledge, not denial, relieves anxiety. (pp. 14-15) He taught his followers to try to understand weather phenomena according to natural laws instead of hearing in a thunderstorm the wrath of the gods:

> For, if we attend to these things, we will give a correct and complete causal account of the source of our disturbance and fear, and [so] dissolve them, by accounting for the causes of meteorological and other phenomena which we are constantly exposed to and which terrify other men most severely. (p. 15)

Laertius recounts a story that Pyrrho, meanwhile, remained calm in a storm at sea by cultivating disbelief in the reality of the storm. Other passengers on the ship were afraid but Pyrrho, "relying on his senses for nothing," was not. He observed a small pig on the boat, happily eating, and resolved to be as incognizant of the storm as was the little pig. (pp. 173-174) It calls to mind Freud in the Adirondacks: Freud found his porcupine; Pyrrho found a little pig. But Freud used the porcupine to buttress his efforts at seeing and saying truth, while Pyrrho used the pig as a role model.

With these two different paths to tranquility, the ancients demarcated the most critical choice facing human beings: to know or not to know. Freud chose knowledge, with all its pressures and pain, and advanced the frontiers of knowledge where no one had previously dared. The postmodernists have chosen the ignorance of Pyrrho and the little pig. Radical disbelief is their own *verum factum*. For *verum factum* applies to postmodernism as well as it does to anything else, and unless postmodernists appeal to reason or experience to contest the assertion, they're in no position to deny it.

Freud Was an Epicurean Enlightenment Thinker

When reality provoked fear, Pyrrho covered his eyes; Epicurus looked and sought to understand. In accordance with that aim, Epicurus used more practical criteria for discriminating truth from error. He wrote in a letter to Herodotus: "[I]f it is testified for or not testified against, truth occurs. One must, then, keep this doctrine too quite firmly in mind, in order to avoid destroying the criteria of clear facts and to avoid having error placed on an equal basis with that which has been established, which would confound everything." (p. 8) Like Wittgenstein, Epicurus pointed out that radical doubt is self-undermining; a total breakdown in the capacity for knowledge makes it impossible to establish the basis for radical doubt in the first place. At the same time, Epicurus didn't overcompensate against doubt with dogmatism. His interest was truth and the avoidance of error, not dogmatic faith: "If, on the other hand, in your conceptions formed by opinion, you affirm everything that awaits confirmation as well as what does not, you will not avoid falsehood...." (p. 27)

Epicurus's embrace of reality endeared him to the poets of the Roman Enlightenment, especially Lucretius, who based *De Rerum Natura* on Epicurean philosophy. Epicurus and Lucretius, in turn, were favorites of the 18th-century *philosophes* who reshaped the world with their secular, scientific Enlightenment ideals. Epicurus, Peter Gay writes, was "the godlike Greek who first dared to defy the powers of superstition and to bring men the gift of freedom." (Gay 1995, p. 101) And here is Gay on the Enlightenment attitude to Lucretius:

Science, and science alone, pitilessly destroying myths, brings the greatest of freedoms, inner peace—this is Lucretius's message and mission, and this is how the philosophes read him…. No propagandist ever conducted the battle of science against religion more exuberantly than Lucretius, nor won it for science with such simple means. In all forms but one, he argues, religion is merely superstition based on ignorance and maintained by terror. Science, by contrast, is right reason offering a complete and coherent account of the universe. The one sensible religion, the Epicurean doctrine of the passionless gods dwelling in indifference in the heavens, does not interfere with true—that is, Epicurean—science. Thus Lucretius admonishes Memmius, to whom he addresses the poem, urging him to listen to "true reason" and glimpse a natural order free from the terrors of true religion. (p. 100)

Freud carried this Epicurean-Lucretian-Enlightenment agenda farther against the tide of religion than anyone. Gay writes, "This is the air that Freud's analysis of religion breathes—the critical spirit of the Enlightenment. There was nothing mysterious or concealed about this intellectual legacy." (Gay 1988, p. 527) As Morris Eagle puts it, psychoanalysis was, before its relational turn, "a quintessential representation of the Enlightenment Vision." (Eagle 2007, p. 13)

Postmodernists sometimes ignore Freud's devotion to Enlightenment ideals. Even as they doubt away their predecessors' achievements, postmodernists also appropriate predecessors like Freud to their own skeptical philosophies. Thus postmodernists claim Einstein and Heisenberg as inspirations to postmodern thought, even though neither scientist could ever accept such anti-scientific ideas.[61] Thus Lacan and Derrida retroactively claim psychoanalysis as a precursor to their radical new (tedious and antediluvian) philosophy of linguistic postmodernism even though the latter contradicts everything Freud stood for.

Everything Freud said and did, he said and did in order to make sense of the psyche. But the postmodernist Lacan turns everything Freud said into an argument for confusion and doubt, as though these were Freud's ends, when in fact they are Lacan's. Lacan seizes upon the unconscious not as an explanation but rather as an exciting epistemic limit that frees him from reality: "Lacan sees [the ego] as a mirage that can never fully know and master the unconscious." (Rivkin and Ryan 2000, p. 122) He looks to object relations to support his view that reality, self, and their relations are linguistically constructed. For Lacan, "It is language that gives us an identity." (p. 123) "[T]he unconscious can never be present to the mind (except through substitute signifiers)" and so "all our desires throughout life will consist of attempts to come to terms with this separation, our 'lack-of-being'," which Lacan called *manque-à-être*. (p. 124) I had a professor in college who used to wrinkle his nose at facile statements and say "High school!" as though he were inhaling the scent of chalk erasers and outdated Mercator maps. I'm inclined to say as much of Lacan's *manque-à-être*.

Harvesting doubts from his misreadings of psychoanalysis, Lacan arrives where he clearly wished to be all along—in the familiar, ancient darkness of radical skepticism: "no signification can be sustained other than by reference to another signification," he writes, reciting almost word-for-word the ancient skeptics' Mode of Infinite Regress.

---

61 The Sokal Hoax, perpetrated by NYU physicist Alan Sokal, famously demonstrated the nonsense and pretense in Derrida's uses of Einstein, and in many other postmodernists' attempts to derive authority from references to recent developments in physics. (Sokal 1996)

THE PSYCHOANALYST'S AVERSION TO PROOF

(Lacan 1966, p. 191) "As a result," Lacan goes on, "we can observe that even a text highly charged with meaning can be reduced, through this sort of analysis, to insignificant bagatelles, all that survives being mathematical algorithms that are, of course, without any meaning." (pp. 191-192). Lacan's nihilistic relativism leaves him as distant as conceivably possible from Freud. In dreams, parapraxes, and symptoms that looked meaningless to everyone else, Freud discovered meanings; meanwhile, in that which appears to have meaning, Lacan discovered underlying indeterminacy. Freud found the signal in the noise; Lacan found noise in every signal.

Freud's aversion to public proof notwithstanding, he furthermore denounced anti-scientific relativism directly and explicitly. For example, he excoriates Adler for espousing "the relativity of all knowledge and the right of the personality to put an artificial construction on the data of knowledge according to individual taste." (Freud 1914, p. 58) Freud diagnoses such relativism as a backlash against scientific progress.

The relativity of our knowledge is a consideration which may be advanced against every other science just as well as against psycho-analysis. It is derived from familiar reactionary currents of present-day feeling which are hostile to science; and it lays claim to an appearance of superiority to which no one is entitled.... The stress on arbitrary personal views in scientific matters is bad; it is clearly an attempt to dispute the right of psycho-analysis to be valued as a science—after that value, incidentally, has already been depreciated by what has been said before [on the relative nature of all knowledge]. Anyone who sets a high value on scientific thought will rather seek every possible means and method of circumscribing the factor of fanciful personal predilections as far as possible wherever it still plays too great a part. (pp. 58-59)

What alarms Freud most, however, is that even though Adler's system of thought is "radically false, it is marked by consistency and coherence," and could therefore deceive people as to its merits. (p. 60)

Here Freud implicitly rejects the coherence theory of truth as the final criterion for accepting or rejecting an idea. As Charles Hanly says: "Freud employed the coherence criterion as a necessary, but not a sufficient, criterion of truth. He used coherence as a logical, methodological tool for discriminating among competing hypotheses." (Hanly 1992, p. 16) Freud used correspondence with reality, not narrative coherence, as the final arbiter of truth. Thus, Hanly says, "Freud takes his place along with other seminal scientists whose thinking was premised upon the correspondence view of truth and empiricist realism." (p. 18)

Paul de Man Was a Pyrrhonian Skeptic

Postmodernists don't confess to their psychological aims in the way the ancient skeptics did. Nevertheless, prominent postmodernists have quite clearly employed radical doubt in exactly the same way as Pyrrho did: in order to purge disturbance from their minds. The salient example may be Yale literature professor Paul de Man, a Derrida disciple and in his time one of the most influential spokespeople for postmodern deconstructionism in the United States. Alvin Kernan writes:

Paul de Man's noted essay "Semiology and Rhetoric" (1979) provides a model of the way deconstructive reading proceeds. Language ... is defined as "pure rhetoric" in which the reading of each word or sign does not lead to "closure" in some truth or fact but only to another word or sign in an endless process of *différence*, by which "one sign gives birth to another." (Kernan 1990, p. 166)

The ancient skeptics' Mode of Infinite Regress once again rears its hoary head. But de Man's career is less remarkable for his ideas and more for the terrible secret he kept, which was exposed after his death. De Man died in 1983 and Kernan tells what happened next like this:

> In 1987, a Belgian student looking for dissertation material turned up a number of journalistic pieces on cultural matters written by de Man in the early 1940s, during the German occupation of Belgium, for newspapers controlled by the Germans and employed for fascist propaganda.... In all these many pieces, there was one particularly terrible essay, "Les Juifs dans la Littérature actuelle," published in the German-controlled paper *Le Soir* on March 4, 1941, in which de Man argued that since the Jews had contributed nothing to European literature, "on voit donc qu'une solution du problème juif qui viserait à la creation d'une colonie juive isolée de l'Europe, n'entraînerait pas, pour la vie littéraire de l'Occident, de consequences déplorables" (it follows that a solution to the Jewish question which envisages the creation of a Jewish colony isolated from Europe would not lead to deplorable consequences for the literary life of the West). (pp. 181-182)

The young de Man in other words publicly endorsed expulsion of Jews from Europe even as the Nazis rounded them up and murdered them, which makes him look like a fiendish Nazi sympathizer. In later life, after the United States had crushed Nazism in a savage war, de Man resettled in America and became a literature professor who denied that words have determinate meanings. Kernan goes on:

"Les Juifs dans la Littérature actuelle" was itself deconstructed by the father of deconstruction and de Man's close friend, the French philosopher-critic Jacques Derrida, to demonstrate that its linguistic contradictions and semantic insufficiencies allowed it to be interpreted as not support for but a demystification of Nazi political positions. Defenders like Derrida were particularly concerned to show that de Man's deconstructive theories about the absence of a definitive meaning in words and texts cannot be taken as a defense erected in later life against the guilt of what had been written in his youth. If words can't mean any definite thing, then de Man's earlier writings never *really* meant any single thing, like solving the "Jewish problem," and therefore no harm was done.

... [De Man's critics argue] that his later literary theories cannot be separated from his earlier life but have to be seen as an elaborate strategy carefully developed over a lifetime to deny to himself and others that he had done anything, or even that anything had happened. (p. 184)

Derrida was himself a Sephardic Jew from Algeria; presumably, he wasn't excusing anti-Semitism—only disbelieving in it.

But Hitler's anti-Semitic words had a determinate meaning because they killed millions of Jews. To argue that Hitler's or de Man's words lack definite meaning or don't lead to consequences in the real world is in the final analysis not only to denigrate science and reason, but to decline moral responsibility and the recognition of other human beings' suffering in the real world. "[D]econstruction has always had a flavor of the satanic," Kernan observes. (p. 185) To de Man's notion of the "myth of semantic correspondence between sign and referent"— another archaic notion originating with the ancient skeptics—Kernan replies that after the Holocaust that correspondence, "far from being myth, became an overwhelming reality." (p. 186)

Defending and attacking him, the scholars described the Belgian concentration camp and the shipments of Jews to it, the numbers in the labor battalions going to Germany and the dates of their departure, the German takeover of the Belgian media, the editorial policy of *Le Soir*, its nickname, *Le Soir Volé*, the politics of de Man's uncle and his place in the government, exactly where de Man lived, how he got his apartment, his relationships with other members of the family, his efforts to escape from Europe in 1940, and on and on. Far from there being nothing outside of the text, everything was out there, waiting to be called back into reality by the power of words. Of all the events evoked by de Man's words, the Holocaust was the most intensely real, of course, and the determination of the Jews that it would not be forgotten, or diminish in memory to some trivial event, ensured that de Man's words about the *problème juif* would not and could not escape what he mocked as the "authority of reference," ensured that his words, whatever their logical status, would forever be tied to and derive their meaning from events in the world.

The de Man case removes deconstruction from the realm of pure intellect and puts the theory, protesting and wriggling, in a full living human context. It confronts deconstruction with the monstrous and passionately felt *fact* of the Holocaust and asks, is this too only a *text*? Can its meaning be endlessly deferred? Can it too be interpreted in any way deemed suitable? To all these questions, of course, despite the staggering revelations of the de Man case, the [postmodernist] logician can and does answer "yes." The deconstructors continue to prove that words are indeterminate, that any text has a surplus of meaning, that interpretations are infinite and arbitrary, and that the world perceived by consciousness is nothing more than a series of ephemeral texts. Examined from this perspective, language is always breaking down, crumbling into nothingness, revealing traces, holes, contradictions, conventionality, infinite regress, tautology, nothing outside the text, ahistoricity, the metaphysics of presence where there is only absence, indeterminacy, logocentrism, différence, the need for supplemention, and numerous other logical weaknesses. (pp. 186-187)

Only powerful psychological forces could support radical self-deception of this magnitude, only a strong unconscious determination to neutralize mental disturbance by denying it, by doubting it away, just as Pyrrho did when he pretended to have the brain of a pig instead of a man.

L'Affaire de Man may very well help to explain why so much radical skepticism came out of postwar France. In 1940 France suffered a humiliating defeat and then signed a deal with its devilish captor. French intellectuals have been clamoring ever since, *Signatures mean nothing! Signatures mean nothing!* Gabriel Josipovici directs our attention to a related instance of postwar postmodernism in Germany:

[In 1951] Theodor Adorno published in Germany the little book of aphorisms and reflections he had written in exile in America as the war was drawing to a close and news of the Nazi atrocities was beginning to emerge. Section 5 of Part I of *Minima Moralia* begins: 'There is nothing innocuous left.... Even the blossoming tree lies the moment its bloom is seen without the shadow of terror.' 'Mistrust', he insists, 'is called for in face of all spontaneity, impetuosity, all letting oneself go....' (Josipovici 1999, pp. 6-7)

For Adorno, guilt necessitates mistrust and doubt. But de Man and Derrida bury whatever guilt they feel much deeper than Adorno, so much deeper that their pain can only be inferred. Were Adorno alive in 2017 when neo-Nazis marched in Charlottesville, Virginia, he surely would have condemned Donald Trump's words of sympathy for the neo-Nazis. What would Derrida have said? That Trump's words were indeterminate? That neo-Nazis with torches are merely being ironic? That Auschwitz is only a text?

3.4. The Secret Desire of Radical Doubt Is Faith

Some postmodernists appropriate Nietzsche to their ancient skeptical agenda, but in fact, in *Beyond Good and Evil*, Nietzsche looks with abhorrence at a new religion of radical skepticism on the rise. He vilifies it with the same fury he reserves for the ascetic idealism of Christianity: "[T]here may actually be puritanical fanatics of conscience who prefer even a certain nothing to an uncertain something to lie down on—and die. But this is nihilism and the sign of a despairing, mortally weary soul—however courageous the gestures of such a virtue may look." (Nietzsche 1989, p. 16) Nietzsche then says of "these skeptical anti-realists and knowledge-microscopists of today":

When they side *against* appearance, and speak of "perspective," with a new arrogance … —who knows if they are not trying at bottom to win back something that was formerly an even *securer* possession, something of the ancient domain of the faith of former times, perhaps the "immortal soul," perhaps "the old God"…. The main thing about them is *not* that they wish to go "back," but that they wish to get—*away*. A little *more* strength … and they would want to *rise*—not return! (pp. 16-17)

Nietzsche trained his own doubt upon *noumena*, Kant's equivalent to Plato's ideal forms, not upon the empirical study of *phenomena*, which is the province of science. Postmodern perspectivists wish to doubt away scientific claims about phenomena and to fly off into the other-worldly noumenal truth of total subjectivity.

Throughout *Beyond Good and Evil*, Nietzsche castigates such thinkers, whom he deems religious at heart. The religious faithful and the radical skeptics together collude against the senses, the body, this world, humanity, in favor of the next world and the spirit. Whoever "takes this world, along with space, time, form, movement, to be falsely *inferred*" is religious and ascetical. Nietzsche's talking to you, Plato, Pyrrho, Kant, Hegel, Husserl, Heidegger, Lacan, Derrida, and all other "skeptical anti-realists" and "cobweb spinners of the spirit!" (p. 36) Whoever doubts reality so pervasively without acknowledging his or her piety is to Nietzsche an "unconscious *advocatus dei*." (pp. 45-46) Doubt of reality, Nietzsche says, is just fear of reality:

[I]t might be a basic characteristic of existence that those who would know it completely would perish, in which case the strength of a spirit should be measured according to how much of the "truth" one could still barely endure—or to put it

227

more clearly, to what degree one would *require* it to be thinned down, shrouded, sweetened, blunted, falsified. (p. 49)

Modern philosophies founded upon epistemological skepticism deny Christ but according to Nietzsche they nevertheless move with the religious spirit:

> It seems to me that the religious instinct is indeed in the process of growing powerfully—but the theistic satisfaction it refuses with deep suspicion…. Modern philosophy, being an epistemological skepticism, is, covertly or overtly, *anti-Christian*—although, to say this for the benefit of more refined ears, by no means anti-religious. (p. 66)

The religious attitude would trade the real hardships of this world for a dream. To accomplish this feat, the pious must first doubt away the reality of this world. Doubt, in other words, serves faith. In the 16th-century Michel de Montaigne described the skeptic thus: "stripped of human knowledge, and all the more apt to lodge divine knowledge in himself, annihilating his judgment to make more room for faith…. He is a blank tablet prepared to take from the finger of God such forms as he shall be pleased to engrave on it." (Montaigne 1976, p. 375) A millennium earlier St. Augustine seemed to grope toward Christian faith in this way when he called ignorance the "mother of admiration" and bid the ministers of Christ: "Contain yourselves from the ungoverned wildness of pride, the sluggish voluptuousness of luxury and the false name of knowledge." (Augustine 1853, p. 297)

When postmodernists use clever arguments to build a case for doubt, using nihilistic doubt to make room for their post-Christian variety of faith in human subjectivity, they seize upon the third rung of what Nietzsche called "the great ladder of religious cruelty":

> There is a great ladder of religious cruelty, with many rungs; but three of these are the most important.
>
> Once one sacrificed human beings to one's god, perhaps precisely those whom one loved most: the sacrifices of the first-born in all prehistoric religions belong here...
>
> Then, during the moral epoch of mankind, one sacrificed to one's god one's own strongest instincts, one's "nature": *this* festive joy lights up the cruel eyes of the ascetic, the "anti-natural" enthusiast.
>
> Finally—what remained to be sacrificed? At long last, did one not have to sacrifice for once whatever is comforting, holy, healing; all hope, all faith in hidden harmony, in future blisses and justices? didn't one have to sacrifice God himself and, from cruelty against oneself, worship the stone, stupidity, gravity, fate, the nothing? To sacrifice God for the nothing— this paradoxical mystery of the final cruelty was reserved for the generation that is now coming up: all of us already know something of this.— (Nietzsche 1989, p. 67)

Postmodernism has all the trappings of religion. It's Nietzsche's Third Rung in the Great Ladder of Religious Cruelty. It's the Third Sophistic Movement. And its many mystical tomes can be distilled down to three words in the poem "Ode on a Distant Prospect of Eton College" by Thomas Gray:

Ignorance is bliss.

The school of "epistemological skepticism" that would later be named postmodernism has indulged in what Nietzsche calls a "decision in favor of ignorance, of deliberate exclusion, a shutting of one's windows, an internal No to this or that thing, a refusal to let things approach, a kind of state of defense against much that is knowable, a satisfaction in the dark, with the limiting horizon, a Yea and Amen to ignorance...." (p. 160) It is everything that a psychologist, whom Nietzsche names the "unriddler of souls" (p. 269), can never be.

And at the end of all Lacan's doubts and obfuscations is not psychology, but something Alan Sokal and Jean Bricmont call "secular mysticism." They comment: "Lacan's writings became, over time, increasingly cryptic—a characteristic common to many sacred texts.... One may then wonder whether we are not, after all, dealing with a new religion." (Sokal and Bricmont 1998, p. 37) Thus relational analysts quail at the scientific community's talk of proof and like Randall Sorensen can argue that "it is a mistake to idealize science or to purge those aspects of psychoanalysis that are based on faith rather than on evidence." (Safran and Aron 2001, p. 574)

4. Conclusion: The Postmodern Aversion to Proof

Resistance to psychoanalysis, proof aversion, and postmodernism seem to me to be three faces of the same protean phenomenon that Freud described: repression. The force of repression in the minds of the public creates undue criticism and doubt of psychoanalysis. Repression inside the expositors of psychoanalysis afflicts them with inhibitions, doubts, and aversions to proving psychoanalytic ideas. The systematized, pious doubt practiced by postmodernists would excuse psychoanalysts from the task of proof on the grounds that proof doesn't exist.

This would appear to be another vicious circle of sorts. Many epistemic difficulties and other factors opened the door to postmodernists' appropriation of psychoanalysis, but Freud's aversion to proof took the hinges off that door. Any discipline that holds itself back from the scientific worldview by denying the possibility of proof becomes vulnerable to an incursion of priests. And once inside, priests will never willingly close the door to "ignorance, mother of admiration," nor bow to the reality principle, as the task of proof requires.

In attempting to shield our much-buffeted and sensitive human consciousness from terrors without and within, repression corrupts knowledge. This was of course Freud's greatest insight. If psychoanalysis as an institution no longer helps people see beyond repression to the truth, because truth is impossible, then what is psychoanalysis doing, exactly? Mills suggests that relational psychoanalysis really has in many ways abandoned the theory of repression. "[F]or many relational analysts," he writes, "the unconscious has become an antiquated category." (Mills 2012, p. 11) But what is psychoanalysis without the theory of repression? I haven't a clue. Until someone can clear this up for me, I see no reason to give up Freud's theory of repression, which has explained myself and other human beings better than any other theory. Until then, I can only think that if psychoanalysis has discarded repression, then psychoanalysis is no longer part of the solution to repression, but merely another symptom of it.

Arnold Richards said in 1990 that theories that "explicate psychoanalysis as an exclusively hermeneutic enterprise are destined to be repudiated." (Richards 1990, p. 360) 1990 happens to have been the year I started college, the year I first encountered what Ricoeur called "the hermeneutics of suspicion." In the 28 years since then, I've sometimes enjoyed the hermeneutics of suspicion as a dark and funny, self-satirical art form—for example in Borges's stories or the Adorno satire in the Twitter feed @NeinQuarterly—but such hermeneutics have not helped me understand anything. Now that racists and ideologues have adopted radical doubt to discredit the free press and deny various dangers facing planet Earth, my patience with postmodernism is wearing thinner than ever before.

I'm inclined to believe postmodernism as a whole is destined to be repudiated. Philosopher Harry Frankfurt tells us that indifference to truth is not the same as lying. It is, in Frankfurt's words, "bullshit." (Frankfurt 2005) And if postmodernism receives its long-awaited comeuppance, we should all be prepared for a variant of its world-denying philosophy to return in another form. Science and religion have clashed since the beginning of human history and they will probably continue to clash to the end, but the overall direction of human history is clear: the scrimmage line moves in the opposite direction from ignorance and doubt, the opposite direction from faith predicated on ignorance and doubt. And if history is to abandon postmodernism, whose backward beliefs and double dedication to the future tense will look risible in the actual future, psychoanalysis might consider unhitching its wagon from this doomed movement.

In conclusion, I would like to recite a fairy tale that is, ironically, all about realism: The Three Little Pigs. The first two pigs in that tale distinguish themselves by their ignorance. Deep down, surely they understood the reality of a wolf's teeth and a wolf's appetite for little pigs. But they settled for shoddy building contractors who worked with straw and sticks. A distant cousin, a porcupine who had once met Freud in the Adirondacks, recommended actual quills instead of defense by the sticks and straw of self-deceit but another cousin, a little pig who had once met Pyrrho on a boat, prevailed on the first two pigs.

Fatefully, they went with Pyrrho and put their trust in postmodern Pyrrhonian skepticism, a philosophy that supplied a radical, but pleasing solution to their anxieties: *There are no wolves because wolves are a cultural construct. Sticks and straw are fine.* While the first two pigs sat in their houses of sticks and straw reading "Semiology and Rhetoric" by Paul de Man and contemplating the unbridgeable divide between "chinny chin chin" and its infinitely deferred referent, the wolf blew the pigs' houses down and deconstructed them with his teeth.

The third pig, however, had a house made of very real bricks. In a cunning exercise of *real politique*, he devised a plot to kill the wolf with the wolf's own ignorance. He deceived the wolf by letting him down the chimney so that the wolf fell into his boiling pot, and he ate the wolf. The moral of the story is: he who's capable of being deceived, whether by himself or by his rival, ends up as dinner.

V. SOLUTIONS TO THE PROBLEM OF PROOF AVERSION

Because I'm not a psychoanalyst, I clearly don't know the exigencies of psychoanalytic practice and professional life in the way that psychoanalysts do. This is both an advantage and a disadvantage in prescribing solutions to the problem of proof aversion. Regardless, the diagnosis of proof aversion suggests to me a few general remedies. I will break down my suggestions into three general categories:

1. Study proof aversion. This would involve psychoanalysts' self-examination and more formal investigations designed to test the hypothesis of proof aversion and to further elucidate its character and its mechanisms.

2. Organize in support of "empirical psychoanalysis." Those who want to advance psychoanalysis with more proof of psychoanalytic theories and efficacy need more institutional and financial support. Develop new plans and institutions to produce more proof and to defend psychoanalysis from unfair criticism. These new plans and institutions need not replace or threaten existing institutions.

3. Conduct new research that aims to validate basic psychoanalytic theories and practices. Use new evidence to construct systematic justifications of psychoanalysis suited for presentation to non-analysts.

1. Further Study of the Hypothesis of Proof Aversion

I can foresee two significant obstacles to further study of my hypothesis: First, people need to hear out my ideas in order to consider whether they have merit, and they may not be willing or able to do this. Second, having considered them, some will deny that they have enough merit to warrant further research. This chapter will treat the subject of resistance to studying proof aversion within the psychoanalytic community. The next will treat the problem of internecine conflict in the field over the pursuit of proof and how to address it.

1.1. The Analyst's Continuing Struggle to Look Inward

The ancient physician Galen took a baby step towards the invention of psychoanalysis[62] when he wrote in the 2nd century that errors come from irrational passions; that we cannot see these irrational passions in ourselves because of narcissism; and that we can only cure ourselves of error by looking to another person who can observe our passions and errors with more neutrality than we can:

> Since errors come from false opinion while the passions arise by an irrational impulse, I thought the first step was for a man to free himself from his passions; for these passions are probably the reason why we fall into false opinions. And there are passions of the soul which everybody knows: anger, wrath, fear, grief, envy, and violent lust. In my opinion, excessive

---

62 Impressive though he is for an ancient physician, Galen's understanding of the psyche looks as primitive next to Freud's as his understanding of nerves does next to that of a modern neurologist. By contrast, postmodern skepticism recapitulates ancient skepticism virtually unchanged.

vehemence in loving or hating anything is also a passion....
[N]o immoderate action is good.

How, then, could a man cut out these passions if he did not first note that he had them? But as we said, it is impossible to know them, since we love ourselves to excess. Even if this saying[63] will not permit you to judge yourself, it does allow that you can judge others whom you neither love nor hate. (Galen 1963, pp. 31-32)

So, Galen advises, find someone else who can judge you neutrally, neither with love nor hate, and ask him or her for feedback.

If you find such a man, summon him and talk with him one day in private; ask him to reveal straightway whatever of the above-mentioned passions he may see in you. Tell him you will be most grateful for this service and that you will look on him as your deliverer more than if he had saved you from an illness of the body. Have him promise to reveal it whenever he sees you affected by any of the passions I mentioned.

It may happen that the other person remains silent, Galen says, "because he's afraid to reproach you, or because he does not wish to be hated, knowing as he does that it is usual, as I might say, with all men to hate those who speak the truth." (p. 33) This was Freud's stated reason for

---

63 Galen was surely aware of the fourth century B.C.E. speeches by Demosthenes known as *The Olynthiacs*. In the third of these speeches, Demosthenes makes the famous statement: "[T]he wish is father to the thought, and that is why nothing is easier than self-deceit. For what each man wishes, that he also believes to be true." http://www.perseus.tufts.edu/hopper/text?doc=Perseus%3Atext%3A1999.01.0070%3Aspeech%3D3%3Asection%3D19, accessed August 8, 2018. Shakespeare in turn quotes Demosthenes almost verbatim in *Henry IV Part 2, Act IV, scene v* when Prince Hal prematurely pronounces his father dead. His father, the king, notices his hurry to succeed to the throne: "Thy wish was father, Harry, to that thought."

THE PSYCHOANALYST'S AVERSION TO PROOF

his "inviolate silence" towards critics—he wished to avoid their hatred—but I have tried to show that he had internal reasons for his reticence as well. I believe he could have used his own "other person," i.e. his own therapist, to help him identify some of those internal reasons.

Though Freud intermittently chose confessors like Fliess, he of course never had his own therapist. When Jung tried to provide therapeutic consultation, the younger analyst found himself with a one-way ticket back to Zurich. And yet no one, Galen says, is free of the irrational passions that lead us into error.

> [E]very day men fall into countless errors and do countless things in passion because they do not understand themselves. Do not, therefore, consider that you are something else and not a human being. But you do judge that you are something other than a human being if you mislead yourself into believing that you have done nothing but good actions for a whole day, much less for a whole month. (pp. 33-34)

Precisely because psychoanalysts' defenses may be responsible for the problem of aversion to proof, an outsider's point of view may be particularly helpful in initiating discussion of the problem. Because I'm not a psychoanalyst, I hope I've been able to do that. At the same time, many psychoanalysts may resist this feedback, whether it comes from without or within the psychoanalytic community. Debate over the merits of proof aversion is of course justified, but resistance to discussing the topic suggests that defenses are at work. I don't want to adopt Freud's defensive method of analyzing my audience's resistance in lieu of arguing my point, but if in fact the task of proof provokes affective resistance, then it's predictable that some analysts should also resist looking at the problem of proof aversion.

It's so far been my experience that some analysts do resist even contemplating this topic. *The Psychoanalyst's Aversion to Proof* began as a paper entitled "The Psychoanalyst's Resistance to the Task of Proof." (Ratner 2018) In the process of submitting, revising, and resubmitting it, I had an informal opportunity to survey some psychoanalysts' responses to the idea. While some reviewers took it in the intended spirit and provided helpful constructive criticisms and suggestions, others reacted with an emotional sensitivity and hostility that genuinely took me by surprise. As I mentioned, *The Psychoanalytic Quarterly* denied it peer review, a particularly concrete example of avoidance.

It wouldn't be the first time psychoanalysts struggled to look inward, of course, since they too are human beings. Consider another example that's created resistance to examination within the psychoanalytic community: countertransference. As early as 1909, when Jung had an affair with one of his patients, Freud recognized that the unconscious emanation of the analyst's feelings about his own family drama was likely to be a universal and permanent hindrance to analysis. (McGuire 1988, pp. 230-231) Yet forty years later Heinrich Racker noted that little had been written about countertransference because analysts resisted talking about it. "It would seem that among analytic subjects counter-transference is treated somewhat like a child of whom the parents are ashamed," he said. (Racker 1953, p. 314) Fear of bad press for the field of psychoanalysis may have contributed to the silence about countertransference (Makari 2008, p. 232), but Racker attributes the silence to psychodynamic resistance, not political secrecy.

If sensitivities arise in connection with the concept of proof aversion, then analysts must be willing to examine those sensitivities. In the table of contents of Ernest Jones's Freud biography, Jones intentionally withholds the end date from one important phase of Freud's life, which he denotes like this: "Self-Analysis (1897-)." It's a charming little homage to Freud's belief that self-analysis is never done. When a psychoanalyst has completed his own analysis, Freud argues, he or she must then "continue the analytic examination of his personality in the form of a self-analysis, and be content to realize that, within himself as well as in the external world, he must always expect to find something new." (Freud 1912, p. 117) By asking psychoanalysts to consider whether they have a psychological aversion to proving their ideas in public, I'm in effect asking them to look inward and find something previously unexamined, which is not easy. Whatever the reactions to the idea of proof aversion, I hope that psychoanalysts will take a moment to examine the emotional content of their reactions before rejecting the idea.

Mills says, "Analysts often have little patience for criticism, especially when one's theoretical orientation or clinical philosophy is intimately tied with one's professional and/or personal self-identity." (Mills 2012, p. xv) Morris Eagle has in passing observed that analysts feel an almost familial protectiveness toward the field of psychoanalysis when confronted with criticism. (Eagle 2007, p. 10) It's a topic that deserves more systematic investigation. Without such investigation, psychoanalysis faces serious emotional obstacles to growth and change, like aversion to proof. And in that case, I'm reminded of what Peter Gay had to say about Ernest Jones's dogged attempts to get Freud out of Nazi-occupied Vienna in 1938. "One of the most tenacious obstacles to the rescue of Freud was Freud himself." (Gay 1988 p. 624)

1.2. Transference in the Presentation-Criticism Dyad

Self-analysis could help analysts consider the idea of aversion to proof in a more neutral light, but it could also help relieve the anxieties attaching to the task of proof itself. To analyze feelings about public presentations of psychoanalytic ideas, it may be useful to consider whether transference is likely to occur in the context of such presentations. Analysis of my own experience with submitting writing to critical editors, reviewers, and readers suggests to me that transference may play a role in the public presentation of ideas before critical audiences, regardless of whether the presented ideas are psychoanalytic ones or not. I draw further support for this hypothesis from Charles Brenner's observation that transference is by no means unique to the analytic situation, that we transfer feelings about the past onto the present all the time, in many situations:

Every object relation is a new edition of the first, definitive attachments of childhood. A patient's relation to his or her analyst is no exception.

… Transference is ubiquitous. It develops in every psychoanalytic situation because it develops in every situation where another person is important in one's life.

… An analyst analyzes a patient's transference instead of responding to it in any other way. It is analysis of the transference that is unique to analysis, not transference itself. (Brenner 1982, pp. 194-195)

A scientist who presents his discoveries to an audience or a journal, or a writer who submits his work to an editor, hoping the editor will publish it, enters into a dyadic relationship with "the authorities." The power differential in this dyad, and the role of unidirectional, unequal judgments in it, confer upon the presenter-critic dyad a special similarity to the relationship between child and parent. A presenter is bound, therefore, to experience acceptance or rejection, praise or criticism, according to childhood feelings about his or her parents. Since any unconscious confusion of critic with parent will inevitably make such presentations feel highly personal, it would benefit the presenter to analyze any such transference.

Consider once again the case of Freud presenting his discoveries to critics. Earlier, I suggested that he perceived the discovery and presentation of psychoanalytic ideas according to an Oedipal template of rivalry with Jacob Freud and disappointment with Jacob Freud; in other words, I've asserted that Freud unconsciously transferred childhood feelings about his own family relationships into the presenter-critic situation. Further analysis of this transference potentially helps create insights into the sources of his irrationality about proof. For example, if in the following passage "the world's opinion" really means "Breuer's opinion" or even "my father's opinion," then the passage takes on new meaning:

> It was hardly to be expected, however, that during the years when I alone represented psycho-analysis I should develop any particular respect for the world's opinion or any bias towards intellectual appeasement. (Freud 1914, p. 24)

To Freud's mind, let's say, Breuer and the rest of the world had spurned him for daring to speak the truth. Perhaps Freud felt in this rejection a personal injury of being denied a father's love, for the unjust reason that he'd uncovered the truth of human sexuality. Then he could feel not just angry, but personally bitter and rejected in the way a son might feel when his father spurns him—when his father rebukes him for ambitiously invading his parents' bedroom and predicts that "the boy will come to nothing." The analysis of transference in Freud's presenter-critic relationships potentially adds more nuance to our understanding of Freud's embittered reactions to his critics.

If Freud's unconscious mind saw in his critics the figure of an abandoning father who judgmentally withdrew affection and condemned him to loneliness, he may have found it particularly painful and vexing to placate such critics by giving them what they wanted— proof. Like an unloving father, they dismiss his brilliant, curious, and ambitious theories, or ask him to jump through hoops to satisfy their petty, ignorant skepticism? When it came to the demonstrations they demanded of him, maybe he felt he would reciprocate and give them what they deserved: nothing.

And if Freud saw his father inside his critics, perhaps he had difficulty ignoring them in a neutral way and carrying on with his work of demonstration. I've suggested that Freud's sensitivity to critics and pessimism about converting them led him to ignore critics when he might have attacked or engaged with them. But in addition, perhaps less sensitivity—an ability to ignore his critics not on a professional level but on an emotional level—could have better equipped him to attack and engage as the particular case required. On an unconscious emotional level, in other words, maybe Freud ignored his critics too little. If ignoring the critics meant ignoring his father, perhaps he felt conflicted about ignoring them. To ignore his critics would have been to silence them, and to silence them, perhaps, was to kill them off in his mind. Perhaps he didn't want to kill off Breuer and his father and to expatiate boldly into the silence they left behind. Perhaps he preferred to silence himself. By choosing not to ignore slights and criticisms, he kept the slights alive in his mind, and with the slights, perhaps, he kept alive the author of the slights—his father. Had he been able to ignore the slights in the first place, maybe they wouldn't have distracted him so much from the job of proving his case.

Freud's obstinacy about giving critics the proof or demonstrations they've asked for reminds me of an elegy from Ovid's *Amores* that describes a man who was angry with his mistress for demanding gifts. At the end of the elegy, the man says:

> It is not my giving but your demand which hurts and repels me.
> You ask for a thing, and I refuse; cease to want it, and I shall give.[64]
> (Quoted in Fränkel 1945, p. 29)

1.3. Formal Investigations into Proof Aversion

Investigations aimed at verifying psychoanalytic claims have taken many forms, and could take many more. Meanwhile, proof aversion itself could be further investigated through case studies, literature review, survey research, social psychology experiments, and even cognitive neuroscience experiments. Because proof aversion happens in public, not in the privacy of the consulting room, it should be more susceptible to formal study. It could be paired with studies of its complementary phenomenon—audience resistance to psychoanalytic ideas—that could in turn supply needed specificity to the theory of public resistance to psychoanalysis.

By literature review, I have two different approaches in mind. One is to review previous work on emotional interferences in job situations, to collate whatever is relevant to assessing the validity of proof aversion, and to gather ideas for methods of studying proof aversion in the future. The other approach is to review efforts at proof and public demonstration of psychoanalytic ideas with the intention of evaluating the interference of defense mechanisms. For example, investigators could collect writings meant to explicate psychoanalysis

---

64 Ovid, *Amores* I, 10.

to laypeople and evaluate them for evidence of proof aversion: how many of them refer to research? How many of them forestall questioning by attacking audience resistance? How many denigrate experimental psychology? How many exaggerate the epistemic difficulties attaching to the study of the unconscious? And so on.

Survey research of the kind undertaken by the Chicago Institute for Psychoanalysis (for example, Schneider et al. 2014, Schneider et al. 2017) could ask psychoanalysts about their experiences presenting psychoanalysis to skeptical audiences. Questionnaires could first of all assess how many times psychoanalysts engage in such presentations. Presumably lectures to medical students constitute one such presentation. The questionnaires could ask psychoanalysts, after lecturing to medical students, to comment on their strategies, their comfort level, their emotional states, their perceptions of the success or failure of the lecture, etc. Questionnaires could likewise ask medical students about their experiences in the audience of such lectures. For comparison, identical questions could be distributed to lecturers and audiences in non-psychoanalytic medical subjects like genetics or heart disease.

Social psychology experiments could take place in which psychoanalysts lecture to psychology students in various formats. Investigators could manipulate the style of presentation, the content, and the lecture conditions and gather useful information about which styles of presentation, which content, and which conditions stimulate and relieve anxieties in the speakers. Questionnaires could measure anxiety, but so could more objective methods such as measuring heart rate, scoring the frequency of slips of the tongue, self-interruptions, etc.

Psychoanalytic researchers have already begun to take account of very specific resistances to research. In advocating the use of computers and statistics in psychoanalytic research, Hartvig Dahl insisted that "to do these things means that we must analyze our resistances to numbers and computers." (1972, p. 256) And Gill et al. report the following about their attempts to record analyses for purposes of validating psychoanalytic ideas:

> To our surprise we found that the patients seemed to accept recording easily and that we ourselves reacted very strongly against it. We turned the machine off instead of on, misplaced wire or tape, plugged an AC machine into a DC outlet, and by these and other less obvious slips demonstrated our real feelings about the procedure. (Quoted in Gill et al. 1968, p. 239)

Evidence of proof aversion comes forth readily once psychoanalysts engage in proving activities. By foreclosing on the pursuit of proof, proof aversion therefore denies the opportunity to observe evidence of proof aversion. In this way it displays one of the trickiest characteristics of defense mechanisms: it prevents itself from being discovered.

2. Organizing in Support of Empirical Psychoanalysis

The "evidence-based medicine" movement, whose first position paper came out in 1992 (Guyatt et al. 1992), set out to shift medical education and practice away from "[t]radition, anecdote, and theoretical reasoning" toward an emphasis on hard statistical data. (Greenhalgh et al. 2014) The American Psychological Association followed suit with criteria for empirically supported treatments and guidelines for evidence-based practice. The evidence-based medicine movement has since been criticized—justly, I think—for robotic treatment algorithms, neglect of theory, overvaluation of randomized controlled trials, undervaluation of individual case studies, and susceptibility to manipulation by powerful corporations and lobbies. (Greenhalgh et al. 2014; Seifter 2015)

These criticisms highlight the dangers of over-prioritizing methodology. Too much focus on epistemic rigor can hamper discovery and explanation, especially where complex phenomena like the human mind are concerned. Studies may inspire false confidence because their methods and results look scientific, when in fact they're flawed either in their design or in their conclusions. Despite their superficial rigor, they may be statistically underpowered, or rely on faulty assumptions or vague definitions, or their results may not support the conclusions their investigators draw. I'm therefore by no means suggesting psychoanalysis rebuild itself in the paint-by-number image of evidence-based medicine.

The goal of "empirical psychoanalysis" would not be to impose authoritarian standards on anyone, nor to invalidate previous work or discredit existing institutions, but rather to advance the interests of psychoanalytic knowledge without the interference of aversions to scientific method. That would mean a systematic effort to prove the validity of psychoanalytic ideas and a campaign to facilitate public comprehension of psychoanalysis, its importance, and its validity. To accomplish this goal, I propose that psychoanalysts create a new institutional organ, namely an endowment to fund empirical psychoanalytic research and to rebrand the field of psychoanalysis. Any psychoanalytic body that does not wish to associate with a new endowment of this kind, of course, doesn't have to.

The new endowment and institution could be established under the auspices of the American Psychoanalytic Association, but I doubt they would welcome such an entity. Joseph Schachter and Horst Kächele report that in 2009 when Irwin Hoffman gave a plenary address to APsaA deriding calls for more scientific research, he received a standing ovation. (I. Hoffman 2009; Schachter and Kächele 2017, p. 246) Furthermore, APsaA's longstanding ambivalence about science has interfered significantly with its stated aims of research, advocacy, marketing, and communications. Schachter and Kächele maintain that "our existing professional system is unable to cope with the exigencies confronting American psychoanalysis and unable to reverse its diminishing status and prestige." (p. 6) It may consequently be easier to create a new institution than to reform an old one, especially one whose history is so deeply entangled with aversion to proof.

2.1. A New Endowment for Psychoanalytic Progress

When I submitted an early draft of my paper on proof aversion to the *Journal of the American Psychoanalytic Association*, some reviewers scoffed at my suggestion that psychoanalysis should consider spending more money on its own advancement. *And just where are the funds supposed to come from?* one analyst hissed. I'm no finance guru, nor am I an accomplished fundraiser, but I think it safe to say: You raise money by asking people for it. Fundraising too can elicit psychological aversion, but the reason to ask for funding is in this case quite clear: to save the great humanitarian institution of psychoanalysis, the product of millennia of enlightened thought without which our species may well go extinct. Especially in an age of nuclear weapons, as Carl Sagan said, Freudian psychoanalysis is necessary to save us from our own irrationality:

> I certainly agree that there is such a thing as the unconscious mind. There is all sorts of evidence for it in our everyday lives,

and Freud provided a compelling argument that it exists. And I think it is essential that we understand it, and I believe that it plays a powerful, maybe even dominant, role in international relations, and that's therefore a very practical reason for understanding it. (Sagan 2006, p. 247)

[E]veryone in this room has felt aggression.... Everyone in this room has felt kindness.... [W]e have two warring principles in the human heart, both of which must have evolved by natural selection, and it's not hard to understand the selective advantage of both of them.... We're talking about adjudicating between conflicting emotions. And you can't have an adjudication *between* emotions *by* an emotion. It must be done by our perceptive intellectual ability.... If we do not, if we cannot manage it, it is clear that we are gone. We are doomed. And therefore we *have* no alternative. Certainly untrammeled, continuing aggression in an age of nuclear weapons is a prescription for disaster. (p. 259)

We ought therefore to be as serious about the validity of psychoanalysis as Giordano Bruno was about Copernicus[65] and as indefatigable, goal-oriented, and fearless in defense of enlightened values as Voltaire.

To break the paralysis that's gripped psychoanalysis as an institution, money is essential. In every branch of science, funding drives the direction of research. Sit around and wait for research to prove the validity of psychoanalysis, and it will come very slowly if it comes at all. Clamor for it till our ears all ring, and still it may not come. Offer grants for that research, and opportunities to publish it,

---

65 Bruno was burned at the stake in 1600 for asserting that the sun was a star like any other.

and people will do it. Schachter and Kächele have proposed practical measures to raise money for research through APsaA (2017, pp. 251-252), but it's unclear that APsaA has the political will to adopt them.

Likewise, if a field wants to promote itself and to defend its values, it's money that empowers the field to achieve its aims. In order to compete with powerful lobbies like the American Psychiatric Association and the American Psychological Association, which together control more than $100,000,000 in assets and spend more than $1,000,000 a year lobbying the federal government,[66] psychoanalysis will need cash in its coffers. And a discipline like psychoanalysis that's dedicated to speaking truth against repressive forces will always have to scrap and claw for resources. It should be no more abashed about doing so than St. Jude's Children's Hospital.

Finally, material reality has a way of resolving controversies. Physicist Alan Sokal has said, "[A]nyone who believes the laws of physics are mere social conventions is invited to try transgressing those conventions from the windows of my apartment. (I live on the twenty-first floor.)" (Sokal 1996) Money is like gravity. It's the material reality that will free psychoanalysis from the endless pessimism and inertia of proof aversion and postmodernism. Freudian-rationalism must empower itself not with more authoritarianism and dogmatism, which have failed psychoanalysis so abysmally, but rather by aggressively funding its own scientific, reality-based initiatives. Those who prefer to preserve psychoanalysis in amber, unchanged, or to pivot to a new postmodern and proudly unscientific psychoanalysis, can't ultimately stop a pro-science movement if they don't have any

---

66 https://www.psychiatry.org/about-apa/read-apa-organization-documents-and-policies/annual-and-financial-reports, accessed February 13, 2018. http://www.apa.org/about/finance.aspx, accessed February 18, 2018. https://www.opensecrets.org/lobby/indusclient.php?id=H01&year=2017, accessed February 12, 2018.

resources. And they don't; their revenue streams are drying up, and their pessimism certainly won't help them raise money for their cause. I invite postmodernists to try and raise money for their systematic brand of denial. In the postmodern era, the humanities have lost students and funding, and the reality-based revolution in the larger culture has only just begun. In the long run, denial of reality is a losing strategy and so is irrationality. When I have the urge to protest others' affection for Lacan and Derrida, I think of what W.H. Auden said: "Some books are undeservedly forgotten; none are undeservedly remembered." (Auden 1989, p. 10)

To avoid an undeserved oblivion, and to equip itself to survive, empirical psychoanalysis needs an endowment, and it will have to look beyond the ranks of psychoanalysts alone to raise capital. It can be done. New York City private schools have smaller constituencies and much larger endowments than APsaA. What's needed is only creativity and willpower instead of pessimism and doubt. Fortunately, psychoanalysis specializes in paralyses of the will.

2.2. Rebranding Psychoanalysis

I would argue that Freud's aversion to proof distorted his efforts at public relations so that he unconsciously identified psychoanalysis with the disconcerting instincts and neuroses he studied. He seems to have insisted on presenting psychoanalysis in connection with sex, and in isolation from medical science, because of irrational projective identifications that helped resolve his own conflicts about discovering and promoting psychoanalysis. This emotional interference has yielded a self-defeating public image of psychoanalysis in connection with *sex* and *pseudoscience*. Freud's nephew Edward Bernays, the father of public relations, is sometimes credited with the adage "Sex sells"; but it evidently doesn't sell psychoanalysis. It's time that the field of psychoanalysis changed the negative narrative in circulation, a narrative that psychoanalysts have in fact co-authored with their critics.

If I were to associate psychoanalysis with one word, it would not be *sex*, but *feelings*. In an age of big data, big impersonal corporations, and expanding automation, I'm certain that people crave someone to listen to their individual voices, individual histories, individual feelings and problems, as much or more than ever. The outpouring of voices into the void of social media seems to me to reflect this desire to be heard. People spend billions of dollars a year on TV and movies, not to hear characters think but to watch them feel and to feel along with them.

Psychoanalysis pays unique attention to people's feelings, and I believe there's a market for that, a hunger for that, stronger than any resistance. Don't people want to be heard and understood, want someone to recognize their private sorrows and struggles, to make sense of their painful childhoods and present worries? Don't they want sage counsel for how to make rational choices about relationships, parenting, and work despite the pressure of irrational feelings? The desire to be understood and the relief of understanding oneself are part of what compels patients to enter psychoanalysis and to continue the hard work that it requires.

The endowment I envision would hire professional consultants to engineer changes in public perception and to measure the results of their efforts. They would shift the public identity of psychoanalysis away from "sex" and "pseudoscience" to "the science of feelings," "listening," "humanity," "child development," "understanding your life story," "making rational choices," "empathy," or other preferable, more positive—and honestly, more accurate—descriptors.

In parallel with efforts to change the public identity of psychoanalysis, the endowment would support improved relations between psychoanalysis and other branches of medicine and mental healthcare. It could achieve that, perhaps, through improved interdisciplinary communication—new colloquia, workgroups, affiliations, invitations to speakers outside of psychoanalysis, social events—and through a stronger embrace of the psychotherapy research community. There are more allies out there among scientific psychologists than Freud would have imagined. If scientists today regard psychoanalysts as "hostile to science," the endowment would aim to change their impressions of psychoanalysis to "newly interested in experimental science" and "gathering new validation from experimental science," etc. Of course, systematic psychoanalytic research would be critical to the success of rebranding within the scientific community.

Refuting Critics

Civil rights groups do not concede to racism because of its implacability or its ubiquity. Psychoanalysis ought to consider emulating those groups in combating slander against psychoanalysis. That would mean refutation of unfair criticism wherever and whenever it arises. Freud sometimes deemed opposition to psychoanalysis too ubiquitous and too inevitable to refute. He preferred the method of "inviolate silence," a method that was partly adapted from Jews' quiet pre-war methods of survival in Gentile Europe. The results of inviolate silence are in at this point and they are unequivocal: silence accomplished little for the Jews and little for psychoanalysis. The ubiquity and strength of public criticism cannot silence psychoanalysis. On the contrary, it demands that representatives of psychoanalysis speak out.

In order to assess the practicality of arguing with anti-Freudian critics, I conducted an experiment in June 2012. I attempted to edit the lead paragraph of Freud's Wikipedia page, which at that time took a decidedly negative view of Freud. The lead then implied that

Freud's influence was now limited strictly to the humanities—a version of the old "Freud is dead" trope. When I attempted to edit the lead to reflect Freud's continuing importance in psychology and psychiatry, an "edit war" erupted. Many of the Wikipedia editors involved were reasonable, but one tenacious adversary reverted all of my changes within minutes and displayed Crews-like irrationality and intense hostility from the first moment. I made a point of staying conciliatory and followed Wikipedia's rules for resolving disputes.

I focused on just this one small aim: to amend the lead to reflect Freud's continuing influence on psychology and psychiatry. If anyone could ever be described as emotionally resistant to psychoanalysis, it was the particular Wikipedia editor to whom I've referred. This editor received automatic notifications from Wikipedia whenever anyone edited the Freud page and at all hours of the night he or she got up and reverted any amendments that cast Freud in a positive light. He or she truly believed that the article would be inaccurate unless it reflected negatively on Freud. When I tried to add Eric Kandel's quote that "psychoanalysis still represents the most coherent and intellectually satisfying view of the mind" (Kandel 1999, p. 505), my opponent reacted with incredulity. The Freud-basher did not believe the quote was accurate and asserted that anyway Eric Kandel was just one man—even though Kandel is not just any man; he is a Nobel-prize-winning neuroscientist and author of the most widely used neuroscience textbook at U.S. medical schools. The Freud-basher questioned the veracity of my source, and complained that it was inaccessible, even though Kandel's article came from the *American Journal of Psychiatry* and is freely available on the Internet in a full-text version.

For a while we debated in the "Talk Pages" attached to the Freud Wikipedia article. I escalated the dispute up the ladder to arbitrators who, like all Wikipedia editors, are uncredentialed, anonymous, and self-appointed. Their decisions ignored content and focused instead on editorial privileges and protocols. I got nowhere. I settled for adding a label to the top of the Freud page stating that its neutrality had been questioned. It was the only edit that remained in my power to enforce; de facto, the page's neutrality had been questioned because I had questioned it. My opponent was so upset that he or she brought in a hand-selected arbitrator who had a track record of resolving edit wars. The Freud-basher clearly thought the arbitrator would vindicate the Freud-bashing perspective just as any sane arbitrator would vindicate negative views of, say, Hitler.

The new arbitrator reviewed our arguments and overruled my opponent, who afterwards stopped editing the page. Today, the Wikipedia lead still underrates Freud's importance and still insinuates that the decline of psychoanalysis is a commentary on its validity, but for the past six years the Freud Wikipedia page also at least acknowledges that Freud's work remains influential in psychology and psychiatry. The Kandel quote I added remains in the body of the article as the final word in a paragraph on controversy over Freud. The arbitrator also amended the lead to conclude with W.H. Auden's laudatory 1940 estimate of Freud's influence on the thinking of all modern people: that he is now a "climate of opinion." It was a small public-relations victory, but a victory nonetheless, and it was achieved by one amateur working alone on the problem for a few days. Imagine what a whole cadre of Freud-defenders could accomplish on that Wikipedia page and beyond.

I must admit that I disliked performing this experiment. Each morning I knew I would face a torrent of irrational hostility from my opponent, directed at me personally and at the science of feelings that had healed my wounds and those of my grandmother. I approached each stage of the altercation with a feeling of dread and, indeed, aversion—an aversion to my opponent's hostility but also to my own aggression, to the retaliations I knew my aggression would provoke and to the damage I imagined it would inflict on my ignorant, and therefore vulnerable, opponent. But the experiment was important because it affirmed my belief that patient, persistent disputation can succeed, even in the context of my own resistance to the task.

Lisa Appignanesi recently demonstrated the value of such disputation when she reviewed Frederick Crews in the *New York Review of Books*. In doing so, she accomplished something that few Freudians have bothered to try: she contradicted Crews directly and publicly instead of treating him with "inviolate silence" or confining her complaints to a psychoanalytic journal. She did not attempt to bludgeon him, but with great finesse merely pointed out that he's obsessed with Freud and in fact paranoid about a Freudian conspiracy that doesn't exist. Through elegant ju-jitsu, she drew forth a reaction from him that proved her point beautifully: he is not rational.[67] Most lobbies and interest groups provide institutional support for this sort of anti-defamation work; psychoanalysis could and should do the same.

The field should likewise support efforts to defend psychoanalysis against its critics at scientific conferences. When Mark Solms debated J. Allan Hobson about the validity of Freud's dream theories at the 2006 Science of Consciousness conference, there was a measureable outcome: Solms won the formal Oxford-rules debate by a 2-to-1 decision. (Solms and Turnbull 2011, p. 140) More of this sort of disputation could have a far-reaching impact, especially as

---

[67] http://www.nybooks.com/articles/2017/10/26/freuds-clay-feet/, accessed February 14, 2018. http://www.nybooks.com/articles/2017/11/09/return-of-the-freud-wars/, accessed February 14, 2018.

more published research becomes available to support arguments in defense of psychoanalysis.

2.3. More Psychoanalytic Researchers

In medicine, some MDs exclusively see patients, while others devote their careers to research, and some do both. Even if the psychoanalytic community embraces extra-clinical research, many psychoanalysts will of course prefer to focus on clinical practice. But the psychoanalytic community can ill afford to continue leaving psychological research to non-analysts. When psychoanalysts don't participate in the evidence-based practice movement, non-analysts predominate there and control the direction of research. It can create a vicious circle in which psychological research looks foreign and unhelpful to psychoanalysts and psychoanalysts continue to turn away from research. Then most of the research that's out there remains ignorant of psychoanalysis and inadequate to its needs. "Surveys indicate that many practitioners [of psychoanalysis] are receptive to empirical data but believe that most studies published in contemporary psychology journals have little relevance for clinical practice." (Bornstein and Masling 1998, p. xxii) The only way analysts can make psychological research relevant to their practices is by participating in research.

Analysts' failure to participate in basic science research also leaves a distorted picture of psychoanalytic validity in the public record. Fisher and Greenberg demonstrate the problem of using non-analytic research to assess the overall empirical evidence for the validity of psychoanalytic theories and therapy. (Fisher and Greenberg 1996) They review experiments that were never really intended to test psychoanalytic hypotheses, so their raw materials are in general not well suited to answering the question of validity of psychoanalytic hypotheses. They have little choice but to review research that lacks analytic and clinical sophistication and that asks the wrong questions, and they amass references of widely varying quality, rationale, design, origin, relevance, reliability, and size. They often review others' reviews. This inevitably haphazard method impairs and sometimes distorts their conclusions.

Exhaustive psychoanalytic reviews of partially relevant and clinically unsophisticated research by non-analysts won't ultimately help to validate or invalidate psychoanalysis. What's necessary is exactly the opposite: research by psychoanalysts meant for review by non-analysts. Only psychoanalytic investigators whose personal and clinical experience has convinced them of the validity of psychoanalytic tenets can design effective research tools and experiments. It then remains for such practitioners to confirm systematically in the laboratory what they know to be true anecdotally. Bornstein and Masling's series reviews studies conducted along these lines; for example, chapter author Drew Westen persuasively highlights the abundance of experimental evidence that supports the core of psychoanalytic theory: repression and the dynamic unconscious. (Westen 1998) That said, many of Bornstein and Masling's chapter authors contribute essays that are excellent in their own right but aim higher than mere literature review. Consequently, they sometimes depart from the prosaic topic of research and how it supports or doesn't support psychoanalytic theory.

In any case, to make use of studies in defense of psychoanalysis, and to produce more systematic studies comprehensible to non-analysts, psychoanalysts must overcome their aversion to experiment and disputation. They must reconceive of that work as an opportunity to spread psychoanalytic knowledge instead of a futile exercise in pleasing hopelessly resistant critics or in throwing unjust experimental doubt upon clinical facts. Of course, if a preponderance of evidence conflicts with an existing theory in a meaningful way (as opposed to many of the contradictory, but flawed and irrelevant, studies cited by Fisher and Greenberg), the theory can be modified. But this is really not the point.

Psychoanalysts have a good theory. Now they must test it in a robust, thorough way and present it with openness, clarity, and a consistent appeal to evidence—not in order to question or change the theory, but in order to prove it. Only then can the general population get access to treatment of defense mechanisms and reap the long-term benefits of self-understanding, instead of solely receiving quick fixes and partial fixes from cognitive-behavioral therapy and psychotropic drugs. Until that time psychoanalysts' failure to pursue research and proof will invite the very academic ostracism that Freud always anticipated.

Where do the new psychoanalytic researchers come from? Schachter and Kächele have suggested changes in psychoanalytic education that could help produce a new cadre of researchers. (2017, pp. 5-6) An endowment to fund new research would also undoubtedly help.

3. New Research Strategies and New Study Designs

"[T]he only effective response [to the decline of psychoanalysis]," Schachter and Kächele write, "will be analytic research programs which by testing the tenets of analytic theory and practice will reestablish respect for the integrity and effectiveness of psychoanalysis in both the general public and in the scientific community." (p. 3) I agree. The ultimate cure for the ills created by proof aversion is proof.

As Westen and others have shown, a solid foundation of research already supports a great deal of psychoanalytic theory, and fine researchers inside and outside the psychoanalytic community continue to build on this foundation. With more funding and leadership behind empirical psychoanalysis, such research could be further systematized and further refined to make sense to non-analytic audiences. Many new avenues of research furthermore still await investigation. In this chapter I will suggest some applications of new technologies that might facilitate expansion and continuation of the work begun by past psychoanalytic researchers.

3.1. Digital Recording

Bellak and Smith made the first audio recordings of psychoanalytic sessions in 1956 and Gill et al. called for more recordings in 1968. Under the supervision of Jacob Arlow, Hartvig Dahl answered the call by recording an entire six-year analysis of "Mrs. C." (Dahl 1972, 1974) This data has been used by later researchers like Enrico Jones to study psychoanalytic processes and outcomes. (Jones and Windholz 1990) "Recordings also have the enormous advantage," Jones wrote, "of opening the door of 'privileged access' to psychoanalytic data and fulfilling the cardinal requirement of science: publicly verifiable data." (1993, p. 94) Luborsky and Mintz (1974) used recorded analytic sessions to study instances of a patient's forgetting so that the instances might be correlated with certain contexts. In this way, they established a scientific basis for inferring the motivation behind the forgetting. The investigators note, "[O]ur study is the first to show systematically that this will-o'-the-wisp recurrent memory dysfunction is closely associated with a recurrent conflict-laden theme of the patient's." (p. 251) More such studies would help solidify the empirical basis of Freud's theory of motivated forgetting.

Digital recording makes such data collection cheaper and easier than in the days when data could only be stored on film and magnetic tape. This makes the acquisition of new case data relatively simple and cheap. Computer analysis of such data is simpler and cheaper than ever before, as well. The new data could be subjected to single-case quantitative analysis and single cases could also be aggregated and compared. As Jones said, "The scientific base for clinical psychoanalysis would be greatly strengthened by a programmatic research effort that would attempt to replicate findings over a succession of studies of individual cases." (1993, p. 105) Digital recording makes this aim suddenly much more attainable.

For the study of psychoanalytic process, Jones argued that nothing could replace recordings of actual psychotherapy sessions. But digital recording could also be applied in other settings in order to gather support for basic psychoanalytic theories, if not for the therapeutic process. Investigators could compile interviews with small children. Has anyone ever asked 700 three-year-old boys whom they would like to marry? Why not? Because it seems shameful to do so? If that is the reason, it indeed speaks volumes about the problem of proof aversion for psychoanalysts. If investigators did ask, it seems to me that "Mom" might not be the only answer but it could conceivably be the most frequent answer, and that would constitute statistically significant evidence of the Oedipus complex. Or has anyone asked 700 three-year-olds for their ideas on where their newborn siblings came from? Their ideas on what should be done with their newborn siblings? I seriously doubt that the repressive picture of childhood innocence in which some critics of psychoanalysis so devoutly believe could hold up to such scrutiny. Childhood sexual theories and aggressive wishes toward siblings would gush into evidence. Opportunities might follow for observing children's anxiety in connection with their own sexual theorizing and in connection with their aggressive wishes toward their siblings. These would be significant findings. To get them all you'd need is an iPhone and enough three-year-olds.

Researchers could likewise attempt to capture video evidence of repression in adults through experiments that use confederates to stimulate anger or sexual desire. The subjects' autonomic responses could be simultaneously monitored. Researchers could ask subjects to write and speak their emotional reactions to the confederate provocations and later give subjects an opportunity to revise what they said initially. How well would most adults do at assessing their own emotional states? Are there differences between what was written and what was spoken? Researchers could compare and contrast objective measures of autonomic arousal and objective video evidence with the subjects' expressions of feeling, in order to look for disjunctions between actual emotions and the subjects' own perceptions of them. Researchers could compare and contrast the subjects' initial expressions with their revised expressions. Do angry and sexual affects provoke more revisions? More disjunctions between what is spoken and what is written? Are there larger disjunctions between objective evidence and self-perception when the subject experiences anger or desire (versus other feelings like boredom or amusement)? Are there more parapraxes during aggressive and sexual arousal? During anxiety? Attempts to measure the accuracy of self-perception such as the Self-Understanding of Interpersonal Patterns Scale (Connolly et al. 1999) are limited by their reliance on subjects' self-reports, but video and linguistic scoring could help provide objective baselines against which self-understanding can be measured.

3.2. Trigger Recording
Digital video caches and trigger recording could also be useful in studying unconscious mental phenomena. Field biologists have successfully applied these technologies in a way that may be

instructive for psychoanalysts. Simon King, for example, a nature photographer for the 2006 nature documentary *Planet Earth*, used trigger recording to capture images that had never been seen before: slow-motion footage of a great white shark breaching the surface in an attack on a seal. Because there's no way to know exactly where and when such a feeding event will occur, it had previously been almost impossible to capture such an event on film, let alone to capture it in slow-motion. Digital video pre-record caches (also called "loops") and trigger recording made it possible.[68]

Here's how it worked. King pointed his video camera at the empty, open water for many hours, waiting for a shark attack on a seal. While filming the empty, open water, a computer held onto the last 5 seconds of video in a temporary cache and continuously purged video data that was any older. When the attack finally came, King triggered the computer to start recording. King of course pulled the trigger just after the attack began, but the computer's video cache had 5 previous seconds of footage stored and the trigger told the computer not to purge the cache this time, but to save it instead, and to keep recording for another 5 seconds. In this way, they got the entire attack on digital video. You can't do this when you're capturing images in analog form on film.

The same technique of continuous storage and cache-purging of video data could enable researchers to observe human beings for long periods of time under natural conditions. When an event of interest occurs, the researchers could trigger the computer to save video data from cache to hard drive and keep recording. If researchers, for example, used continuous digital video in a children's classroom, they

---

68 https://www.thetimes.co.uk/article/lights-cameras-action-filming-natures-finest-c9wwt7fmdfr, accessed March 1, 2018.

could probably capture a lot of Freudian phenomena.[69] Researchers could start the digital video rolling and await behavior that Freud has described anecdotally, like regression (e.g. an older child's use of baby talk) or obvious, childlike instances of denial—like when my son accidentally spilled a container of blackberries all over the floor of a supermarket, looked up at me, and said instantly, "That didn't happen."

Child psychologists like Jean Piaget have studied children at play, and later psychologists have used videos of children at play to help train teachers and clinicians, but to my knowledge no one has ever attempted systematic video documentation of children at play specifically in order to corroborate Freudian observations. Researchers could apply digital video, trigger recording, and psycholinguistics to the study of children at play in order to produce hard data in support of psychoanalytic theories.

Other phenomena could be studied systematically in the same way—parapraxes, for example. Like shark attacks, parapraxes are hard to predict. But using trigger recording, they could be captured on video and compiled into a database. They could then be analyzed in context in order to test the Freudian theory that slips are meaningful against the null hypothesis that slips are random. Online games with a social dimension also provide easily recordable opportunities to study unconscious slips and mistakes in aggressive gameplay. Anonymous sexual behavior on the Internet provides another potential trove of data that could be analyzed to test Freudian assumptions.

3.3. Quantitative Psycholinguistics

Feelings, memories, and affectively determined thoughts—the phenomena that psychoanalysis takes for its subject matter—are

---

69 Parents and teachers would obviously have to opt into an observational study of this kind.

expressed in words, and words are at the same time the lens through which psychoanalysis observes the mind. Postmodernists have invoked linguistics irrationally in order to undermine the scientific belief in objective reality, but linguistics has also aided the scientific verification of psychoanalytic theories. Such aid has by no means been exhausted.

The earliest experimental data in support of psychoanalytic ideas were derived from linguistic research—Jung's studies of word-association groups, which he called *complexes*. Later psycholinguistic studies have compared individuals' word associations to group norms in order to show a subject's capacity for unconsciously pondering subliminal stimuli (Shevrin and Fritzler 1968), to measure correlations between various clinical phenomena and word frequencies in a recorded analysis (Dahl 1972), and to show that psychoanalytic treatment augments a patient's ability to free-associate. (Spence et al. 1993)

Advances in computing power now make it possible to record, transcribe, search, and analyze human speech in ways that were unavailable to previous generations and ways that could be particularly useful to psychoanalytic researchers. Over a half-century ago, child psychoanalyst Ishak Ramzy speculated that computers might one day "permit psychoanalysis to take its place in the procession of accurate sciences." (1963, p. 67) Dahl predicted, "The consequences of getting reliable data through recording, of using computer-based content-analysis procedure, and of applying sophisticated statistical and mathematical analyses to our data will be, I believe, a revitalization of our field." (1972, p. 256)

That time has come. Not only is a speech-to-text function freely available in a computer that fits in your pocket, but technological developments like the Internet and social media have enabled cognitive scientists to apply quantitative linguistics with greater ease than ever before outside the lab or the consulting room. As a recent study put it: "We are in the midst of a technological revolution whereby, for the first time, researchers can link daily word use to a broad array of real-world behaviors." (Tausczik and Pennebaker 2010, p. 24)

Linguistic-frequency analysis could provide an alternative to self-report questionnaires filled out by subjects who are not reliable commentators on their own thoughts and feelings (since no one is). Except perhaps at the end of an analysis, one can hardly ask a patient to say whether or not he's in the midst of an unconscious transference that casts his analyst in the role of his father. But linguistic-frequency analysis bypasses self-reports and converts patterns of word usage into hard data, as Dahl's research has done. Given a study subject's free associations in the lab or in a recorded psychoanalytic session, a linguist can score the frequency of father-related words, for example, and look for divergences from average frequencies, either above or below. Oblique references and unconscious associations in human speech and texts can in this way be converted into measureable data comprehensible to non-analysts.

Frequency analysis can also enable psychoanalytic researchers to make specific, testable predictions. Suppose I wanted data to confirm the Freudian proposition that the conscious experience of chronic worries often correlates with an unconscious feeling of guilt. I could fashion my hypothesis in the form of a word-frequency prediction: *I predict that if I ask a subject to speak on his worries for X amount of time, the subject's speech will contain a higher-than-average frequency of words or phrases associated not just with worry but with guilt, regret, self-reproach, etc., even if the subject denies a conscious feeling of guilt.* I could draw up a finite list of self-reproachful words and phrases before the experiment, then ask the subjects to speak or write about their worries. Then I could compare the measured frequencies of the guilt-words with the predicted guilt-word frequencies on my list. The measured frequencies of guilt-associated words would either match my prediction—in which case the measured frequency of guilt-related word-usage would be higher than the guilt-word frequency in general speech—or the measured frequencies would reflect the average word-usage frequency. A higher-than-average guilt-word frequency in connection with worry would be grounds for rejecting the null hypothesis and accepting the Freudian hypothesis of a connection between worry and an unconscious sense of guilt. An average guilt-word frequency would not support the Freudian hypothesis.

After using quantitative linguistic analysis to show that worries correlate with guilt-associated ideas and words, I could conduct another study to show that after subjects' conscious reflection on their guilt-words and feelings, they use fewer worry-related ideas and words. Perhaps quantitative linguistics could provide a new outcome measure: the frequency of usage of worry-words or other negative-affect words and phrases. This could be another way around the use of crude self-report questionnaires in measuring outcomes.

3.4. Conclusion: Presenting Evidence to Critics

Given the inevitable aversions to psychoanalytic proof and criticism, the presentation of evidence is of course bound to raise tensions for the presenter, but historical experience suggests that presentation and disputation often go better than expected. If psychoanalysts can analyze their proof aversion and recover their sense of optimism, curiosity, and ambition, such presentations could be less fraught and more effective. The main thing, however, is that once proof aversion is laid aside, such presentations could occur more often.

The truth is that the possibilities for proving and presenting psychoanalysis are endless: Invite critics to join in repeating experiments that successfully demonstrate psychoanalytic ideas. Explain the experiment in terms of the hypothesis, the predicted outcomes that would confirm it, and the conceivable outcomes that would disconfirm it. Show that psychoanalytic ideas are "falsifiable." Given a well-designed experiment, critics may find themselves as surprised and disappointed as the Freud-bashing Wikipedia editor who was overruled by his own arbitrator. If the experiment fails, repeat it, or do another. If the result truly conflicts with psychoanalytic theory, revise the theory, and do another experiment. If the experiment succeeds but doesn't impress the critics in attendance, then it's an opportunity to show others the biases that psychoanalysis faces. There is nothing in reality for psychoanalytic researchers and expositors to fear. The fear is an irrational, psychological construct.

Having assembled systematic research in support of psychoanalysis, present it in a form comprehensible to non-analysts. Create the first evidence-based psychoanalytic textbook. Reinvent Freud's *Introductory Lectures* with citations of studies. Edward Glover, Director of Research of the London Institute of Psycho-Analysis for 16 years, long ago called for exactly such a book:

[T]he whole future theory and practice of psycho-analysis depends on making, as soon and as thoroughly as possible, a complete survey of the subject—as it were, a Domesday Book of the science.... [To create it, we must first] settle down to the long and arduous task of defining terms, verifying criteria and developing reliable statistics. (Glover 1952, p. 403)

Systematic research culled into a textbook makes it that much easier to defend psychoanalysis, whether in person, in letters, in articles, or in editorials.

George Washington said that the best defense is a good offense. In order to counterattack critics, it will be necessary for psychoanalysts to resolve their conflicts over the aggression in such counterattacks and over the aggression inherent to the act of proof. Many fields and phenomena outside of psychoanalysis are vulnerable to attack and psychoanalysts must not be afraid to administer those attacks when deserved and necessary. Psychologists who strictly treat behavior and not feelings, psychiatrists who use self-report questionnaires and pills but not insight, insurers and drug companies who demand quick-fix treatments, practitioners who ignore childhood, gatekeepers who formulate reimbursable diagnoses by checklists and not etiology, resistant irrational critics of psychoanalysis: this crowd has been dishing it out to psychoanalysts for a long time without the least awareness of how vulnerable they themselves are to criticism in the eyes of the public. Time to turn the tables and give criticism back to those who have unjustly dealt out so much of it. This needn't be anxiety-provoking. It can be gratifying. And it's certainly for a good cause.

VI. CONCLUSION

1. Looking Back

Freud's theory of public resistance to psychoanalysis has for over a century covered over a deeper problem with the transmission of psychoanalytic knowledge: psychoanalysts' aversion to the task of proving their ideas. Once the ill-fitting blanket of "public resistance" is drawn back, however, it seems obvious; psychoanalytic ideas are as hard for the psychoanalyst to transmit as they are for the psychoanalyst to discover in the first place. Public expression of repressed emotional subject matter brings with it inevitable tension in the form of shame, anxiety, and guilt. All of these emotions hinder the public exposition of psychoanalytic ideas. Defenses like projection, avoidance, reversal, and pathological doubt would rescue us from such tension by excusing us from the task of proof, but neglect of proof and public exposition in the end brings worse consequences down on our heads: it inflames public hostility to psychoanalysis outside the field while inflaming dogmatism and dissidence within it.

There is no way out of the predicament except to understand the psychological connections between knowledge, power, and guilt. These connections evade awareness, perhaps, but have persisted since the beginning of human history, as our common language attests. *Proof* in English, *Probe* in German, and their common root, *proba* in Latin, all carry both a scientific meaning and a criminal justice meaning. We *submit* papers and data, and we *submit* to our masters. The word *science* stares back at us from within the word *conscience*, just as the German word for *conscience (Gewissen)* embeds within it the German word for *knowledge (Wissen)*. These double meanings hide the fact in plain sight: the business of knowing is entangled with human relationships, power, and guilt.

Some of our oldest myths attest to the powerful connection between knowledge and guilt as well. Adam and Eve's acquisition of knowledge made God fear and revile them, and cast them out of Eden. Zeus resented humanity for learning the secret of fire, and he punished them with Pandora's box; curiosity in turn made Pandora open it. Lot's wife looked back at a city of sin and turned into a pillar of salt. Orpheus looked back at his beloved Eurydice as he walked out of Hell and lost her forever. The message is clear: Don't look back. But anyone who wishes to live a rational, decent life must be able to do just that, and Freud provided the best means we have for looking back and understanding what we left behind.

2. You're Allowed to Cry There

It's March 6, 2018, and I'm finishing a draft of my book *The Psychoanalyst's Aversion to Proof*. The past is with me as always: I got a message today from my cousin Jeremy, who is forever linked to my father's death. He was born the day my father died, on December 4, 1974, eleven days before I turned three. For many years, I was not able to remember to wish Jeremy a happy birthday. I would try to remember and fail. Since my psychoanalysis, I've been (mostly) able to remember. Jeremy's message to me contained a link to an essay that was published just today.

The essay is by professional basketball player Kevin Love, the starting forward for the Cleveland Cavaliers. It's called "Everyone Is Going Through

Something." And it happens to be about how he overcame his resistance to talking therapy. Love tells of a panic attack he had during a game this season and of how his masculine self-concept made him ashamed to talk about his feelings. He never thought he'd see a therapist. Love says:

> I went to my first appointment with the therapist with some skepticism. I had one foot out the door. But he surprised me. For one thing, basketball wasn't the main focus. He had a sense that the NBA wasn't the main reason I was there that day, which turned out to be refreshing. Instead, we talked about a range of non-basketball things, and I realized how many issues come from places that you may not realize until you really look into them. I think it's easy to assume we know ourselves, but once you peel back the layers it's amazing how much there is to still discover.[70]

Love says he's aware there's a stigma around talking about mental health but he decided to follow DeMar DeRozan's example and speak out in order to help others feel less ashamed about their own inner struggles and about seeking help; DeRozan is a fellow NBA all-star who has publicly acknowledged his depression. Within hours of Love's posting his article on Twitter, it got tens of thousands of retweets, and earned multiple headlines like this one from *USA Today*: "Sports world applauds Kevin Love."[71]

---

70 https://www.theplayerstribune.com/kevin-love-everyone-is-going-through-something/, accessed March 6, 2018.

71 http://www.sportingnews.com/nba/news/kevin-love-players-tribune-mental-health-pan-ic-attack-demar-derozan-depression-cavs-raptors-news/1wg2bt0hge55h13jbgc9s0y7s4, accessed March 6, 2018. https://www.usatoday.com/story/sports/ftw/2018/03/06/kevin-love-opened-up-about-his-mental-health-and-the-sports-world-applauded/111134104/, accessed March 6, 2018.

What the essay shows is that talking about feelings—talking about your own feelings, but also *talking about the general topics of feelings, mental health, and psychotherapy*—is much harder than listening to others talk about it. Love was ashamed to talk about the importance of psychotherapy and the importance of feelings, but the public was perhaps less resistant to hearing it. On the contrary, he spoke for thousands of people who also feel ashamed of their feelings and their need to talk about them. They thanked him for doing it on their behalf.

The essay also shows that Freud is wrong when he argues that only laborious efforts can break down resistance to psychoanalytic ideas. So are critics who imagine that all Freudians have been brainwashed by their analysts. Love is a veteran of the NBA, not of years of analysis. This is an all-star athlete who's unaccustomed to looking inward and has met with a therapist a handful of times. And yet he spoke out because it was a relief to him to shed some of his machismo, and with it the stigma of getting help, and to reflect on his feelings.

This brings me back to my own history once again. My mother says that when people asked me as a small child how I liked my nursery school Hanna Perkins, the one founded in Cleveland by psychoanalysts, I said it was good because "You're allowed to cry there." Psychoanalysis at its best creates this environment of toleration for the expression of emotion. This is what psychoanalysis has to offer, and in the end, *everyone* wants it. I suspect it's that atmosphere of understanding that psychoanalysts themselves have long craved. They've sought it out by avoiding a public that does not understand feelings and talking instead to themselves.

ACKNOWLEDGEMENTS

Without Arnold Richards, this book would never have come to be. I thank him for his wisdom, guidance, and support. I am also grateful to the *International Journal of Psychoanalysis* whose anonymous reviewers displayed unusual openness to considering my ideas and who helped me to refine and reformulate them.

REFERENCES

APA Presidential Task Force on Evidence-Based Practice. (2006). Evidence-Based Practice in Psychology. *Amer Psychol.* 61(4):271-285.

Arlow, J. (1993). Discussion: A Clinician's Comments on Empirical Studies of Psychoanalysis. *J Amer Psychoanal Assn.* 41S:143-152.

Auchincloss, E. and Kravis, N. (2000). Teaching Freud To Undergraduates. *Int J Psychoanal.* 81(4):753-770.

Auchincloss, E. and Samberg, E. (2012). *Psychoanalytic Terms and Concepts.* New Haven: Yale.

Auden, W. (1989 [1948]). *The Dyer's Hand and Other Essays.* New York: Vintage.

Augustine. (1853 [c. 400]). *Confessions.* London: Oxford.

Bair, D. (1990). *Samuel Beckett: A Biography.* New York: Summit.

Barnett, A. The Psychoanalytic Review: 100 Years of History. *Psychoanal Rev.* 100(1):1-56.

Bellak, L. and Smith, M. (1956). An experimental exploration of the psychoanalytic process: exemplification of a method. *Psychoanal Q.* 25:385-414.

Blass, R. (2003). The Puzzle of Freud's Puzzle Analogy: Reviving a Struggle with Doubt and Conviction in Freud's Moses and Monotheism. *Int J Psychoanal.* 84:669-682.

Bloch, R. ed. (2013). Introduction to *The Fabliaux: A New Verse Translation.* New York: Liveright.

Bloom, H. (1973). *The Anxiety of Influence.* New York: Oxford.

Bloom, H. (1994). *The Western Canon.* New York: Riverhead.

Borck, C. (2001). Electricity as a Medium of Psychic Life: Electrotechnological Adventures into Psychodiagnosis in Weimar Germany. *Science in Context*. 14(4):565-590.

Borges, J. (1964). *Labyrinths: Selected Stories and Other Writings*. New York: New Directions.

Bornstein, R. and Masling, J. eds. (1998). *Empirical Studies of Psychoanalytic Theories, Volume 7: Empirical Perspectives on the Psychoanalytic Unconscious*. Washington D.C.: APA.

Bornstein, R. and Masling, J. eds. (2002). *Empirical Studies of Psychoanalytic Theories, Volume 10: The Psychodynamics of Gender and Gender Role*. Washington D.C.: APA.

Brabant, E. et al. ed. (1993) *The Correspondence of Sigmund Freud and Sándor Ferenczi Volume 1*. Cambridge: Harvard.

Brenner, C. (1968). Psychoanalysis and Science. *J Amer Psychoanal Assn*. 16:675-696.

Brenner, C. (1973). *An Elementary Textbook of Psychoanalysis*. New York: Anchor.

Brenner, C. (1982). *The Mind in Conflict*. Madison: International.

Breuer, J. and Freud, S. (1893). On the Psychical Mechanism of Hysterical Phenomena: Preliminary Communication. S.E. 2:2-17.

Breuer, J. and Freud, S. (1893-1895). Studies on Hysteria. S.E. 2.

Carroll, J. (2001). *Constantine's Sword: The Church and the Jews: A History*. New York: Houghton.

Casanova, G. (2011 [1797]). *The Duel*. New York: Melville House.

Ciardi, J. (1978). The Lungfish. *Poetry*. August. 269-270.

Cicero. (1951 [1st century BCE]). *On the Nature of the Gods; Academics*. Cambridge: Harvard.

Connolly, M. et al. (1999). The Reliability and Validity of a Measure of Self-Understanding of Interpersonal Patterns. *J Couns Psychol*. 46(4):472-482.

Custers, R. and Aarts, H. (2010). The Unconscious Will: How the Pursuit of Goals Operates Outside of Conscious Awareness. *Science.* 329:47-50.

Dahl, H. (1972). A Quantitative Study of a Psychoanalysis. *Psychoanal Contemp Sci.* 1(1):237-257.

Dahl, H. (1974). The Measurement of Meaning in Psychoanalysis by Computer Analysis of Verbal Contexts. *J Amer Psychoanal Assn.* 22:37-57.

Depue, B. et al. (2007). Prefrontal Regions Orchestrate Suppression of Emotional Memories via a Two-Phase Process. *Science.* 317:215-219.

Derrida, J. (1968). Différance. In: Rivkin, J. and Ryan, M. eds. (2000). *Literary Theory: An Anthology.* Malden: Blackwell. 385-407.

Doolittle, H. (1974 [1933-1948]). *Tribute to Freud.* New York: New Directions.

Eagle, M. (2007). Psychoanalysis and Its Critics. *Psychoanal Psychol.* 24(1):10-24.

Eagle, M. et al. (2001). The Analyst's Knowledge and Authority: A Critique of the "New View" in Psychoanalysis. *J Amer Psychoanal Assn.* 49(2):457-488.

Eagleton, T. (1983). *Literary Theory: An Introduction.* Minneapolis: Minnesota.

Eisold, K. (1998). The Splitting of the New York Psychoanalytic Society and the Construction of Psychoanalytic Authority. *Int J Psychoanal.* 79:871-885.

Erreich, A. (2002). Empirical Studies of Psychoanalytical Theories, Volumes 7 and 8. Review. *J Amer Psychoanal Assn.* 50(2):657-663.

Falzeder, E. ed. (2002). *The Complete Correspondence of Sigmund Freud and Karl Abraham 1907-1925.* London: Karnac.

Fisher, S. and Greenberg, R. (1977). *The Scientific Credibility of Freud's Theories and Therapy.* New York: Basic.

Fisher, S. and Greenberg, R. (1996). *Freud Scientifically Reappraised*. New York: Wiley.

Fitzpatrick, T. et al. (2015). Establishing the Reliability of Word Association Data for Investigating Individual and Group Differences. *Appl Linguist*. 36(1):23-50.

Fonagy, P. (2001). The Talking Cure in the Cross Fire of Empiricism— The Struggle for the Hearts and Minds of Psychoanalytic Clinicians. *Psychoanal Dial*. 11(4):647-658.

Fonagy, P. et al. (2015). Pragmatic randomized controlled trial of long-term psychoanalytic psychotherapy for treatment-resistant depression: the Tavistock Adult Depression Study (TADS). *World Psychiatry*. 14(3):312-21.

Foucault, M. (1966). The Order of Things. In: Rivkin, J. and Ryan, M. eds. (2000). *Literary Theory: An Anthology*. Malden: Blackwell. 377-384.

Fränkel, H. (1945). *Ovid: A Poet Between Two Worlds*. Berkeley: California.

Frankfurt, H. (2005). *On Bullshit*. Princeton: Princeton.

Freud, E. ed. (1961). *Letters of Sigmund Freud 1873-1939*. London: Hogarth.

Freud, S. (1895 [1894]). On the Grounds for Detaching a Particular Syndrome From Neurasthenia Under the Description 'Anxiety Neurosis.' *S.E.* 3:85-117.

Freud, S. (1895). A Reply to Criticisms of My Paper on Anxiety Neurosis. *S.E.* 3:119-139.

Freud, S. (1896). The Aetiology of Hysteria. *S.E.* 3:187-221.

Freud, S. (1899). Screen Memories. *S.E.* 3:299-322.

Freud, S. (1900). The Interpretation of Dreams. Part I. *S.E.* 4:1-338.

Freud, S. (1900). The Interpretation of Dreams. Part II. *S.E.* 5:339-625.

Freud, S. (1901). On Dreams. *S.E.* 5:633-686.

Freud, S. (1905). Three Essays on the Theory of Sexuality. *S.E.* 7:123-246.

Freud, S. (1908). On the Sexual Theories of Children. *S.E.* 9:205-226.

Freud, S. (1909). Analysis of a Phobia in a Five-Year-Old Boy. *S.E.* 10:1-150.

Freud, S. (1909). Notes Upon a Case of Obsessional Neurosis. *S.E.* 10:151-318.

Freud, S. (1910). Leonardo Da Vinci and a Memory of his Childhood. *S.E.* 11:57-138.

Freud, S. (1912). Recommendations to Physicians Practising Psycho-Analysis. *S.E.* 12:111-120.

Freud, S. (1913). On Beginning the Treatment (Further Recommendations on the Technique of Psycho-Analysis I). *S.E.* 12:121-144.

Freud, S. (1914). On Narcissism. *S.E.* 14:67-102.

Freud, S. (1914). On the History of the Psycho-Analytic Movement. *S.E.* 14:1-66.

Freud, S. (1916). Some Character-Types Met with in Psycho-Analytic Work. *S.E.* 14:309-333.

Freud, S. (1916-1917 [1915-1917]). Introductory Lectures on Psycho-Analysis. Parts I and II. *S.E.* 15.

Freud, S. (1917 [1916-1917]). Introductory Lectures on Psycho-Analysis. Part III. *S.E.* 16.

Freud, S. (1917). A Difficulty in the Path of Psycho-Analysis. *S.E.* 17:135-144.

Freud, S. (1918 [1914]). From the History of an Infantile Neurosis. *S.E.* 17:3-122.

Freud, S. (1925 [1924]). An Autobiographical Study. *S.E.* 20:1-74.

Freud, S. (1925 [1924]). The Resistances to Psycho-Analysis. *S.E.* 19:211-224.

Freud, S. (1926). The Question of Lay Analysis. *S.E.* 20:177-258.

Freud, S. (1931). The Expert Opinion in the Halsmann Case. *S.E.* 21:251-253.

Freud, S. (1933 [1932]). New Introductory Lectures on Psycho-Analysis. *S.E.* 22:1-182.

Freud, S. (1936). A Disturbance of Memory on the Acropolis. *S.E.* 22:237-248.

Freud, S. (1937). Constructions in Analysis. *S.E.* 23:255-269.

Freud, S. (1938). Anti-Semitism in England. *S.E.* 23:301-302.

Freud, S. (1939 [1934-1938]). Moses and Monotheism. *S.E.* 23:1-137.

Freud, S. (1950 [1892-1899]). Extracts from the Fliess Papers. *S.E.* 1:173-280.

Friedländer, A. (1911). Hysteria and Modern Psychoanalysis. *The Journal of Abnormal Psychology.* 5:297-319.

Friedlander, H. (1995). *The Origins of Nazi Genocide.* Chapel Hill: North Carolina.

Frosh, S. (2005). *Hate and the 'Jewish Science.'* Houndmills: Palgrave.

Gabbard, G. et al. (2002). The Place of Psychoanalytic Treatments Within Psychiatry. *Arch Gen Psychiatry.* 59:505-510.

Galen. (1963 [2nd century CE]). *On the Passions and Errors of the Soul.* Columbus: Ohio State.

Gay, P. (1988). *Freud: A Life for Our Time.* New York: Norton.

Gay, P. (1995). *The Enlightenment: The Rise of Modern Paganism.* New York: Norton.

Gerber, A. et al. (2011). A Quality-Based Review of Randomized Controlled Trials of Psychodynamic Psychotherapy. *Am J Psychiatry.* 168:19-28.

Gibbons, M. et al. (2016). Comparative Effectiveness of Cognitive Therapy and Dynamic Psychotherapy for Major Depressive Disorder in a Community Mental Health Setting: A Randomized Clinical Noninferiority Trial. *JAMA Psychiatry.* 73(9):904-11.

Gill, M. et al. (1968). Studies in Audio-Recorded Psychoanalysis—I. General Considerations. *J Amer Psychoanal Assn.* 16:230-244.

Glover, E. (1952). Research Methods in Psycho-Analysis. *Int J Psychoanal.* 33:403-409.

Govrin, A. The Dilemma of Contemporary Psychoanalysis: Toward a "Knowing" Post-Postmodernism. *J Amer Psychoanal Assn.* 54(2):507-535.

Greenberg, J. (2013). Reflections on Object Relations in Psychoanalytic Theory. *Contemp Psychoanal.* 49(1):11-17.

Greenberg, J. (2016). Editor's Introduction: Is Truth Relevant? *Psychoanal Q.* 85(2):269-274.

Greenhalgh, T. et al. (2014). Evidence based medicine: a movement in crisis? *BMJ.* 348:g3725.

Greenson, R. (1969). The Origin and Fate of New Ideas in Psychoanalysis. *Int J Psychoanal.* 50:503-515.

Grunbaum, A. (1984). *The Foundations of Psychoanalysis.* Berkeley: California.

Guyatt, G. et al. (1992). Evidence-Based Medicine: A New Approach to Teaching the Practice of Medicine. *JAMA.* 268(17):2420-2425.

Hanly, C. (1992). *The Problem of Truth in Applied Psychoanalysis.* New York: Guilford.

Hauser, S. (2005). The Legacy of Enrico Jones. *J Amer Psychoanal Assn.* 53(2):535-539.

Hempel, C. (1965). *Aspects of Scientific Explanation.* New York: Free Press.

Hoffman, I. (2009). Doublethinking Our Way to "Scientific" Legitimacy: The Desiccation of Human Experience. *J Amer Psychoanal Assn.* 57(5):1043-1069.

Hoffman, L. (2010). One hundred years after Sigmund Freud's lectures in America: towards an integration of psychoanalytic theories and techniques within psychiatry. *Hist Psychiatry.* 21(4):455-470.

Holt, R. (2002). Quantitative Research on the Primary Process: Method and Findings. *J Amer Psychoanal Assn.* 50(2):457-482.

Holt, R. (2015). On Freud's Authoritarianism. *Psychoanal Rev.* 102(3):315-346.

Huprich, S. ed. *Personality disorders: Toward theoretical and empirical integration in diagnosis and assessment.* Washington D.C.: APA.

Husserl, E. (1970 [1907]). *The Idea of Phenomenology.* Hague: Nijhoff.

Ibsen, H. (1882). *An Enemy of the People.* In: Sharp, R. trans. (1981). *Four Great Plays by Henrik Ibsen.* New York: Bantam. 129-215.

Inwood, B. and Gerson, L. (1988). *Hellenistic Philosophy: Introductory Readings.* Indianapolis: Hackett.

Jelliffe, S. (1933). Address—Glimpses of a Freudian Odyssey. *Psychoanal Q.* 2:318-329.

Jones, E. (1920). Editorial. *Int J Psychoanal.* 1:3-5.

Jones, E. (1922). Mysticism, Freudianism and Scientific Psychology. *Int J Psychoanal.* 3:387-394.

Jones, E. (1953). *The Life and Work of Sigmund Freud, Volume 1.* New York: Basic.

Jones, E. (1955). *The Life and Work of Sigmund Freud, Volume 2.* New York: Basic.

Jones, E.E. and Windholz, M. (1990). The Psychoanalytic Case Study: Toward a Method for Systematic Inquiry. *J Amer Psychoanal Assn.* 38:985-1015.

Jones, E.E. (1993). How Will Psychoanalysis Study Itself? *J Amer Psychoanal Assn.* 41S:91-108.

Josipovici, G. (1999). *On Trust: Art and the Temptations of Suspicion.* New Haven: Yale.

Jung, C. (1913 [1912]). The Theory of Psychoanalysis. *Psychoanal Rev.* 1(1):1-40.

Jung, C. (1989 [1962]). *Memories, Dreams, Reflections.* New York: Random House.

Kandel, E. (1999). Biology and the future of psychoanalysis: a new intellectual framework for psychiatry revisited. *Am J Psychiatry.* 156(4):505-24.

Kaufmann, W. (2017 [1980]) *Discovering the Mind, Volume 3: Freud, Adler, and Jung.* Abingdon: Routledge.

Kenny, A. (2004). *Ancient Philosophy: A New History of Western Philosophy, Volume 1.* Oxford: Oxford.

Kernan, A. (1990). *The Death of Literature.* New Haven: Yale.

Kernberg, O. (1986). Institutional Problems of Psychoanalytic Education. *J Amer Psychoanal Assn.* 34:799-834.

Koch, S. and Leary, D. eds. (1985). *A Century of Psychology as Science.* New York: McGraw-Hill.

Kravis, N. (2013). The Analyst's Hatred of Analysis. *Psychoanal Q.* 82(1):89-114.

Kriegman, D. (1998). Interpretation, the Unconscious, and Analytic Authority: Toward an Evolutionary, Biological Integration of the Empirical-Scientific Method with the Field-Defining Empathic Stance. In: Bornstein, R. and Masling, J. eds. (1998). *Empirical Studies of Psychoanalytic Theories, Volume 7: Empirical Perspectives on the Psychoanalytic Unconscious.* Washington D.C.: APA. 187-272.

Lacan, J. (1966). The Instance of the Letter in the Unconscious or Reason since Freud. In: Rivkin, J. and Ryan, M. eds. (2000). *Literary Theory: An Anthology.* Malden: Blackwell. 190-205.

Lacan, J. (1966). The Mirror Stage as Formative of the Function of the I as Revealed in Psychoanalytic Experience. In: Rivkin, J. and Ryan, M. eds. (2000). *Literary Theory: An Anthology.* Malden: Blackwell. 178-183.

Leichsenring, F. and Rabung, S. (2008). Effectiveness of Long-term Psychodynamic Psychotherapy: A Meta-analysis. *JAMA.* 300(13):1551-1565.

Leichsenring, F. and Rabung, S. (2011). Long-term psychodynamic psychotherapy in complex mental disorders: update of a meta-analysis. *Br J Psychiatry.* 199(1):15-22

Leichsenring, F. et al. (2015). Psychodynamic therapy meets evidence-based medicine: a systematic review using updated criteria. *Lancet Psychiatry.* 2(7):648-60.

Levy, R. ed. (1991). *Antisemitism in the Modern World: An Anthology of Texts.* Lexington: Heath.

Lifton, R. (1988). *The Nazi Doctors.* New York: Basic.

Luborsky, L. and Mintz, J. (1974). What Sets Off Momentary Forgetting During A Psychoanalysis? *Psychoanal Contemp Sci.* 3(1):233-268.

Mahon, E. (2015). Insight as Defiance: A Neglected Aspect of Self-Awareness. *Psychoanal Q.* 84(1):169-174.

Makari, G. (2008). *Revolution in Mind: The Creation of Psychoanalysis.* New York: Harper.

Masling, J. (1999). An Evaluation of Empirical Research Linked to Psychoanalytic Theory. Paper presented June 11, 1999 at the Annual Meeting of the Rapaport-Klein Study Group. "http://www.psychomedia.it/rapaport-klein/masling99.htm" Accessed December 2, 2016.

Masson, J. ed. (1985). *The Complete Letters of Sigmund Freud to Wilhelm Fliess.* Cambridge: Belknap.

McGowan, K. (2014). The Second Coming of Sigmund Freud. *Discover.* 24(3):54-61.

McGuire, W. ed. (1988). *The Freud/Jung Letters.* Cambridge: Harvard.

McHugh, P. (2006). *The Mind Has Mountains: Reflections on Society and Psychiatry.* Baltimore: Johns Hopkins.

McHugh, P. and Slavney, P. (1986). *The Perspectives of Psychiatry.* Baltimore: Johns Hopkins.

Mills, J. (2012). *Conundrums: A Critique of Contemporary Psychoanalysis.* New York: Routledge.

Mitchell, S. (1993). Reply to Bachant and Richards. *Psychoanal Dial.* 3(3):461-480.

Modlin, I. et al. (2004). Siegfried Oberndorfer: origins and perspectives of carcinoid tumors. *Hum Pathol.* 35(12):1440-51.

Montaigne, M. (1976 [1580]). *The Complete Essays of Montaigne.* Stanford: Stanford.

Nakhnikian, G. (1970). Introduction to: Husserl, E. (1970 [1907]). *The Idea of Phenomenology.* Hague: Nijhoff.

Nietzsche, F. (1989 [1886]). *Beyond Good and Evil.* New York: Vintage.

Pagels, E. (1995). *The Origin of Satan*. New York: Random House.

Parsons, M. (2006). The Analyst's Countertransference to the Psychoanalytic Process. *Int J Psychoanal*. 87:1183–98.

Racker, H. (1953). A Contribution to the Problem of Counter-Transference. *Int J Psychoanal*. 34:314-324.

Ramzy, I. (1963). Research Aspects of Psychoanalysis. *Psychoanal Q*. 32:58-76.

Rangell, L. (1985). On the Theory of Theory in Psychoanalysis and the Relation of Theory to Psychoanalytic Therapy. *J Amer Psychoanal Assn*. 33:59-92.

Ratner, A. (2018). The Psychoanalyst's Resistance to the Task of Proof. *Psychoanal Rev*. 105(2):157-186.

Redmond, J. and Shulman, M. (2008). Access to Psychoanalytic Ideas in American Undergraduate Institutions. *J Amer Psychoanal Assn*. 56(2):391-408.

Richards, A. (1990). The Future of Psychoanalysis: The Past, Present, and Future of Psychoanalytic Theory. *Psychoanal Q*. 59:347-369.

Richards, A. (2009). The Need Not to Believe: Freud's Godlessness Reconsidered. *Psychoanal Rev*. 96(4):561-578.

Richards, A. (2014). Freud's Jewish Identity and Psychoanalysis as a Science. *J Amer Psychoanal Assn*. 62(6):987-1003.

Richards, A. (2015). Psychoanalysis in Crisis: The Danger of Ideology. *Psychoanal Rev*. 102(3):389-405.

Richards, A. (2016). The Left and Far Left in American Psychoanalysis: Psychoanalysis as a Subversive Discipline. *Contemp Psychoanal*. 52(1):111-129.

Ricoeur, P. (1977). The Question of Proof in Psychoanalytic Writings. *J Amer Psychoanal Assn*. 25:835-871.

Rivkin, J. and Ryan, M. eds. (2000). *Literary Theory: An Anthology*. Malden: Blackwell.

Rosenzweig, S. (1985). Freud and Experimental Psychology: The Emergence of Idiodynamics. In: Koch, S. and Leary, D. eds. (1985). *A Century of Psychology as Science*. New York: McGraw-Hill. 135-207.

Rosenzweig, S. and Mason, G. (1934). An Experimental Study of Memory in Relation to the Theory of Repression. *Br J Psychol.* 24:247-265.

Safran, J. and Aron, L. (2001). Introduction. *Psychoanalytic Dialogues.* 11(4):571-582.

Sagan, C. (2006). *The Varieties of Scientific Experience*. New York: Penguin.

Sandler, J. (1962). Research in Psycho-Analysis—The Hampstead Index as an Instrument of Psycho-Analytic Research. *Int J Psychoanal.* 43:287-291.

Schachter, J. and Kächele, H. (2017). *Nodal Points: Critical Reflections on Psychoanalytic Therapy*. New York: IPBooks.

Schlessinger, N. (1985). Empirical Studies of Psychoanalytical Theories, Volume 1. Review. *Psychoanal Q.* 54:97-101.

Schneider, J. et al. (2014). Psychoanalytic Training Experience and Postgraduate Professional Development: A Survey of Six Decades of Graduate Analysts. *Int J Psychoanal.* 95(6):1211-1233.

Schneider, J. et al. (2017). Psychoanalytic Training Experience and Postgraduate Professional Development, Part II. *Int J Psychoanal.* 98(5):1385-1410.

Seifter, J. (2015). Don't Abandon the Case Report in the Race for Big Data. *Medscape.* Sep 03, 2015. https://www.medscape.com/viewarticle/850365#vp_1, accessed February 10, 2018.

Shamdasani, S. (2012). Introduction to: Jung, C. (2012 [1912]) *Jung Contra Freud*. Princeton: Princeton.

Sharp, R. trans. (1981). *Four Great Plays by Henrik Ibsen*. New York: Bantam.

Shedler, J. (2002). A New Language for Psychoanalytic Diagnosis. *J Amer Psychoanal Assn.* 50(2):429-456.

Shedler, J. (2010). The Efficacy of Psychodynamic Psychotherapy. *Am Psychol.* 65(2):98-109.

Shedler, J. (2015). Integrating clinical and empirical perspectives on personality: The Shedler-Westen Assessment Procedure (SWAP). In: Huprich, S. ed. *Personality disorders: Toward theoretical and empirical integration in diagnosis and assessment.* Washington D.C.: APA. 225-252.

Shevrin, H. and Fritzler, D. (1968). Visual Evoked Response Correlates of Unconscious Mental Processes. *Science.* 161(3838):295-298.

Shevrin, H. (1998). The Freud-Rapaport Theory of Consciousness. In: Bornstein, R. and Masling, J. eds. (1998). *Empirical Studies of Psychoanalytic Theories, Volume 7: Empirical Perspectives on the Psychoanalytic Unconscious.* Washington D.C.: APA. 45-70.

Sokal, A. (1996). A Physicist Experiments with Cultural Studies. *Lingua Franca.* May/June. http://linguafranca.mirror.theinfo.org/9605/sokal.html, accessed February 2, 2018.

Sokal, A. and Bricmont, J. (1998). *Fashionable Nonsense: Postmodern Intellectuals' Abuse of Science.* New York: Picador.

Solms, M. and Turnbull, O. (2011). What is Neuropsychoanalysis? *Neuropsychoanalysis.* 13(2):133-145.

Spence, D. et al. (1993). Impact of Interpretation on Associative Freedom. *J Consult Clin Psychol.* 61(3):395-402.

Tausczik, Y. and Pennebaker, J. (2010). The Psychological Meaning of Words: LIWC and Computerized Text Analysis Methods. *J Lang Soc Psychol.* 29(1):24-54.

Van Helden, A. (1995). Christoph Scheiner. The Galileo Project, Rice University. "http://galileo.rice.edu/sci/scheiner.html" Accessed April 18, 2014.

Wampold, B. et al. (2017). In pursuit of truth: A critical examination of meta-analyses of cognitive behavior therapy. *Psychother Res.* 27(1):14-32.

Wallerstein, R. (2006). The Relevance of Freud's Psychoanalysis in the 21st Century: Its Science and Its Research. *Psychoanal Psychol.* 23(2):302-326.

Westen, D. (1998). Unconscious Thought, Feeling, and Motivation: The End of a Century-Long Debate. In: Bornstein, R. and Masling, J. eds. (1998). *Empirical Studies of Psychoanalytic Theories, Volume 7: Empirical Perspectives on the Psychoanalytic Unconscious.* Washington D.C.: APA. 1-43.

Westen, D. (1999). The Scientific Status of Unconscious Processes: Is Freud Really Dead? *J Amer Psychoanal Assn.* 47:1061-1106.

Wittgenstein, L. (1972 [1951]). *On Certainty.* New York: Harper.

Yerushalmi, Y. (1991). *Freud's Moses: Judaism Terminable and Interminable.* New Haven: Yale.

CPSIA information can be obtained
at www.ICGtesting.com
Printed in the USA
FSHW021837150119
55040FS

9 781949 093025